BEYOND DIXON OF DOCK GREEN

For Alexander Burnett

BEYOND DIXON OF DOCK GREEN
Early British Police Series

Susan Sydney-Smith

I.B.Tauris *Publishers*
LONDON • NEW YORK

Published in 2002 by I.B.Tauris & Co Ltd
6 Salem Road, London W2 4BU
175 Fifth Avenue, New York NY 10010
www.ibtauris.com

In the United States of America and in Canada distributed by
St Martins Press, 175 Fifth Avenue, New York NY 10010

ISBN 1 86064 790 1 hardback
ISBN 1 86064 824 X paperback

A full CIP record for this book is available from the British Library
A full CIP record for this book is available from the Library of Congress

Library of Congress catalog card: available

Project management by Steve Tribe, London
Printed and bound in Great Britain by MPG Books Ltd, Bodmin

Contents

Illustrations

Acknowledgements

My sincere thanks and appreciation to Charles Barr and Jon Cook, who saw this book through its doctoral thesis stage. In terms of its research, the staff at the BBC Written Archives Centre were superb: thanks in particular to Trevor White, for unstinting support and suggestions and, latterly, to Jeff Walden. Thanks also to Colin Francis King, for sharing his knowledge and showing me around the Robert Barr archive at Exeter University.

A special note of gratitude should also be recorded for Mark Glancy's highly congenial Issues in Film History Seminar at the the Institute of Historical Research in Senate House, where I have learned a great deal from leading exponents, especially from James Chapman and Jeffrey Richards, without whose encouragement this project would not have come to fruition. In terms of completing the project, I am grateful for the helpful criticism of my friend and colleague Mary Ellen. Steve Tribe completed this process, probably later in the day than he'd have liked. To him and his patience I am indebted. I would also like to thank Jan Read, for giving me information about the true beginnings of *Dixon of Dock Green*, and Robert Barr, sadly no longer with us, for his invaluable and amusing insights into life at the BBC and about the 'real' Fabian of 'the Yard'. Thanks also to Joe Pope of the Department of Historical and Critical Studies at Preston for allowing me an early Sabbatical. Finally, well done and love and thanks to Alex Burnett who has successfully graduated from Durham as this book nears completion, and to friends and colleagues for seeing it through.

The illustrations were provided by the Stills, Posters and Designs Division of the British Film Institute and the BBC Photograph Archive, copyright of the BBC. Details in the appendices are taken as entered on the published as broadcast (psb) records at the BBC Written Archive, Caversham.

INTRODUCTION
Casing the British copshow

George Dixon would not recognise many aspects of modern
police work, but he would still find there the 'old-fashioned'
values of commitment, responsibility and teamwork …
From what the Government is saying, you'd think the last
big change in the police service was when *Dixon of Dock
Green* changed his whistle for a walkie talkie.

Guardian, 1993[1]

In 1993, the Sheehey Committee put forward radical suggestions for
modernising the British police force, including the carrying of firearms.
Arguing against its recommendations, the Police Federation inserted a full-
page advertisement in the national broadsheet press, illustrated by a portrait
of Jack Warner, in the role of the eponymous protagonist of *Dixon of Dock
Green* (BBC, 1955–1976), the earliest British television police series to remain
solid in the popular imagination. The advertisement – cited above – claims
'commitment', 'responsibility' and 'teamwork' as the British police force's
traditional attributes. Following charges of corrupt practice and institutional
racism within the police force – in the oft-recited litany of the Guildford
Four, the Birmingham Six and the more recent Steven Lawrence case – there
ought to be cause for scepticism at so blatant a fictional appropriation. Nonetheless, five decades after his first appearance in the Ealing film *The Blue
Lamp* and subsequent 'resurrection' on British TV, 'Dixon' remains the embodiment of an ideal British policeman. His continuing status as the iconic
British Bobby of, and for, all time exemplifies that process so memorably
cited by Roland Barthes, where, by a sleight of hand, 'myth' is turned into
nature.[2]

Another reason for the Dixon character's enduring popularity lies in the
formulaic nature of the series itself. As Horace Newcomb has stated:

> The television formula requires that we use our contemporary historical concerns as subject matter. In part we deal with them in historical fashion, citing current facts and figures. But we also return these issues to an older time, or we create a character from an older time ... That vaguely defined 'older time' becomes the mythical realm of television.[3]

Such a circumstance helps to explain why Police Federation spin-doctors so easily play upon our unsullied conception of the 'olden days', a mythical time during which everything seems – and in television terms, literally was – more black-and-white. Working upon a consolidated sense of the collective memory, the 'Dixon' image is able to transcend the often less than pleasant 'real life' facts of today's policing methods. Embedded within this whole trajectory is a strongly evidential relationship between past and present missing from those synchronic methods of 'semiotic' analysis following on from Barthes' work, whose limitations will shortly be discussed.

In British television scholarship, there has to date been little written about the 'beginnings' of popular generic forms. It is, for example, not widely known that early British television possessed none of the soaps and series – 'Cops', 'Docs' or 'Vets' – that we recognise today as so familiar a part of the television landscape. By comparison with the United States, there is little written in terms of a television-centred analysis of the emergence of early British television's *popular* forms: nothing comparable to Eric Barnouw's foundational *Tube of Plenty* (1975), or Robert Allen's important *Speaking of Soap Opera* (1985). What has arisen in the interim is a version of television history constructed by television itself.

Although anniversary series such as *Auntie: The inside story of the BBC* (1998), a series of weekly programmes about the BBC up to the present day, undoubtedly complement the established institutional and technological historiographies that do exist (Asa Briggs's magnum opus, for example), the same cannot be said for the recent trend for compilation editions featuring past programmes.[4] A plethora of 'recycled TV', taking the form of repeats, themed evenings and anthologies from past shows has become an integral part of programming. In recent years, archive footage has entered the schedule, 'strip-scheduling' Saturday evenings Channel 4's; from *Top Ten* series to the BBC's *I Love the 1970s*, TV fiction jostles with TV fact. As Tim O'Sullivan argues, 'Repeats of early *Coronation Street* episodes ... notably one of the weddings of Elsie Tanner (1967), coincide with actuality celebrations', including that foundational television 'event', the Coronation of Elizabeth II (1953).[5] From the Royal Family to *The Royle Family*, programmes and families, past and present complete for equal attention. This seamless television text of fictional and actuality narratives is part and parcel of today's postmodern television world, whose 'TV on TV' knowledge base is tested in 'numerous quizzes, on chat shows and in other formats of popular programming'.[6] The problem with such productions is that they arise from a historical vacuum and are frequently characterised by a lack of 'balance'. An appropriate case in point was *Cops on the Box* (BBC, 1993). Despite the significance of its title, this anthology programme failed to make the distinction between the Scotland Yard detective, whose literary antecedents are well-known, and the ordinary 'cop' of the television originated police show.[7] What this indicates is not only a lack of content, but of historical *context*.

The problems which arise where there is an inadequate historiography set into place based upon primary evidence may be further illustrated by the normative account of the origins of the British police series itself. This, as previously mentioned, traces its genesis from the Ealing film *The Blue Lamp* (1950), written by Jan Read and Ted Willis, in which the 'Dixon' character, played by the well-known actor Jack Warner, arises, only to meet – by 1950s standards – a shocking demise. He is executed at point blank by a dangerously virile young Dirk Bogarde, in what has become a classic cinematic moment.[8] A salutary, if diversionary, example of the ways in which secondary sources following each other in unchecked error can achieve factual status is provided by the varying accounts of the timing of Dixon's death. He is not killed, as many critics have described it, only 20 minutes after the film's opening. As Charles Barr pointed out during the 1970s, 'in round figures, he is shot after 40 and dies after 45 minutes of an 80-minute film'.[9]

Dixon's weekly resurrection on the small silver screen during the programme's 21-year run between 1955 and 1976 meant that by the time Warner died, in 1979, character and individual had become virtually synonymous. Even after the actor's death, Dixon was kept alive by endless repeats, the moment of his demise constantly replayed on television, most notably after Sir Dirk Bogarde's death in 1999. One outcome of this common-sense account, which sees *The Blue Lamp* as the British television police series' sole point of origination, is that it has consolidated the idea that the genre is predicated upon film. With this in mind, *Beyond Dixon of Dock Green* offers a revisionist account of the British televison police series, suggesting that the relationship between film and television, and that within television itself, is of greater complexity than has previously been acknowledged. In so doing, it seeks to contribute to a scholarship that is now only beginning to establish televison history as an important subject in its own right.

In order to set out the issues, this introduction first provides a discussion and overview of existing British television scholarship, together with its short-comings and elisions, before moving into a discussion of general issues pertaining to the development of the British television police series. Subjects which form a central point of reference are included, such as the development of early video-recording technology (VTR), BBC Audience Research methods and the creation of new, modernist forms of documentary practice. It is these which television accepted from its film and radio predecessors and out of which BBC television's earliest popular fictions arose, including the police series. Finally, for clarity's sake, a chapter-by-chapter breakdown is provided.

Overview

As far back as the mid-1980s, Barr himself issued a specific plea for a thoroughgoing television scholarship, stating that 'between the blocks of dated raw material and the institutional and technological histories, bridges need to be built'.[10] While progress is being made with particular reference to 'serious drama', there continues to be the need for a satisfactory account of the development of British television's popular fictions. Part of the problem it that early British television studies tended to be organised through ideas of authorship, where the writer or dramatist was important. Critical method here was extrapolated from traditional literary and dramatic criticism, as in George Brandt's edited volume *British Television Drama* (1981).[11] During the 1980s, television studies, influenced by Stuart Hall's seminal article, 'Encoding/decoding in television discourse' (1973) moved the debate away from textual analysis to issues of audience reception. In the 1980s, John Fiske introduced Americans to the subject of British cultural studies with *Television Culture*, and his concept of 'the resistant spectator' opened up the possibility that, taken to its logical extremes, a text could mean almost whatever anyone wished it to mean.[12] The trajectory through the earliest audience and ethnographic studies began with David Morley's *The Nationwide Audience* (1987) and a feminist scholarship including Ien Ang's *Watching Dallas* (1985) and Christine Geraghty's *Women and Soap Opera* (1991). The turn to soap opera, a previously derided 'low' form, in contradistinction to the serious current affairs programme, emphasised the gender divide within television studies itself.[13]

In a 1984 *Screen* article, significantly titled 'Television Criticism: "A Discourse in Search of an Object"', John Caughie critiqued a television scholarship whose discursive theories tended to dissolve what may be constituted as its 'object' of enquiry; or rather, as he further implies, lets it slip between the cup of semiotic analysis and the lip of reception theories.[14] As Jerry Palmer has also observed, the problem is that such methods tend to be 'essentially static, or synchronic: genre is defined as such and such and the definition is thought to obtain in a certain number of cases whose distribution through time is non-relevant'.[15] This methodology, locked into a closed circuit of competing truth identities and paradigms, disallows intersecting economic and technological factors. According to structuralist precepts based upon a system of difference, a copshow is a copshow because it is not a soap opera. Such methods can only say *what* is there, they cannot say *why* it has come about.

Generic forms, such as the television police series, do not just arrive 'ready-made', they are historically contingent. Part of the reason for the delay in constructing a comprehensive history of television programmes is that whereas in the subject which we constitute as film studies, links have been forged between history on the one hand and theory on the other, in British television studies there has, until very recently, between the two disciplines. As John Corner and Sylvia Harvey emphasised during the mid-1990s, there needed to be some new thinking about television, for:

> When theoretical developments disconnect themselves entirely from enquiry into the historical and the particular, their ability both to yield explanatory models and to develop rapidly deconstructs.[16]

Today, British television studies is producing a new scholarship which is breaching this traditional divide, although there is still some way to go.

In what constitutes a brief overview of the *historical* scholarship that does exist on British television, and by way of breaching the history/theory divide, I have adapted James Chapman's differentiation between 'the old historians, the empiricists and the theorists, as applied to the Second World War'.[17] Of the 'old historians', Asa Briggs's monumental five-volume *History of Broadcasting in the United Kingdom* (1961–1995), Bernard Sendall's account *Independent Television in Britain* (1992), Cardiff and Scannell's *A Social History of British Broadcasting* (1991) and Curran and Seton's *Power Without Responsibility* (1998) offer the most thorough social and institutional histories of broadcasting to date.[18] Set against such established and 'official' television histories (Briggs's has been described in these terms), are those celebratory memoirs by practitioners and writers. These include such examples as Maurice Gorham's *Broadcasting and Television since 1900* (1952), Grace Wyndham Goldie's *Facing the Nation* (1977), Michael Barry's *From the Palace to the Grove* (1991) and Arthur Swinson's *Writing for Television* (1995). In terms of an empiricist television history, there has been some timely and exemplary work, including the *Oxford Television Studies* edited by Charlotte Brunsdon and John Caughie, combining historiographic with conceptual approaches. In particular, Caughie's *Television Drama* (2000) and Jason Jacobs' *The Intimate Screen*(2000) offer detailed, scholarly work on early television drama.[19]

The plea for a written history is at last being met by the new television scholarship, such as the *Oxford Television Studies*, which embraces both theory and empiricist history, thereby breaching the traditional divide. However, this scholarship tends to be angled towards what John Caughie, and others, characterise as 'serious' drama. Excellent as these studies are, their prioritisation of the single play is in danger of reviving the Leavisite values of early television studies. As Jason Jacobs has recently stated in *The Intimate Screen*, 'television drama is the form that is typically foregrounded, rightly or wrongly, as emblematic of the aesthetic state of the medium as a whole'.[20] While both Caughie and Jacobs discuss both series and *serial* production, they tend not only to treat these latter terms as interchangeable but also to elide them with the single play. Further, Jacobs sees the lack of any scholarship on series forms as connecting to their actual absence. In a footnote, he states that:

> what is missing in these early ideas about television is a notion of television's seriality: although early serials did exist, seriality was not a major characteristic of television before 1955.[21]

Although he is referring to dramatised forms here, it should be noted that seriality as such was a central component of all broadcasting media, whose very function was premised upon their constant updating. Television's *Picture Page* (1936), inherited from a radio magazine programme, provided an early template for iterative, collaboratively produced forms. In connection with the move away from discrete modes of production, as Raymond Williams has stated:

> until the coming of broadcasting the normal expectation was still of a discrete event or a succession of discrete events. People took a book or a pamphlet or a newspaper, went out to a play or a concert or a meeting or a match, with a single predominant expectation or attitude.[22]

In this context, television's serial nature is indicative of an entirely new mode of cultural practice, premised upon collaborative, mass-produced forms. It is these which have been seen in some way as threatening and have therefore been relegated as subjects for serious study. Yet it is these series and serial forms which are arguably the very stuff of television. As Stuart Hall has discussed, when writing during the early seventies, there has always been in television:

> a continuum or spectrum which impinges directly on the domain of culture. It seems to be a general rule that the more serious, 'high-brow' or 'high culture' in orientation the production is, the less it will be conceived *ex novo* for television – the more it will borrow from other media. The Shakespeare play will tend, on the whole, to be either a straight relay from the Stratford stage, or a production in studio which is subordinate in form, setting, acting technique, rhythm and staging to theatrical forms. The closer we get to the popular end of dramatic productions – popular plays, serials, series – the stronger will be the medium elements, the more distinct they will be from theatrical conventions.[23]

From this perspective, popular genre series, including the British television police series, are arguably more 'leading edge' than the single play and therefore at least as deserving of consideration.

Although a body of interdisciplinary scholarship has grown up around the British television police series, none looks closely at the context of its origins within television itself. In terms of sociological debate, there has been much written about the 'effects' of television violence.[24] The 1990s witnessed an increased consideration of the viewer's experience of televised crime and law enforcement, which led to concerns about disparities between the degree of fearfulness experienced and actual risk. Whilst there have been individual monographs on police series, such as Alan Clarke on *Dixon of Dock Green*, Stuart Laing on *Z Cars* and, most notably, an entire *Screen Education* issue devoted to *The Sweeney*, these anthologised chapters and articles tend towards a sociological point of view.[25] A notable exception is Jeffrey Richards' chapter, written from a cultural history perspective, in *Best of British* (1999), which persuasively argues that the British television police series' point of origin is to be found in *The Blue Lamp*.[26]

More generally on the British television series, there are several monographs on individual British series or genres, from John Tulloch and Manuel Alvarado's cultural studies-based *Doctor Who: The Unfolding Text* (1983) to James Chapman's *Saints and Avengers* (2002). Historical scholarship on the *origins* of popular British series forms is generally underdeveloped: either collapsed into 'serious' drama or elided with American development, as self-evidently displayed by David Buxton's otherwise exemplary *From the Avengers to Miami Vice: Form and ideology in television series* (1990).[27]

Whereas American series-drama during the late fifties and early sixties is defined by its film base, in Britain most dramatic output, including that of popular series drama, was premised upon live television. The different utilisation of technology, in both America and Britain, means that it is imperative that each country's television histories need to be studied separately before the construction of comparative accounts can occur: they just do not cross over from America so easily as is implied by present accounts. Whilst there was a period of 'live' television and a 'golden age' across both sides of the Atlantic, these developments were far from concurrent. In the USA, it lasted barely a half-decade and was famously exemplified by the anthology play series, including Paddy Chayevsky's influential *Marty* (1953).[28] However, the system of commercial sponsorship proved incompatible with the aims of US producers. Although *Marty*, the story about an ugly man finding love was morally worthy, advertisers saw it as lacking commercial potential. This factor, along with the acquisition of video-recording technology and the breaking of the previously-held embargo by the Hollywood film industry, led to the anthology play's abrupt demise – and with it, the era of live television.[29] By contrast, the period of live television in Britain was prolonged beyond the point of necessity: here, it was not film which first provided a means of recording the image, but the access to video-recording technology, developed in the USA.

These differences had to do with factors specific to each country. First and foremost was each country's very different relationship with the film industry. Hollywood was long aware that television could be extremely useful to advertise its own products via the television equivalent of the film-trailer. Philco was the first to produce series and then Warner Brs, who produced experimental runs based on old films and stock, including *Cheyenne* (1955). This series spun off endless lookalikes; some like *Gunsmoke* are still transmitting today either side of the Atlantic. TV films dominated from 1956 onward and Hollywood TV took over from live television practice centred upon New York. Its dominant form, the Western, was undoubtedly influential, of which the US police procedural may be considered an urban relocation.

In contrast to that of America, early British television had a far more uneasy relationship with the film industry, in particular, the actors' unions, which were at least partly responsible for its late access to video-recording technology.

The ability to record programmes on video, when the technology arrived, did not solve the problem. Because of a lack of space, videotapes were constantly re-used. In addition, there was no coherent archiving policy, as has been well documented by Steve Bryant.[30] Film, of course, had been used by British television from the start, in particular in newsreels and outside broadcasts (OBs). However, it was not used in programmes of entertainment, mainly because of the need to recoup costs from the expensively re-equipped television studios, symbolically acquired from the film industry (Pinewood, 1949; Ealing, 1955). This factor alone is suggestive of the way in which the film industry felt threatened by the new medium of television, such that it put up obstacles in its path. In terms of programmes, since there was no BBC film unit in existence until 1953, the first ever British-made film series, *Fabian of the Yard* (1954), starring Bruce Seton, was shot by Trinity Productions, an outside film company, and consisted of 39 black-and-white, 30-minute episodes. It was syndicated to the USA and may be seen, in cultural and economic terms, as reciprocating the 12-part American import, *I Am The Law*, transmitted during the same year, thereby initiating a process of international exchange.

The use of filmed inserts, although widely used within British television drama was hotly debated, because, the electronic image was deemed more 'pure'. However they were vital in introducing extra-diegetic space particularly in the British television police series which aimed in aesthetic terms to reproduce the effects of film, within the television studio. They also acted as a cover, like 'the wings' in theatre, allowing space and time for the actors to change costumes, and for scenery and light changes. Peter Nichols' gives some idea of 'those prehistoric days' with his recollections of working on *Pilgrim Street* (1952):

> For a few months in the Fifties I played a constable in an early precursor of *The Bill*, repeated a few nights later, which meant we all schlepped back to Lime Grove Studios and did the show again, dashing from set to set, changing costumes on the way.[31]

Here, the connection between *The Bill* and its ancestor, *Pilgrim Street*, is made by a first-hand witness of television's early constraints, imposed by the very conditions of its 'liveness'.[32]

Video-recording technology

The ability to record a television signal electronically rather than photographically was first demonstrated in 1951 in the USA, when the Electronic Division of Bing Crosby Enterprises developed the first black-and-white video-recorder, itself as cumbersome as the earliest computers. However, it was highly advantageous because the performance could be replayed instantly and recorded over and used again: it also took the television product outside the tyranny of the schedule, especially important in the USA where time-zones were being crossed. A new method, developed by Ampex, also in the US involved a cylindrical head which took up far less space. It was this model that was eventually adopted in the UK, although British television did not use videotape until 1958 when Richard Dimbleby demonstrated an early model of Vision Electronic Recording Apparatus, named VERA, by the cunning expedient of a clock on *Panorama*.[33] The BBC's desire to educate its audience, with regard to technological developments, is absolutely in line with its public service remit. It was also part of an ideology in which the corporation always sought to declare the truth status of its productions.

Editing videotape initially was problematic: it could not be cut like film, so it was used – often in conjunction with live performances – simply as a backup. However, it was soon realised that video-recording technology enabled a way of controlling the schedule, for it allowed programmes to be made before transmission. This method of video-recording followed the 'live' performance, cueing in filmed inserts, as previously, via telecine. Because it so closely followed the original studio performance, this mode of transmission was known as broadcast 'as if' live.

An agreement with the actors' unions meant there was a four-week gap between original transmission and recorded repeat, repeat fees equalling 100 per cent of the performance fee, provided it took place within the first month. Finally, telerecordings were made, but only of repeat performances. For example a recording of the Thursday night repeat of a Sunday play would guarantee actors the equivalent of two paid performances, an important con-sideration in remunerative terms (actors being paid for each performance). All this was to change with the arrival of Independent Television, 1955), but even when the restrictive practices of the unions disappeared, dramatised series such as *Z Cars* (1962) continued to be transmitted 'live'. As Caughie has argued, this practice was because dramatists and producers clung to a belief in the efficacy of 'live' production, and thereby preserved it as 'effect' long after the necessity for doing so had passed.

Another reason why popular forms such as the soap opera and series did not occur in British television until as late as the fifties was that a clearly defined public service remit sought to define the new medium's practices away from what were held to be 'low' cultural forms. This occurred just when American television production, contingent upon sponsorship, was embracing commercialism. Despite an animus against what neo-Reithians saw as populist or 'tabloid' tendencies, producers were determined to experiment – often against the wishes of their superiors – with television's potential as a story-telling medium. It was, therefore, no accident that the British television police series, along with other forms of institutionally based or derived series, hospital and legal dramas for example, emerged from a pivotal form of modernist practice. This was the so-called television 'story' or 'drama-documentary' programme, an adopted but radically *adapted* form of the public service film.

As John Ellis has argued, commercial entertainment cinema today is a *narrative* fiction medium. This holds true for both America and Britain. Each country – as does Europe – carries large amounts of non-fiction such as news, documentaries, announcements and weather forecasts. As he further discusses, any model of televisual narration would have to give pride of place to the division of TV products, between fiction and non-fiction. However, this hasn't quite happened in the UK, where a new relationship between fiction and non-fiction is subjected to ongoing analysis.[34]

Shifting truths: the story-documentary

The prototype for the television version of the story-documentary – from which the British television police series grew – was inherited from its predecessors during a pre-television period, first by BBC radio-features and subsequently by a sponsored form of documentary film practice.[35] In a key *Screen* article, entitled 'Progressive Television and Documentary Drama', John Caughie, addressing the so-called 'drama-documentary debate', asserted that the 'formula' of mixing fact with fiction is not new. He connected this development to:

> an important cinematic antecedent … found in the various ideologies and practices which were circulating in the documentary movement in the 1930s and 1940s … from *Fires were Started* to Ralph Bond and the Co-operative Society films.[36]

What Caughie first identifies here is not just the advent of the documentary movement, problems associated with the 'ideologies and practices' of a modernist innovation that Hayden White, in 'The Modernist Event', calls 'a founding presupposition of Western realism': namely, 'the opposition between fact and fiction'. The 'marriage' of the feature film with documentary and the subsequent transformation of the British film during the wartime years has been much discussed.[37] Public service films, such as Harry Watt's *Target for Tonight* (1941), about the airforce, were exemplary in bringing new techniques which incorporated story-telling techniques, whilst also retaining some aspects of documentary practice. It was the application of new, up-to-the-minute original documentary subjects, rather than those of literary derivation, which made these fact/fiction cultural productions so novel. Arthur Swinson has usefully taxonomised the television documentary as possessing three categories: the dramatised documentary, the magazine documentary and the actuality documentary.[38] The dramatised or story-documentary accepted from film practice was by far the most important category in terms of establishing new forms of self-originated, series-produced drama for television.

To return to the 'realist problem', in terms of describing the considerable historical impact of documentary techniques, and associated issues of modernism, Ellis' conceptualisation of 'Witness' is extremely useful. Witness, he describes, as 'a new modality of perception', one which implicates the viewer via a 'quasi-physical documentation of specific moments in specific places'.[39] In this statement, we are reminded of various remarks about documentary as a new lingua franca, like print, or later television. As Ellis himself states, this formulation shifts the debate away from the knotty issues of realism which:

> conflate questions of mechanical reproduction: (as in 'the camera doesn't lie') with questions of the adequacy of the representation (as in '*Apocalypse Now* is more realistic than *The Green Berets*') and questions of verisimilitude (as in 'Stephen Fry looks just like Oscar Wilde').[40]

Such claims can be conflicting and reductionist, in terms of rendering realism down to an ethical category whereby it is judged by its 'truth' status (the closer it is to the referent the more 'real' it is). They also ignore factors of determination in terms of audience composition, and reception contexts.

Ellis' perception, informed by William Urrichio, of the way in which cinema's particular relationship to Witness anticipates the desire for simultaneity *realised* by television, is extraordinarily prophetic:

> Both cinema's difficulties and its strengths come from its special inadequacy in relation to a desire for witness which it had itself stimulated, and which had called it into existence. … 'a look at broader cultural practices, at the telephone, at ideas sparked by electricity, at fantasies of the new media, all suggest that *simultaneity* stood as a powerful anticipation which film could

stimulate but never deliver. And there is reason to believe that film audiences understood these limits.' [my italics][41]

It was television, with its ability to 'see it now', which realised the 'desire' for instaneity, that cinema, being a recorded medium, could not. Because of its immediacy aesthetic, documentary informed most of television's proto-generic output. Indeed, it was the story-documentary which negotiated the spectrum between factual and fictional forms. As Caughie himself identifies, these forms included diverse topics 'on Scotland Yard, on bankruptcy, on the town vet, on a doctor struck off the medical list, or the immigration service'.[42] They constituted the earliest prototypes of the particular form of critical realism which was to inform both popular series fiction, and the single play. Just as in the public service war films, television story-documentaries focused upon ordinary people and, once more, like their predecessor the documentary feature, became absorbed into the mainstream, in what can be seen as amounting to a second phase of documentary assimilation. From correspondence on file at the BBC Written Archive, it is evident that BBC story-documentarists were indeed aware that they were pioneers of a new hybrid. By comparison to theatre which was still, according to this view, confined to the middle-class drawing room, the television story-documentary depicted:

> police, welfare workers, neglected children, alcoholics and marriage problems and created a school of writers who were beginning to write realistically about society (admittedly from the viewpoint of Us looking at Them) while the curtains were still rising on French windows and butlers answering telephones.[43]

Most importantly these forms, unlike the valorised single play, were *allowed* to be technologically innovative. Their increased use of film inserts freed up the medium from its dependency upon studio sets, as well as introducing contemporary themes. Yet despite being 'television's most important contribution to serious entertainment', the forms had a short life, 'vanishing altogether at the end of 1962'.[44] The reason they did so was that, just as in the case of their radio and film forbears, story-documentaries, as previously indicated, became absorbed both into the mainstream, and in particular, into the institutional series, including the copshow, their innovative, radical qualities transferring into the single play.

Not only does the British television police series participate in these debates, it is also implicated in one about national and regional identity. For, as this book also traces, whilst the earliest versions were London-centred, there was a move north associated with that simultaneously developing in film. This was connected to notions of a critical new realism and, as *Beyond Dixon of Dock Green* argues, this trajectory was arguably anticipated by drama-documentaries.

Methods and contexts of audience research

In endeavouring to provide my own contribution to a written television historiography, I have first of all had to decide what kind of history I should endeavour to write; should it be conceptual or empiricist? As I have already indicated, I discovered how difficult it seemed in British television studies to marry the two approaches. As Harvey and Corner state:

> In the future, thinking about television will need to keep up a dialogue with 'lower' level analysis. It will need to be more explicit about its precise aims than it has often been in the past, and it will also need to be clearer; the sheer obscurity of much theoretical writing on television has put off many readers.[45]

What I want to do in this book is to situate my own study both at a 'lower' or micro-level, engaging with empiricist methodology at the same time as building-out from some of the work that has been done in conceptual terms.

Whilst my book discusses technology, looking at technological change with regard to both television and its predecessors, it is not a work about technology as such. I shall nonetheless, at appropriate points, be referring to key developments in this respect. Similarly, although it analyses programmes in some detail where they exist, it does not set out to be about textual analysis. However, where apposite, I shall examine programme content, picking out ideological themes and stylistics, especially where these are seen to articulate wider cultural processes, such as the hegemony of the BBC's public service remit during the immediate post-war period. The approach can best be defined as endeavouring to situate the discussion concerning the nascence of the uniform police series within its social, cultural and institutional conditions of production, as well as those of its reception. Once again, the balance of these will be weighted according to individual need, as they arise, rather than meted out to a regular formula. Finally, since my book is concerned with 'beginnings' it does not seek to follow any one series across its vicissitudes, so much as to trace its emergence.

What has informed my work most of all is the concept of 'genealogy', which has become dominant over the more commonly used trope of 'archaeology'. Douglas Couzens Hoy deciphers the difference between the two terms by stating that:

Unlike archaeology, which avoids casual explanation of social change by restricting itself instead to the identification of self-contained discourses demarcated by abrupt discontinuities, genealogy can pay attention to gradual, continuous processes of social change. Genealogy charts the emergence and growth of social institutions as well as the social-scientific techniques and disciplines that reinforce specific social practices.[46]

Of course, as Foucault has warned, there are difficulties in writing genealogies. It is all too easy to make assumptions of intentionality, so as 'to discover already at work in each beginning, a principle of coherence and the line of future unity'.[47] I do not therefore want to base my approach on a 'Rise of the Police Series' trajectory, as if its formation outlined in the rock-face, is ready and waiting to be liberated by earnest scholars. Nonetheless, the archaeological metaphor is not without significance. Caughie, for example, has stated that it is the potsherds and fragments which – in the absence of recorded material – become crucial to the endeavour.[48] In these terms, the BBC Written Archive at Caversham Park, Reading, is a veritable treasure trove. It includes written material on programme and policy documents, as well as details on 'programmes as broadcast' in the form of annotated scripts and Audience Research Reports. All these helped enormously in the process of constructing an object where there was no recorded programme. Other primary sources I have consulted include programme information and editorial discussion from the *Radio Times*, the *Listener*, *BBC Quarterly* and *Sight and Sound* from the 1940s, 1950s and 1960s.

Audience research

Since I draw on Audience Reports held at the Written Archive in Caversham it is necessary to discuss the way in which these relate to the BBC's earliest attempts at discovering the hitherto 'nameless aggregates' which comprised its listening and viewing public. In order to clarify my approach here, as well as the appearance of Audience Research material throughout the book, it is worth offering a preliminary discussion of the background history of BBC Audience Research.

Because television was merely a department of the BBC until 1950, little thought was given to considerations of its audience. Early audience research was conducted in an amateur fashion through the correspondence columns of the *Radio Times*. Val Gielgud, whilst still an assistant on the magazine – he was to become Head of BBC Radio Drama in 1950 – voiced a dissenting opinion when he complained after a meeting of the Programme Board (1939) that 'a very great deal of our money and time and effort may be expended on broadcasting into a void'.[49] A popularity poll conducted in 1939 placed Drama in front of Sport and only slightly behind Variety. In the Autumn of 1948, after post-war television's third year of resumption, the BBC initiated its first inquiry into the nature of the television public and the impact of the new medium upon its leisure habits. One thousand randomly selected television households were chosen. Details were taken of the age and nature of the TV set owned by the family concerned, together with the family's socio-economic status, its size and predominant gender. Special log books were supplied in which each evening's viewing activities were to be recorded. The final Report and Enquiry revealed that television was not 'a rich man's toy'. More than half the homes with television sets were found to be lower-middle, or working class. Furthermore, there was evidence to suggest that television was spreading downwards through the social pyramid. Thus, whereas 57 per cent of those families which possessed TV sets when the Television Service was resumed in 1946 were well-to-do or upper-middle class and the remaining 43 per cent lower-middle or working class, the corresponding proportions of 1948 buyers were 39 per cent and 61 per cent.[50]

Stephen Tallents, Controller of Public Relations (1935) had earlier advocated the setting up of a Consumers' Council to guide the policy of BBC programmes. As Asa Briggs argues, this was just what Reith and his cohort did not want. The *Yorkshire Post* (10 July 1935) wrote:

> The BBC ought never to be too anxious to please the public at all costs. The promoter of entertainment who tries slavishly to follow public taste is always left behind.[51]

Undaunted, Tallents submitted a paper to the General Advisory Council of the BBC in January 1936, entitled 'Listener Research'.[52]

The Broadcasting Committee of 1951 shows a demonstrable shift from such reactionary post-Reithian attitudes when it states that 'Broadcasting without a study of the audience is dull dictation'.[53] Its main announcement carries details of a new Audience Research Department which is 'to provide the BBC with all manner of information about its public'. Describing the function of the Audience Research Department as running 'a continuous Survey of Listening and Viewing', it observes:

> Every day, BBC interviewers scattered all over the United Kingdom question some 2,800 people, a sample or cross section of the public, asking them

what broadcasts they listened to or viewed on the previous day. The results of each's interviewing reach the Department in the form of 2,800 log sheets, each the record of a completed interview.[54]

The report goes on to describes the work of the Listening and Viewing Panels which give information about public opinion concerning specific broadcasts. Extrapolating from a count made with the 'aid of mechanical devices ... thanks to the laws of sampling', it goes on to state that the results can be applied to the population as a whole.

Whilst the Listening Panel comprised about 4,200 listeners, the Viewing Panel consisted of a mere 600 families with television sets. All volunteers expressed willingness to answer questions about broadcasts they normally hear or see. They were drawn from all parts of the country, and every effort was made to see that all shades of opinion and levels of brow were represented. Questionnaires were sent to panel members on a weekly basis relating to a wide variety of forthcoming broadcasts. All the answers on the completed questionnaires about a broadcast were tabulated, analysed, and summarised in an Audience Research Report which aimed to give a fair and balanced picture of Panel members' views. In 1955 about 60 sound programmes and every television item was covered each week by the Panel method. Finally, Audience Research findings were considered in conjunction with other factors, such as critical professional judgement, the exercises of taste, and conformity to the Corporation's conception of its responsibilities under the Charter.[55]

Since my book traces the genealogy of a specific genre, I must fully identify and try to place it in context with other identifiable programme cycles. First and foremost, the British television police series is a self-originating genre, distinguished from *literary* adaptations of earlier published texts, such as Conan Doyle's Sherlock Holmes series. There is a proliferation of 'heritage' detective series whose roots derive from the golden-age detective novel; productions like *Poirot*, *The Wexford Files* and *Miss Marple*, which seem as nostalgic today as Basil Rathbone's portrayal of Sherlock Holmes was to the previous generation. Second, the British television police series is also differentiated from the dramatised memoirs of living ex-police officers, usually featuring the figure of the élite Scotland Yard detective, for example the filmed series *Fabian of the Yard* (1954) or the made-for-television *Course of Justice* (1951) series by Robert Barr. Both these procedural type programmes were based on real crimes, or stories from the police files centred upon Scotland Yard.

As Jason Jacobs has noted, the very first representations of Scotland Yard seem to begin with a series of 15-minute dramatisations called 'Telecrimes', where a Scotland Yard inspector would introduce true crimes from the casebook. The 'Scotland Yard' genre continued a month later with a production of *The Murder Rap*, described as a 'full-blooded Scotland Yard piece'.[56] In June 1947, Robert Barr produced *Armed Robbery*, a reconstruction from a real-life Scotland Yard arrest. Notable later examples include the 13-part series *Scotland Yard* (BBC, 1960). Such productions contain documentary realism, in that they are concerned to show a degree of procedural activity, but are not yet concerned with the ambiguities of day-to-day police procedure.

The British television police series emerged from, and defined itself against the Scotland Yard genre, in terms of featuring uniformed officers, and depicting non-serious crime (although increasingly, plain-clothes, CID officers and uniformed men feature together, as in *Z Cars* and *Softly, Softly*). It was similarly derived from scripts written specifically for television claimed as 'real' but often loosely based on sources from authentic police files (*Pilgrim Street, Dixon of Dock Green*). All these programmes about the institution of the police connect closely to the public service films of the documentary movement in showing the minutiae and paperwork of everyday police procedure.[57]

On a more general note regarding the origins of terms relating to 'the referent', the real-life British police force, it is well-known that the sobriquet 'bobby' connotes the ordinary Police Constable (PC) and derives from the name of Sir Robert Peel, who established today's modern police force in 1829 in the face of protracted and widespread opposition. As Robert Reiner remarks, whilst the middle and upper classes had little experience of 'the plague of blue locusts', their machinations were far more likely to regulate the lives of the working class, who held 'more negative attitudes towards them'. The forces expanded from the Metropolitan heartland established by Peel in 1829 to encompass the whole of England and Wales and gradually, if unevenly, began to cultivate increasing public consent and support.[58] Of especial interest here is that the terms 'Jacks', 'Knaves', 'The Bill' and 'Copper' are, in fact, all *regional* variants. Prior to the advent of the Second World War, policemen, along with servants and the working classes, tended to be portrayed as stereotypical figures of fun. If the police were represented at all, it was the glamorous crime-busting detective or superior Scotland Yard detective. In no other country at any other time has the ordinary beat-pounding patrol officer been seen as a national hero. The enormous influence and popularity of the Dixon character speaks volumes about the peculiarity of the English veneration of their police in what is often described as the 'Golden Age' of policing.[59]

Beyond Dixon of Dock Green, as its title implies, is concerned not only with early television, but with a pre-television period and that 'beyond' the early period which I designate the professional period, for reasons which will shortly be discussed. In terms of the first, because television accepts from its film and radio predecessors their techniques and modes of address, especially that of documentary practice, it is necessary to examine these main influences both during a pre-television period and at a time when television itself was off the air. According to Jason Jacobs' study, the era of early television is seen to run between 1946 and 1955: this periodisation fits the present study. As Jacobs quite rightly states, 'it is important not to collapse early and transitional periods together, just as much as it is vital to recognise the various continuities they share'. Nonetheless I designate the subsequent period, running from 1955 to 1966 – being that which spans the so-called 'Golden Age' – the era of Professional Television.[60] I have done so for two main reasons. First, it was during this era that the BBC moved away from what Caughie has aptly described as its 'wizard prang' amateur efforts, towards a more industrialised process, one impelled by the arrival of independent television.[61] Second, the period coincides with one in which the police themselves took on a more professional public relations role, being keen to collaborate with television producers. That the 'Golden Age' of policing so nearly coincided with the 'Golden Age'of television may be another reason why the advertisement used by the Police Federation against the Sheehey report resonates so strongly: a case of serendipity.

So as to more easily situate the reader, I have set out the book below, chapter by chapter. In addition there are two appendices, the second in three parts. Appendix 1 gives details of the Bibliography. Appendix 2a consists of a chronology of the story-documentary. Appendix 2b provides an alphabetical list of the police programmes themselves, restricting transmission details to their first two or three seasons (further published as broadcast details (psb's) are available at the BBC Written Archive at Caversham).

Chapter by chapter

In the interests of setting out what constitutes a pre-history of the British television police series, Chapter One, **Telling stories of the realm**, traces the British police series' origins in the public service films and radio documentaries produced between the two wars and during the Second World War, when television itself was off the air. Central to this discussion was both the 'documentary idea' and the creation of a powerful new consensual audio-visual discourse whose articulation of new story-telling forms came to prominence during the Second World War, for purposes of both propaganda and morale. New forms of narrativised documentaries on the one hand, such as *Target for Tonight* (1941) on the one hand and documentary-features, including the later but appropriate example of *The Blue Lamp* (1950), on the other, represented a first phase process of documentary assimilation: one which was to be accepted and reinvented by television during the post-war period.

Chapter Two, **New forms for old**, traces the vicissitudes of the television story-documentary and its articulation within the small BBC Documentary Unit, consecutively under Robert Barr (1947) until his departure in 1953, when documentary filmmaker Paul Rotha was appointed Head of a newly promoted Television Documentary Department. During the post-war period, the consensus ideology employed to win the propaganda war became redeployed in the interests of winning the peace. Although television's earliest perception was as a mediator, encapsulated by the phrase 'we bring you live pictures', television documentarists – often against the wishes of the authorities – quickly began experimenting with innovative dramatised forms of entertainment, produced in series formats. Central to this development was the nascent British television police series. The chapter traces its emergence from the earliest 'Scotland Yard' narratives, in monthly programmes such as *War on Crime* (1950), through *I Made News* (1951), which introduced the weekly 'strike' (a stage-derived name taken from striking the set) to *Pilgrim Street* (1952), the first ever series featuring the ordinary, uniformed police officer. It describes the way in which a Reithian version of 'public service culture', as broadcast by radio and television, folds into post war television.

Entertaining Lightly: *Fabian of the Yard* **to** *Dixon of Dock Green*, the third chapter, traces the accession of the foundational *Dixon of Dock Green* series (1955–1976), within the context of BBC Television Light Entertainment, whose aims were self-evidently different to those of the small Documentary Department. Yet, as will become apparent, this department was also concerned to develop new forms that would not only entertain, but also fit in with post-war consensus values. It was *Dixon of Dock Green* which began the process of achieving cachet for the Light Entertainment programme, with its judicious mix of public service and entertainment values. Far from breeding contempt, it was discovered that the familiarity of a repetitive formula, with its familial ethics and interpellatory mode of address, helped establish a new sense of community and nationhood within the private space of the home. This chapter analyses the emergence of this central programme within the context of Light Entertainment generally.

Chapter Four, **Jacks, Knaves and the 'other' north**, looks at the reformulation of the Documentary Department under BBC Drama and the aegis of Michael Barry until the arrival of Sydney Newman in 1962. The period is characterised by a new *zeitgeist*, influenced by the Suez crisis, the advent of the teenager and an orchestrated rebellion by the 'angry young men', whose ire manifested itself in narratives projecting a critical new realism. Colin Morris and Gilchrist Calders' dramatisations in *Tearaway* and *Who, Me?* are examined both in relation to their influence, not only upon the British police series and the construction of the Northern policier realised in *Z Cars*, but also in terms of the single play, in particular Ken Loach's *Cathy Come Home* (1966). *Jacks and Knaves*, the four-part series which builds out from the two single productions of *Tearaway* and *Who, Me?*, is innovative both in its introduction of humour and its new series format. Meanwhile, 'back at The Met', *Scotland Yard* (1960) the 13-parter, sometimes considered *Z Cars*' most immediate predecessor in terms of its demonstrating new police technology, provides a point of comparison from a Southern, and more elitist viewpoint.

Chapter Five, calling '**Z Vctr 1**' and '**Z Vctr 2**' discusses how *Z Cars*' first season brings the trajectory of the story-documentary's dramatisation and series production to full fruition. In many ways, *Z Cars* was a documentary return, produced by 'the remnants' of the old Documentary Department, now under the aegis of BBC Drama (Series). *Z Cars*' committed form of social realism represented a departure from its famous predecessor, *Dixon of Dock Green*. Its re-location was indicative of how documentary drama became fully integrated into mainstream television. In the very first episode, 'Four of a Kind', we meet its two protagonists, the irascible John Barlow and his sidekick Frank Watt who are stalking each other in a graveyard scene following the death on duty of one, Reggie Farrow, a 'Dixon' type of beat policeman.

However, the inhabitants of the modern new, eponymous cars are no angels but, after all the fuss has died down, seem to be near normal 'lads'. However, *Z Cars*' authenticity was found offensive by those it claimed to represent. Once more, the chapter examines the discrepancy in terms of the programme's local and national reception. It also looks at the methods of writers and directors in obtaining their documentary effects, at the same time examining why the series form itself seemed to prohibit development. Associated with this was the so-called 'Naturalist Debate' about the destination of television drama in which, as the chapter further investigates, *Z Cars*' producers were implicated.

The final chapter, **Softly, Softly, back-pedalling south**, discusses *Softly, Softly* (1966) in its context as British television's first 'spin-off', and the way it revives Southern values, symbolically despatching those associated with Northerness, both by its geographical relocation south and the 'softening' of Barlow, the irascible central protagonist who, together with Watt, crosses over from *Z Cars*. In particular, it examines the way in which the critical new realism which emerged from within the Documentary Department and found its 'moment' in *Z Cars*, moves across from series formats to the single play. This shift is exemplified by Ken Loach's *Cathy Come Home*, produced the same year as *Softly, Softly*. *Softly, Softly*'s spin-off status, is an indicator of the more commercial television values within British television. Nowhere is this more evidently deciphered than in the trajectory of the British television police series which monitors 'a thin blue line', not only between the state and commerce, but also between fact and fiction, North and South, collaborative and individual processes.

1. Percy Grainger, the Lord Mayor's coachman, being interviewed for the magazine programme *Picture Page*, on the evening of Television's official opening day (1936).

1

Telling stories of the realm

This is an Age of News, all over the world they seem to be
turning from Fiction to Fact.

StephenTallents[1]

British television opened, if the words of Adele Dixon's song in the opening
programme are at all representative, on 2 November 1936, 'in a mighty
maze of mystic rays all about us of blue'.[2] The rhyming phrase nicely conjures
up the modernist ambience which surrounded the new medium's accession.
Despite its auspicious start, television, an offshoot of BBC sound broadcasting,
was ended only three years after it began. On 1 September 1939, the eve of
the Second World War, it was unceremoniously shut down, halfway through a
Micky Mouse cartoon.[3] Unlike the cinemas, which were also closed but
quickly re-opened, television remained silent for the duration. Since its
outreach was limited to London and its technology experimental, 'radio-vision'
had some way to go in achieving its own, self-defining characteristics. Because
of television's early perception as a 'live' medium, documentary formed the
spine of much of its output. Indeed, it was in television that John Grierson,
'Father of the British Documentary Movement', saw documentary's final
destination.

In order to substantiate the claim that new forms of post-war popular
television – including the British television police series – were closely related
to those documentary forms developed earlier by film and radio, the main
thrust of this first chapter is to offer a revisionist reassessment of the 'documentary idea'. It examines the documentary achievement not so much in
establishing, in the words of that famous documentary exponent Paul Rotha,
'a truly British cinema', as in its contribution to new, non-*literary* narrative
forms. It was these, developed earlier by documentary practitioners, which
television was to adapt and extend when it resumed after the end of the Second
World War (1946).

The hybridity of television was therefore related to, and accepted from, a conflation of discourses which took place across an extended era. For the purposes of convenience, my first chapter analyses this development across two consecutive periods, that between the Great Wars (1918–1939) and during the Second World War itself (1939–1945). Whereas the inter-war period, as we will see, projects a version of broadcasting which strictly demarcated class divisions, the Second World War brings about a far wider consensus. The more inclusive definition – that of a common culture[4] – is advanced by a process of collaboration within and across the media, often through apparently oppositional cultural discourses: progressive versus reactionary; entertainment versus education; popular and elite.[5] Taking into account this increasing confluence, this chapter further examines the role of what can be construed as a culture of public service, in homogenising disparate discourses. In particular it looks at how a strengthening audio-visual discourse begins to develop its own calendrical function, through the introduction of regular slots such as the News.

The documentary film's gradual assimilation into the mainstream was a crucial development in the process of developing forms that were highly original based upon, or featuring, living characters, either in the sense of 'the real', as in the story-documentary *Target for Tonight* (1941), or dramatised, as in the feature-documentary, *In Which We Serve* (1942). To some critics these productions caused discomfort: they seemed not quite 'fact', nor yet fully 'fiction'. Nonetheless, it was the very ambiguity of story-documentaries and documentary-features which enabled a new dramatic space, thereby allowing a far wider range of narrative possibilities than previously. Further-more, the iterative, series forms of television dramatised documentaries were also, arguably, developed by sound broadcasting across the same period. A secondary aim of this chapter, therefore, is to examine the way in which what constituted a total system of sound and vision began to develop its own chronotope in which radio – and later television – was absorbed into the texture of everyday life.

In the making of a British audio-visual culture, there was, from the first, the strongest demarcation between commercial interests and those of the state. The pull towards political and social consensus was reinforced during the 1920s and 1930s by the threat of hunger marches, strikes, and 'red united fronts', protesting against the effects of the Depression. A pro-monarchical and pro-imperial discourse, promulgated by the BBC Empire Service (1933), by the BBC itself and, to a certain extent, by the British Documentary Movement, kept dissent at bay.[6] Fears of a form of internal colonisation,

American cultural imperialism, also kept the potentially rampant forces of commerce in check. Cultural leaders feared the social consequences of what they saw as a debased and pervasively transatlantic form of culture. As one contemporary observer wrote in the *Radio Times*:

> The American invasion of the entertainment world is responsible for many things, for changes of taste, for the blunting of dialect ... for new manners of thinking, for higher pressure of living, for discontent among normally contented people, for big ideas, and for 'Oh yeah!'.[7]

In these terms at least, the project owed its success at being perceived by critics like Rotha as a counteractive to Hollywood's 'dream machine'. Despite documentarists' initial posturing about the need to 'show the other half' – the unrepresented ordinary working people – documentary's potential to promote the state was quickly realised. However, it soon became evident that the 'classic' documentary film with its voice-over narrative and montage techniques, whilst fascinating a few aesthetes, could not hold the public imagination in the same way as did the feature film. A growing awareness arose that, in order to render the Government's 'message' palatable, it was necessary to borrow techniques from mainstream entertainment. At the same time, regularised sound broadcasting formats and routinised procedures were key to an emergent broadcasting schedule, as was the introduction of the radio personality. Influences from music hall gave rise to repetitive comedic forms, from Arthur Askey's sketches in *Band Waggon* to *ITMA* reached their full potential during the Second World War. Finally, those great Lancashire stars, JB Priestley and Gracie Fields, instituted a new tradition of 'the personality'. This chapter follows the trajectory by which, across the two consecutive periods under consideration, a new, democratised image of the public sphere came into being, one which represented the interests of 'ordinary' people.

Performing the public sphere

In order to trace the vicissitudes across which the new public realm was mediated, it is important to note an institutional juxtaposition: that of the British Broadcasting Corporation (BBC) and the General Post Office (GPO). This came to be an allegiance cemented by the common interests of Sir John Reith (later Lord Reith), first Director General of the BBC (1927), Sir Stephen Tallents – consecutively Director of the Film Unit at the Empire Marketing Board (EMB, 1927) and GPO (1933) – and John Grierson. All three leaders were bound together by their antipathy towards commerce and their belief in the State as the best means by which to serve the public interest. A hierarchy of taste cultures underwrote the BBC's three-tiered public service remit of 'information', 'education' and 'entertainment', with the latter being seen as third and last.[8] The ideas of nineteenth-century educationist and poet, Matthew Arnold, assimilated to Reithian practices in terms of reproducing 'the best that has been thought and written in the world'.[9] However, at the same time as espouring such traditional precepts, it was necessary to look forward for it was indisputably an age of The New. As Tallents, then First Press Officer of the BBC, was to state after reaching agreement with the press to extend the BBC's News broadcasting hours where his predecessor had failed, it was also an 'age of News'.[10]

Reith and Grierson have frequently been compared as cultural leaders. Apart from their Christian names and Scottishness, they had much in common. Both were prolific self-publicists. In creating 'the performative' space of a new, public sphere of information, this trio of key players were of fundamental importance. Grierson, writing in new journals such as *Cinema Quarterly* (1932), *World Film News* (1936) and *Documentary Newsletter* (1940), addressed a narrow critical margin and stressed the educational and instructional potential of the documentary film. From the first, Tallents, that 'remarkable public servant', was aware of the public relations potential of documentary, putting it to work first at the EMB, and subsequently at the GPO. Whereas Grierson and Reith both strongly denounced any notion of the box office as a determining standard of value, it was Tallents who realised that it was no use preaching to an empty church. A pivotal figure, migrating between the BBC and the British Documentary movement, Tallents was concerned to 'entertain', in both senses of that word, the previously neglected notion of 'the audience'.[11] Tallents' introduction of the new-fangled public relations concept was to add another dimension to the key discourses of public service and public information. So far as documentary practitioners on the left were concerned, this was to prove something of an unholy alliance.

Both the British Documentary Movement and the BBC aspired to similar notions of public responsibility in terms of constructing a public realm. As Lord Reith stated of the latter, 'The BBC had founded a tradition of *public service* and devotion to the highest interest of community of nation'.[12] Reith's notion of public service broadcasting, in line with the times, was one of cultural improvement. He famously specified:

> It is occasionally indicated to us that we are apparently setting out to give the public what we think they need – and not what they want, but few know what they want, and very few what they need.[13]

This high-handed attitude needs to be understood in its historical context during a time when working-class children left school at 14 and 'those temples of high art', the concert halls, opera houses and theatres, were beyond the reach of ordinary people.[14] It is also important to remember that, as critics have discussed, the history of public service differs from that of public information.[15]

Whereas the concept of public service has traditionally been linked to the reproduction of 'high culture', that of public information was more closely associated with the history of news production and the creation of the public sphere as defined by Jurgens Habermas, in relation to the nineteenth-century printing press.[16] Reith was always aware of broadcasting's potential as a purveyor of public information, and how, if it continued to be curbed by an anxious press, it could never be fully realised.

Nonetheless Reith's conceptualisation of the democratic process was somewhat different from Grierson's messianic project, influenced by the ideas of Walter Lippman, which he had studied during his post-graduate career in the US.[17] The BBC's first Director General's notion of bringing mass enlightenment has frequently been criticised for attempting to 'level up the masses'.[18] It was arguably the case that it was as much to gain legitimation for sound broadcasting's news potential that Reith instituted the BBC's (in)famous 'arts and music' programme as for its own sake. Following its transition from company to corporation, the BBC's first outside broadcast feature (OB) was notably not that of a popular sporting event, as might have been expected given the excitement about radio's new technology, but a live performance of Mozart's *The Magic Flute* (1927).[19]

So far as radio arts were concerned, the culturally respectable West End play was indeed 'the thing'. Asa Briggs states that during the 1920s the BBC sponsored over a hundred theatrical productions a year, live from the theatre.[20] Soon it was realised, as in television later, that radio had the ability to produce its own, self-originated narratives inside the studio especially once the ability to record sound on disc was developed. Lance Sieveking's *Kaleidoscope* (1928) was a typically modernist feature production, billed as a 'rhythm representing the life of man from the cradle to the grave'.[21] Stylistically, the production took the form of a melange of close-ups, dissolves, slow-motion and montage, influenced by Soviet techniques. An exponent of 'pure radio' Sieveking was concerned at:

> the curious habit that exists in England of presuming and asserting that any attempt whatsoever at doing anything in a new way proclaims its author

as a member of some political party of the left. Modern painters, sculptors, poets, architects and composers are all supposed by popular opinion to be paid to do what they do by cheque from Moscow.[22]

This assumption was not without foundation. Exponents of the new documentary forms of cross-cultural practice had been influenced by the Russian Revolution. In particular, the Workers' Theatre Movement (WTM) reflected the political aspirations of its founders rather than their class background, consolidated its interests during the years following the General Strike (1926).[23] Similar to Brechtian theatre, the WTM used montage, voice-overs and on-stage slogans as an antidote to 'documentary' realism, whose seamless transcription of reality might lull an audience into a false belief of its transparency. Such developments anticipated the so-called 'naturalist' debate, taken up in television during the 1960s.[24]

Although 'Living Theatre' self-evidently had an advantage over the printing press in terms of dramatising the public realm, it did not reach a wide audience. 'Blind radio' despite its obvious disadvantage, could nonetheless reach those parts that the other media could not, deep into the privacy of the home. From the first, Reith was fully aware of sound broadcasting's political power, but he was also aware that in order to realise its potential, he first needed to gain acceptance for it in the face of considerable opposition from a jealous printing press. As he later opined, the microphone was able to succeed:

> where print and the philosophic formulation of doctrine had failed ... Not the printable scheme of government but its living and doing, the bringing of the personalities of the leading figures to the fireside, which could unite governments and governed in democracy as in dictatorship.[25]

Critics have variously documented Reith's rite of passage after the closure of the printing presses during the General Strike, which allowed the BBC to broadcast the news for the first time.[26] It is worth briefly mentioning that the event was successful in two other respects: first, it established radio's independence from the printing press and second, it paved the way for the inauguration of the BBC. Reith was created its leader as first Director General, and simultaneously awarded a knighthood.

During the 1920s, new types of radio programme were developed that capitalised upon radio's immediacy aesthetic, realised by the news, whilst for the first time, allowing editorial commentary. 'Talks' were a form of extended editorial about ordinary, everyday subjects organised by Hilda Matheson (Head of Talks, 1927–32), whose brief was for the creation of 'a new genre to interpret the vast field of interests and knowledge which is happily beyond the frontiers of acute current partisanship'.[27] Simon Frith describes the new strategies required to broadcast Talks as the projection of 'a particular sort of voice – intimate and authoritative – and a particular sort of personality – relaxing and knowable ... The radio star was public figure as private friend'.[28] Such a phenomenon was very different to the distantly worshipped film star and the new term 'radio personality' became a reality during the war with JB Priestley and Richard Dimbleby.

Meanwhile, with the expansion of sound broadcasting into the regions, the key concept defining the development of what became known as the Regional Scheme, was that of centralisation. This constituted a policy which imposed upon the margins from the centre in a thoroughly arbitrary way and resulted in a persistent dichotomy between them. Part of the problem was Reith's own contradictory stance. On the one hand, he stipulated that it was the business of radio broadcasting to represent the regions, whilst on the other hand, he spoke of it as making the nation 'as one man'. In terms of their distribution, broadcasting 'regions' were assigned according to the BBC, rather than for their true geographical identity. As a result, they were not representative. As Crissell states:

> the distinctiveness of each region was not immediately and authentically expressed but only gradually and somewhat artificially achieved: the West Region pioneered agricultural programmes, the Midlands industrial documentaries and variety shows, the North 'features'.[29]

Features, somewhat misleadingly, was the term used to describe the radio equivalent of the documentary-drama. These were the forms which first represented ordinary people. However, attempts to allow them to speak before the microphone were frustrated because BBC policy-makers were nervous of granting the male working-class subject a voice. As Peter Lewis puts it, 'That he should actually use broadcasting to express his own opinions in his own unvarnished words was regarded as the end of all good social order'.[30] Thus it was that 'Talks' – a misnomer if ever there was one – tended to present a safe scripted formula, spoken by a single narrator. Presented by the National Programme, Talks portrayed working people either as 'victims' (as occasionally uncomfortable reminders of how the other half lived), or as stereotypes of 'the man in the street'. *Other People's Houses* (1933), about life in a deprived area on Tyneside, is exemplary of the way in which such programmes were framed by a form of paternalistic anthropologism. Howard Marshall, the well-known narrator, likens a respectable sounding Cornwallis Square to 'a collection of mud huts in an African swamp', the region is implicitly likened to 'the dark continent' (the darkness within). More 'Out of Africa', than in Britain.[31]

It was against such condescending portraits of the working class, that BBC Northern Features endeavoured to portray genuinely 'rounded' characters. Geoffrey Bridson's popular BBC North series, *Harry Hopeful* (1936), cleverly circumnavigated the prohibition on *vox pops* by creating 'sound pictures' in the studio of people and places, as if they had been shot on location.[32] When Bridson went on to make his first big feature, *Steel* (1937) – influenced by the earlier documentary film *Coalface* (1935) – the audience found its modernist mode risible. As the *Daily Independent* stated, 'Sheffield Laughed when BBC Went Poetic Over Steel'.[33] Taking the point, Bridson and his colleague, the then little-known Joan Littlewood, endeavoured to make documentaries more directly aimed at reflecting the lives and opinions of the North.

After a month of living and working shifts with the miners, *Coal* (1938) was well received. *They Speak for Themselves* followed a year later, and was produced by Olive Shapley, whose reportage and 'feel' for her subjects equates with Elizabeth Gaskell's novels of Manchester life in the 1840s.[34] However, this development was short-lived. With the outbreak of the Second World War, the Regional Scheme was suspended and the National Programme renamed the Home Service. For a few months, this was the only channel available to the public. In much the same way, at around the same time as early radio features, film documentarists were experimenting.

Flagging the nation

Grierson's inaugural *Drifters* (1929), which set out to show a day in the life of ordinary fishing folk off the Shetland Islands, claimed to be 'the first picture of the working classes'. As was Sieveking's radio features work, it was influenced by Soviet film practice, in particular that of a new method of editing by cutting across shots.[35] As Rotha put it, 'It was not just movement of action within the screen-frame or movement of the camera itself, but the all important movement created by editing shot after shot'.[36]

So as to contextualise the documentary film's aesthetic relative to that of the ordinary feature, it is worth citing the difference between the two 'looks'. As Caughie has argued, that of documentary institutes 'a system of looks which constructs the social space of the fiction, a social space which is more than simply a background, but which, in a sense constitutes what the documentary drama wished to be about'.[37] By contrast, that of the dramatic constitutes:

> the system of looks and glances which is familiar from fictional film, and which works to produce the consistency and movement of the narrative, placing the spectator in relation to it – the rhetoric, that is, of narrative realist film.[38]

Partly as a result of the film's montage techniques (during the sea-storm, close-ups of wild seas alternate with images of fishermen struggling to keep hold of their nets) critics complained that the film's formalist aesthetics outweighed its social purpose.[39] This was true, it seems, of much documentary product. Even the well-known film *Song of Ceylon* by Basil Wright for the tea-industry, has been seen as 'pure pastorale'. The problem was, that whilst being influenced by modernist aesthetics and avant garde social theories, both documentarists and sound features directors were discursively enclosed within an all-pervasive imperialist ideology. John Mackenzie nicely demonstrates an example of the collusion between the BBC and the EMB in his observation that while the British documentary film movement:

> treated Empire as an existing commitment, open to reform perhaps, but offering the British public excitement (imperial air routes and the like) and valuable products (Ceylon tea, etc.) Reithian broadcasting sought to educate the public to a national consensus which included a royal and imperial ethos as part of an immutable order.[40]

As we have seen, a hierarchical mindset was institutionalised in the BBC's own public service remit: Reith himself was mindful of the importance of royalty in terms of constituting a family of nationhood, with the monarch at its head.

Despite documentarists' grandiose claims that 'the old flags of exploitation' were being substituted for 'the new flags of common labour', they often produced the same old themes, only re-wrapped. Documentary practioners' attempts to represent 'the other' from within a circle of ideological determination in which they were themselves implicated, was one of the Documentary Movement's many paradoxes.

The Griersonian 'project' was undoubtedly guided away from its early democratic mission by Tallents, who, as First Secretary of the EMB (1927), saw its potential in ousting the hegemony of American film product. By the mid-1920s, only five per cent of films shown on Imperial cinema screens were made in Britain, due to the way in which the USA maintained a stranglehold through a blind and block booking system until there was scarcely a system to show British films. A fellow diplomat summed up the 'official' attitude to this sorry state of affairs:

> It is horrible to think that the British Empire is receiving its education from a place called Hollywood. The dominions would rather have a picture with a wholesome, honest British background, something that gives British sentiment, something that is honest to our traditions, than the abortions we get from Hollywood.[41]

Critics argue that the British public found an excitement in American cinema, lacking in the home-grown variety. Peter Stead remarks that audiences felt less patronised by US movies than British ones when 'only very occasionally did the ... sermonising of the commentators give way to a vox populi'.[42] For Tallents, this circumstance provided a major incentive for the making of British films with an emphasis upon the 'projection' of national identity.

In a subsequent publication, judiciously named *The Projection of England* (1932), Tallents sought to provide something of a manifesto for film-makers. Today, *Projection* reads like a recipe for the 'heritage film'. National institutions such as the Monarchy, Parliament and the British Navy rub shoulders with national sporting events including the Derby, the Grand National, the Boat Race, Henley, Wimbledon, the Test Matches and the Cup Final. The first of its kind, the publication evokes a common national identity and sought to invent timeless and incontestable national traditions, even where these did not exist.[43] As Jeffrey Richards so accurately comments, 'some of these recommendations merely endorse the class-biased image which already emerged clear and fully formed from the British cinema ... there is no mention here of unemployment'.[44] While Reith and Grierson, in their own ways, sought to expand the new technology and, at the same time, bring about a form of enlightened democracy through their practices, Tallents was far more concerned to exploit it to propagandist ends. During the Second World War, *Projection*'s tenets were to become an institutionalised part of propaganda policy.

After the EMB Film Unit was abolished in 1933, the role of disseminating official imperial propaganda, was assumed by both the British Council and the GPO. (The BBC's Empire Service also began at around this time.) However, in terms of its mass projection, the act of publicising the British Empire was by default, and somewhat ironically, left to British commercial film-makers whose activities had been stimulated by beneficial quotas with the introduction of the Cinematograph Films Act (1927).

What Jeffrey Richards nominates as Alexander Korda's 'notable trilogy of imperial dramas', *Sanders of the River* (1935), *The Drum* (1938) and *The Four Feathers* (1939), were stirring adventures of 'derring do', all very popular with the public.[45] In particular, they emphasised the individualistic qualities of 'character and spirit' which Richards sees as being central to Korda's 'imperial vision'. *Sanders of the River* and *The Drum* evoked the imperial mythology of Africa with its *Heart of Darkness* connotation; a vast continent peopled by intrepid whites and child-like Africans. Sanders himself is endowed with the public-school attributes, and 'charisma' of those who take up occupation with the Colonial services. He is one of the 'pioneers who laid the foundations of the British Empire'.[46]

It is of interest to contrast this individualist 'gung-ho' production with that of an earlier Gaumont-British film, produced by Michael Balcon. *The Good Companions* (1933) describes the journey of the zanily named 'Dinky Doos', a disparate troupe of vaudeville players. As Barr himself has recently argued, *The Good Companions* notably brought together JB Priestley, famed for his wartime *Postscripts*, Michael Balcon and Ian Dalrymple, who was to become Supervising Producer at the Crown Film Unit.[47] Charles Barr has maintained that *The Good Companions* stands 'as the prototype of the wartime national epic' in its dramatisation of consensus through teamwork:

> the teamwork of the key collaborators, their individual functions effaced in a joint credit matches the teamwork celebrated on screen through the *Good Companions*, the theatrical troop within which a disparate collection of individuals find fulfilment.[48]

Barr further sees *The Good Companions* as establishing an important 'bridge' between popular cinema and documentary, thereby anticipating the wartime marriage which emerged during the Second World War, between the British documentary and feature film.

Balcon's Ealing films are often seen as a fulfilment of his own personal ambition of 'Putting the real Britain on the Screen'. Barr cites the typical Ealing plot in *Cheer Boys Cheer* (1939):

> To make this really Ealing, lay on the contrasts. The brewery names: Ironside against Greenleaf. Grim offices and black limousines against country lanes, ivy covered cottages, horses, bicycles.[49]

Rooted in the notion of an idealised community, whether town – *It Always Rains on a Sunday* (1947); *Passport to Pimlico* (1949) – or country, Ealing films identify the state with the family. Barr further argues that, 'If at one level Greenleaf is England, a second correspondence is equally striking, the Greenleaf Brewery is like Ealing Studio'.[50]

Famously, of course, Ealing was the studio with 'the team spirit'. 'Greenleaf' ideology offers a retreat from the city to the suburb; neither fully in a state of nature, nor of nurture. The films themselves were shown to people who actually lived in them, part of the growing population constituting the growing middle-class group of middle-brow cinema. During the post-war period, television not only took over the Ealing Studios in 1955, but also began to erode its regular audience. Barr argues that despite the onslaught, the values of the studio, along with personnel nonetheless 'infiltrated the conqueror'. As will become evident, 'Greenleaf' ideology became absorbed and deeply embedded in television, as indicated by the pastoral connotations of soaps like *The Grove Family* and the police series, *Dixon of Dock Green*.

Imperial to public relations

After their transference to the GPO Film Unit, documentarists too projected a more internal sense of Britishness.[51] Here, under the auspices of the Post Office, their brief was to 'bring alive' the institution, just as they had done for Empire. In Stephen Tallents' estimation:

> Lack of knowledge made the daily work of thousands of men and women, large bodies of them working remote from contact with the public less interesting to them than it really was. They suffered from the lack in the public mind of an understanding of what they were doing.[52]

The erstwhile diplomat's skills in public relations, imported from the United States, are here made fully manifest.[53] Utilising the language of democracy, as theorised by Walter Lippman and others, in the interests of public relations represents a cunning manoeuvre to win over those who previously doubted what they saw as the potentially specious use of 'publicity'. Tallents saw documentarists as occupying a useful threshold between Government and private enterprise and aimed to establish 'a school of national projection to maintain close contact with the various existing publicity bodies and with the press, the BBC, the news agencies and the film industry'.[54] This threshold or borderland was never 'a degree zero', however, especially after documentarists joined the GPO, when their outside contracts dried up completely.[55]

On arrival at the GPO, documentarists discovered that pre-commissioned GPO films including *Cable Ship* (1933), *Six-Thirty Collection* (1934) and

Weather Forecast (1935), used the standard Voice-of-God narration techniques of the instructional film. After Grierson's departure for Canada in 1939, Alberto Cavalcanti took over the documentary film unit and, according to some critics, propelled the GPO Film Unit back towards the narrative techniques of the commercial film industry (from whence he came).[56] Assisted by the availability of synchronised sound, documentary practitioners increasingly retrieved traditional methods of story-telling and applied these to their portrayals of the civil service, using real-life personnel. This can be seen in *Big Money* (1938), a documentary piece which demonstrated how the Accountant General's Department controlled the country's finances with the Accountant General re-enacting his 'real life' role. A second film, *Health for the Nation* (1939), featured the Minister of Health himself taking measures to provide good housing, water supply, sanitation and drainage, as well as the whole health service, was similarly criticised.

As Rotha declared, *Health for the Nation* 'left one with the impression that there was nothing the Ministry wouldn't do to improve the lot of the working man'.[57] Whereas the presence of ministers and public servants might be tolerated as voice-overs, in *person* they were not. To some critics the documentarists' collusion with the state, looked like like a complete sell-out. According to Arthur Calder Marshall for example:

> Mr Grierson may like to talk about social education, surpliced in self-importance and social benignity. Other people may like hearing him. But even if it sounds like a sermon, a sales talk is a sales talk.[58]

The return to 'story' has been an engrossing preoccupation in all histories of the British documentary movement, especially in terms of its precise genealogy. In tracing the provenance of the 'story film' – or story-documentary – some critics argue that the earliest exponent was *Night Mail* (1936).[59] Others assert this production, with words by WH Auden and music by Benjamin Britten, to be a mechanistic dramatisation of post-office communications with a dearth of human characterisation, or 'people'. In Pat Jackson's words, 'You never heard how they felt and thought and spoke to each other, relaxed. You were looking from a high point of view at them'.[60] Yet others, including Harry Watt (its maker), cite the character-led *Saving of Bill Blewitt* (1937) as primary. Then there are those who are adamant that *North Sea* (1938) is the definitive example.[61] Although lineages are undoubtedly important, there has perhaps been too much time spent barking up this particular documentary 'tree'. 'Story' had never been exactly abandoned from the documentary project. Even in *Drifters*, boats go out to sea, 'fish' and return with their catch: a sequence which fulfils the standard Aristotelian narrative requirement of a beginning, middle and end.

Whilst Grierson famously stated that he wished to 'abandon story', his early development was influenced by the American 'yellow press', whose strong desire for human interest stories were produced – in a format we today would call tabloid – for a largely immigrant consumption.[62] As he later recalled:

> What fascinated me as a European was the way the Hearst press and its imitators on every level of journalism had turned into a 'story' what we in Europe called a 'report'. They had in fact made the story – that is to say, a dramatic form – the basis of their means of communication ... All I did in my theory of documentary film was to transfer that concept to film making.[63]

The idea of documentary as animated photo-journalism is striking, and was to be most fully realised by the television story-documentary, with frequent accusations of its deferral to tabloid interests.

War: last resort of the popular

It was in order to create an 'optical illusion' of consensus that when the Second World War eventually did break out, maximum effort was expended on the Home Front, turning film cameras and sound radio into 'the public eye' and 'voice of Britain'.[64] In Antonia Lant's words:

> A new ministry was created, the 'Ministry of Home Security', responsible for planning and supervising ARP services with the Home Secretary at its head. The 'Home Guard', 'Home Intelligence Units' and the BBC Home Service' were all instigated in the first few months of war.[65]

The concept of the Home Front, appropriated from the First World War, was a potent symbol of national unity despite the absence of mobilised women. As Lant further notes, in all Second World War propaganda, the word 'home' is interchangeable with 'nation'. If England is Home and the Nation, then Germany is the 'Other': the unhomely, or, *unheimlich*. During the post-war period, television was to shift the prevalent discourse away from war, to that of law and order. From this perspective, television, police-series' narratives may be seen as a replacement for those of the public service film.

Because it broadcast on a low frequency, the BBC could continue to broadcast during bombing raids without giving away its geographical locations (unlike television with its extremely high mast). Both in the BBC and the films division of the GPO, the government had a ready-made propaganda facility at its disposal, however, it was slow to use the documentarists. According to Lant it was:

> Radio [which] seemed to bring the nation together through a mechanism unavailable to the enemy. The government certainly preferred radio over cinema as its main communication channel to the nation in wartime.[66]

Notwithstanding this partiality, the coalition between film and broadcasting in the national interest, is frequently cited in films with scenes of families clustered around the home set, such as *In Which We Serve*, which replays the announcement of the start of the war. The BBC is writ large in Humphrey Jenning's *Listen to Britain* (1942), featuring Dame Myra Hess performing at a lunchtime concert, intercut with scenes from radio comedians, Flanagan and Allen.

In 1940 the GPO Film Unit was symbolically renamed the Crown Film Unit (CFU). Following the MOI's own commercially sponsored effort at propaganda, the aspirationally named *The Lion Has Wings* (1939), produced by Alexander Korda, which turned out (at the risk of a mixed-media metaphor) to be more like a book with legs, documentarists were called up. Although described in glowing terms by some reviewers, with its newsreel clips, documentary clips and material from *Fire Over England*, the film was assembled in a hotchpotch, incoherent fashion. Its Manichean depiction of good and evil was deemed unconvincing by the left-wing press, who saw the Nazi pilots stereotypically all portrayed as 'cowardly morons'.[67]

At this stage the expertise of the documentarists ranged widely. Whilst Humphrey Jennings continued experimenting with modernist aesthetics, incorporating music and montage, by far the majority of practitioners retrieved narrative or story-telling, techniques. However, it was not a case of 'either/ or', so much as a mutual exchange of ideas engendered by an increasing sense of collaboration. An informal exchange between the mainstream film industry and documentarists known as the Ideas Committee was set up, which, according to Rotha, consisted of a fortnightly get-together over beer and 'rather lousy sandwiches' throughout the war.[68] In each direction the exchange of personnel catalysed the cross-fertilisation which had commenced during the inter-war period. New forms of 'documentary realism' occurred across all genres and were furthered by an exchange of personnel from the feature film industry into documentary and vice versa, as in the case of Alberto Cavalcanti and Harry Watt's transfer from the GPO Film Unit to Ealing Studios. Meanwhile, Ian Dalrymple, previously a scriptwriter for MGM and Alexander

Korda, whose work included *The Lion Has Wings*, became the CFU's Director. The different ways in which public processes were dramatised and projected resulted in an eclecticism of documentary and story-film techniques – location-shots in narrative films and studio-shorts in documentary – as well as the use of actors in documentary films and non-actors in features.

It has been suggested that Britain entered the Second World War with a more sophisticated notion of propaganda than previously recognised. A War Office 'secret' memo observed: 'The highest art in propaganda is to maintain the appearance of impartiality while securing the wholehearted adoption of the view propagated'. It suggests 'glorifying' the Royal family and 'idealising' national heroes.[69] A subsequent document entitled *The Projection of Britain* (1943), published by the MOI, strongly echoes Tallents' earlier pamphlet. The replacement of 'England' by 'Britain' is demonstrative of a felt need to portray national over sectional interests. Very specifically, the memo instructs that:

> In presenting this image it is essential that we should give full emphasis to the cultural aspect; and by 'cultural' in this context is meant much more than the contents of our art galleries, museums and old country houses ... Our culture is embodied in every phase of our national life and institutions, social and economic, industrial and scientific.[70]

Just as the assimilation of narrative modes by film documentarists was to be matched by an absorption of documentary itself into the feature film, radio features were also given a substantial boost in terms of advancing radio journalism from its earliest news forms. Writers such as Robert Barr, EAF Harding (previously Head of Imperial Communications) and Cecil McGivern contributed to these new programmes, and were to cross over to post-war television. *Shadow of the Swastika* (1944), a series produced by McGivern, marked a turning-point in the narrativised radio-feature and was highly popular. Priestley's earlier *Postscripts* slot, just after the nine o'clock news, has been described by Tony Aldgate and Jeffrey Richards as the 'harbinger of the new consensus'. This was to be realised in the Beveridge Report (1942), with its promise of full employment and security 'from the cradle to the grave'.

The radio news, in whose interests Reith had struggled against press and state was valued as never before during the Second World War. A vanguard of the Home Front's 'war of words', it became memorably transformed into the 'shock troops of propaganda'. Nonetheless, at the outset of the war, it was found to be plain boring.[71] Part of the problem was that the 'BBC Voice' was still associated with the upper classes, and of the five main 'menaces' to public calm identified by a Home Morale Emergency Committee meeting, 'class feeling' was considered the most pernicious in undermining morale. (This was a fact which Lord Haw-Haw, alias William Joyce, a German counterfeit who presented himself as an Englishman broadcasting from Radio Hamburg, so effectively played upon.)[72] Remedial action resulted in the employment of Wilfred Pickles, a Yorkshire character actor, as the first newsreader with a regional accent. Pickles was to go on to become Billy Welcome in a series of industrial features live from the factory, all designed to maintain morale and demonstrate the importance of the industrial front to the nation.[73] Newsreaders, who had hitherto been anonymous, were for the first time named for security reasons to avoid the kind of confusion instigated by Lord Haw Haw. This began a move towards greater individualism, and the construction of the radio personality, of which JB Priestley was a great exponent.

Involved with Hollywood, the British Documentary Movement and two Gracie Fields films, Priestley spanned the divide between popular and élite culture. When people referred to his populism as 'his roast beef and beer attitude', he countered that the BBC's Arnoldian ideals lacked the common touch. Never before had the 'received pronunciation' of the metropolitan BBC been placed in stronger opposition to the 'local' than in Priestley's amusing posturings. It is perhaps unfortunate that the latter's comments about the BBC's 'amateurish and patronising' paternalism, 'As if the charitable lady of the manor had got up an entertainment to keep the men of the village out of the public houses' together with his stridently left-wing views, precipitated the demise of the *Postscripts* slot.[74] Ever an advocate of the popular and debunker of the BBC's supposed impartiality, Priestley went on to become a champion of the democratic possibilities of post-war television during a time when there was on the parts of novelists and film-makers alike a considerable animus against it.

War Report replaced *Postscripts*, taking the microphone to places where things were happening and 'let it listen as one would one's self like to listen to the sounds of battle, to the daily voices of men just returned from the fighting line'.[75] Richard Dimbleby, its presenter, although more robustly Middle England than Priestley, nonetheless addressed a large constituency. Witnessing at first-hand the Bombing of Duisburg (1941) and the Normandy Beach-head (1944), Dimbleby acted as a mediator for the listener, crossing the divide between the Home Front and the Front Line. The great turning-point, in terms of a move towards populism during the war, was the advent of the Forces programme. This service arose in response to competition provided by Radio Normandy, a commercial popular station, broadcasting off mainland France and successor to Radio Luxembourg (which closed down during the war).[76] It has been variously argued that this move represented 'the clearest expression of the reversal of pre-war values in broadcasting'.[77] As one BBC authority commented:

> If we give them serious music, long plays, or peace-time programme talks, they will not listen. Our peace-time argument (which we shall never I trust surrender) completely breaks down when faced with the conditions prevailing over this new programme.[78]

Despite this avowal, the reversal was to remain. During the post-war period, in the tripartite reconfiguration of radio broadcasting, the Forces programme became the new Light Programme. Its arrival, encouraged by competition from Radio Normandy, meant that the terms of the BBC's public service remit were forced to become more inclusive, a circumstance paralleled during the post-war period, with the arrival of Independent Television (ITV, 1955). Radio programmes such as *Workers Playtime* (1942) and film titles like *Millions Like Us* (1943), with their self-evidently populist titles, shifted the hegemony of the BBC's Arts and Music 'high-brow' definition of culture towards a more consensual version. The provision of programmes for factory workers was especially important, both in maintaining the morale of the workforce and to speed up factory production. 'Calling all Workers' was the theme tune of *Music While You Work*, whose magazine format featured well-known variety performers like Gracie Fields, the original Lancashire Lass, as well as the ubiquitous Priestley.

Asa Briggs has seen the war as important in terms of consolidating and extending 'a weekly round' already in existence, a pattern television would later follow. People 'listened in' to *Monday Night at Eight*, 'with the certain draw of Inspector Hornleigh', and *Puzzle Corner*. On Tuesday, *ITMA* (1939) built up the largest war-time audience and was beloved for its irreverence in'Funf' (Hitler) and towards the MOI (the 'Ministry of Aggravation'). Wednesday featured an alternation of single shows like *Kentucky Minstrels* (1933) and *For Amusement Only*, with Robb Wilton (from Liverpool) in *Mr. Muddlecombe JP*, the first ever sitcom to appear on British radio as a series of 15-minute programmes. Thursday featured *Songs from the Shows*, *At the Billet Doux* and *Henry Hall's Guest Night* (1935).[79] According to Briggs, the latter could provide greater continuity than anything which yet existed on Fridays, 'the bits and pieces day of the week'.[80] On Saturdays, *Band Waggon* (1937) was followed by *Garrison Theatre*, 'a music-hall programme with trimmings', based on recollections of the Northern Command Garrison Theatre during the First World War. Series programmes to build up the schedule were developed, and with them fears of increasingly industrialised methods of production that lacked the 'shaping vision' of the individual writer or producer. As Scannell argues:

> this regularity enabled performers to perfect their characterisations without repeating their acts; enable writers, once they have established a familiar set of characters in a stock situation to explore the permutations of the formulae, develop running gags and catch phrases and at the same time to assimilate a wide range of social and topical references.[81]

Such 'serial' forms of reproduction gained acceptance during the war and were to become an increasingly important part of television production during the post-war period. Meanwhile, many of the radio programmes, not altogether successfully, became films, including *Inspector Hornleigh Goes to it* (1941), *Band Waggon* (1940) and *ITMA* (1942).[82]

Propaganda and pleasure

It was inevitable that during the Second World War British feature film-makers should turn to stories of men at the front as a form of propaganda. As James Chapman states:

> It was the commercial feature film industry which led the way in the production of war narratives, though the Crown Film Unit also made an important contribution to the representation of men at war through its feature-length documentaries. The story of the British war film has usually been described in terms of a gradual shift from false heroics and jingoism in the early war years to the emergence of a mature realism in the representation of men in battle by the middle of the war. It was a process which reflected the trend towards realism which characterised the British cinema as a whole during this period. This trend was mirrored by a shift in the narrative interest in service films, from a focus on dashing officers-and-gentlemen in the early war years to a greater emphasis on the ordinary enlisted men in the later years.[83]

Harry Watt's *Target for Tonight* (1941) is often held up as the acme of wartime story-documentary style. It describes an important mission over Germany (it was actually three-quarters made in the studio), the RAF personnel play themselves and the film announces its own raison d'être:

This is the story of a Raid on Germany – how it is planned and how it is executed. Each part is played by the actual man or woman who does the job from Commander in Chief to Aircraft Hand. In order however, not to give information to the enemy all figures indicating strength have been made purposely misleading.

The story, concerning a Wellington bomber's execution of a one-night bombing raid on Germany, applied the same authenticating techniques which had been used to publicise the Post Office. That is, the film used actual airforce personnel and acknowledged the assistance of the Royal Airforce in the titles. In Grierson's estimation, *Target for Tonight* was important because it gave Hollywood 'an idea, the idea of teamwork in action, the excitement of the administrative factor in modern action and the value of spotlighting the contribution of the ordinary'.[84] It showed the crew of 'F for Freddie' involved in a raid on an oil depot at 'Friehausen' in Germany. It was the first major British film to show Blighty on the offensive, rather than just 'taking it'.[85] Tragically, shortly after its exhibition, all the personnel were killed.

As Tony Aldgate and Jeffrey Richards have noted, it was apparent from the first that ordinary people preferred popular narratives, based upon the old premises of individualism and single authority, to documentary films.[86] During war-time conditions, familiarity, far from breeding contempt, was found reassuring, especially by Stars, portraying acts of heroism. Documentary features, such as *In Which We Serve*, whilst looked down upon by the critics, were great box office hits.[87] The portrayal of real-life events by actors added an extra frisson of meaning to the text, even more so when they were stars like Noël Coward.

Michael Balcon's *In Which We Serve* – despite early disclaimers – was based upon the real-life experience of Louis Mountbatten whose ship was torpedoed. At first Coward was deemed highly unsuitable to portray a famous Royal Navy Captain. Coward's own protestation that he was only portraying 'to the best of my ability … an average naval officer' was given scant credence. The *Daily Express* put the press position:

There are the two schools of thought on the position: 1. those who support Mr Coward; 2. those who think that a film about the Navy should be produced in the same way as the RAF film *Target for Tonight*, with real naval men in the leading parts.[88]

The second comment is of interest in terms of anticipating the later documentary drama 'debate' that occurs in television, especially over real-life events, such as *Death of a Princess* (1980).[89]

In Which We Serve was to prove a box office sell-out and was described by *Newsweek* as 'One of the screen's proudest achievements at any time in any country'.[90] This was the film which inaugurated the technique known as Independent Frame (IF), a method of rationalised production techniques and special effects introduced by David Rawnsley: in this instance, involving the illusion of a storm created by a 'rocking process screen' behind the ship. This mixed economy of studio and location shooting introduced by the early documentary films, anticipated the methods of mass production adapted by early television.[91] Balcon's later films such as *San Demetrio-London* (1943), were proof of his determination to 'grasp with both hands the opportunity of putting every phase of the war on the screen'. *The Next of Kin* (1941), about the dangers of unwitting betrayal through careless talk, was taken as being 'so explicit that it sobered the troops who saw it and sickened many of the civilians, some of whom were carried out in a dead faint'.[92] Never before had death been depicted on the screen to the same degree: in the interests of preserving morale, official policy had been to avoid showing casualties whether 'feature, documentary or newsreel'.

British films of the Second World War show a tendency not only to dramatise but to interrogate class difference. During *In Which We Serve*, the doomed ship's three survivors swim to a raft whilst being strafed by German aircraft. In rapid succession three different Christmas dinners are portrayed. First, a working-class family Christmas, followed by an officer's (uppercrust) Christmas and a middle-of-the-road, middle-class Christmas. As Barr argues, unlike earlier naval dramas such as *Convoy* and *Ships with Wings*, which concerned themselves exclusively with officers; the story of Coward's Captain Kinross (aka Mountbatten) is involved with his lower-deck shipmates.[93] Such a dispersal of the class hierarchy dramatises a more inclusive social definition. Whether the new consensus can last or not is the question put by Charley, the working-class factory foreman, in *Millions Like Us*, in a defining moment as he asks Jennifer Knowles, the upper-class woman he has come to love, 'What's going to happen when it's over? Shall we go on like this or are we going to slide back?'

Films about the People's War, cut right across the social classes, and were characterised by qualities of 'comradeship and cooperation, dedication to duty and self-sacrifice, a self-deprecating good humour and unselfconscious modesty'.[94]

Commentators are divided as to the real nature and degree of class change effected in Britain by the Second World War. Whilst historians Paul Addison and Arthur Marwick argue that there was substantial social and political alteration, Angus Calder and Henry Pelling state that in social terms the war made little difference. On the one hand, the post-war implementation of the Beveridge Report and guarantee of full employment augured a profound political and social shift; on the other, the retention of the monarchy, public schools and House of Lords signified class stasis. However, whilst there is agreement that some of the hegemonic structures remained, there was at least a new awareness of class inequality. As noted by George Orwell, although the:

> essential structure of England is still almost what it was in the nineteenth century ... real differences between man and man are obviously diminishing and this fact is grasped and even welcomed by people who only a few years ago were clinging desperately to their social prestige.[95]

Significantly, there is no mention here of women. During the late forties, there was a discernible shift towards the domestic values of the feminine, exemplified by the story-documentary *Diary for Timothy* (1945). Jennings' film marks a moment when the war is coming to an end and is centred upon the figure of a baby boy. As Wendy Webster has argued, the space marked by the film is a transitional one between war and post-war. This is symbolised by the domestic image of baby Timothy lying asleep in his cot; the men's public activities, as they 'hew coal, drive trains and fly fighter planes'; and the women's, as they nurture and encourage the progress of the protagonist's convalescence. In this sense:

> Timothy is also transitional between female and male worlds. His present is female as he lies warm and comfortable in his mother's arms but his future is in the world of men who speak to him and the story he is told is one where he will grow into manhood, away from mother and nursery.[96]

Jim Cook notes that although women are portrayed during the war, in such films as *The Gentle Sex*, *Millions Like Us* and *Listen to Britain*, there is an overriding sense of their work being temporary. As he states, 'whilst the male discourse of *The Gentle Sex* struggles to keep women in their place ... *This Happy Breed* shows women in their place'. Queenie Gibbon's father tells her, when she gets notions of grandeur and getting out, 'We're as we are and that's how we're going to stay. And if you don't like it you can lump it ... there are worse things than being just ordinary and respectable and living the way you've been brought up to live'. Despite its anticipation of woman's *re*-placement during the post-war period, *This Happy Breed* does renegotiate notions of class for the central family. 'The Gibbons' are indeed a 'happy

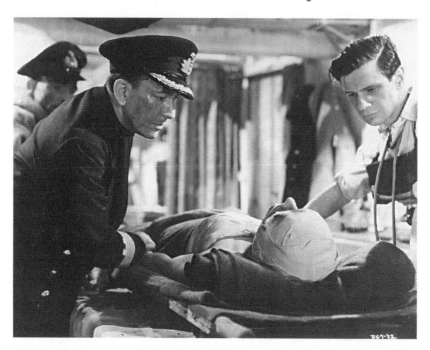

2. All classes pulling together. Noël Coward tending a casualty as Captain Kinross, standing for Louis Mountbatten, in *In Which We Serve* (1942).

breed' of respectable working-class people and, as such, are new protagonists, ones that will infiltrate television, from *The Groves* (1954) onward. The film charts the whole of the inter-war period through their lives from the end of the 1914 war, the British Empire Exhibition of 1924, the General Strike of 1926, right up to the Munich Crisis of September 1938.

Ordinariness and respectability, decent working class values. The post-war world was one in which feminine identity was securely returned to the domestic realm. By contrast, that of the masculine was less certain, for de-mobilisation brought with it uncertainty in terms of employment and consequently in gender definitions, as may be seen in the so-called, 'problem films'.

'Huggetry' to problem families

At a more local level, the post-war film series which more than any other anticipates the 'ordinariness' of the television soap opera family, is 'The Huggetts'. The eponymous protagonists have been characterised by Andy

Medhurst as 'an endearing set of Cockney stereotypes that appear in a sequence of post-war comedies beginning with *Holiday Camp* (1947)'.[97] After three follow-up films – *Here come the Huggetts*, *Vote for Huggett* and *Huggetts Abroad* – 'Huggetry' became a derisive byword for working-class domestic comedy. Jack Warner played the Joe Huggett character and Robert Murphy has referred to the later, Dixon incarnation as a sort of Joe Huggett in uniform. Yet, as he has also noted, Jack Warner's George Dixon cum Huggett persona has tended to obliterate the fact that he played some memorable villains in 1940s films.[98]

Towards the end of the 1940s, and during the post-war period, there was an acknowledgement that war-torn families were not all as cohesive as either the Gibbons or the Huggetts. What John Hill has designated the 'problem film' came to prominence just after the end of the Second World War in films that no longer presented families valiantly struggling to 'cope'. Whilst crime had been high during the period of the war itself, for the sake of morale and propaganda very little was ever represented. Public service films such as the Crown Film Unit short *War and Order* (1941) 'sought to reassure the public that though the ranks of the police were depleted, gaps were being filled by keen amateurs whose odd appearance (initially they had no uniform and their status was insecure) did not necessarily mean that they were ineffective'.[99] In the Gainsborough film *My Brother's Keeper* (1948), Warner significantly (in terms of his subsequent canonisation) played the character of George Martin, a hardened criminal, who escapes prison.[100]

At the same time as early television was reinventing the documentary wheel, feature films were producing the earliest institutional narratives on the police, borstal and law courts. According to Hill, *Children on Trial* (1946) set the agenda for post-war documentary features centred upon social issues. In ideological terms, the film presented a benevolent state, epitomised by 'understanding' Juvenile courts and concerned approved schools and dealt with an assortment of social problems as personified by deviant adolescents, young spivs and 'good-time girls'. The ominous figure of the spiv arises earlier in a film that was initiated by the MOI. Launder and Gilliat's *Partners in Crime* (1942) created a characterisation more sinister than the cardboard cut-outs of early comedy thrillers. Unlike George Formby's *Spare A Copper* or Harker and Simms' 'Inspector Hornleigh' films, this evil protagonist is not varnished with any legacy of music hall or vaudeville, whose 'coating' of humour, as Medhurst has so nicely argued, tended to deflect the censor's eye.[101]

A major reason for the newly realistic depiction of 'these relentless opportunists' was that, prior to the war, censorship rules prohibited the direct

3. Jack Warner as Joe Huggett in *Huggetts Abroad*, with Petula Clark, Jimmy Hanley and Dinah Sheridan (1942).

portrayal of crimes, any reference to drugs and prostitution or prison scenes. Although crime films were one of the staples of the 1930s, the British Board of Film Censors (BBFC) made it clear that these must be about the detection and punishment of crime, showing neither criticism of the authorities nor sympathy for the criminal. Films attacking capital punishment, prison conditions and the administration of justice were given short shrift. However, the war – and in particular the incorporation of documentary techniques – moved the boundaries of what might be represented. Producers realised that in the post-war climate it might be possible both to promote reconstruction and attract a box-office following by showing previously banned scenes, allowable in a public service context. Although Muriel Box has been quoted as stating 'We were not under contract to Rank to make films with overt statements on social problems', her statement is somewhat belied by *Boys in Brown* (1949), a film about boys in Borstal.

In public relations terms, *Boys in Brown* did for Borstal what Ealing's *The Blue Lamp* (1950) did for 'the Met'; it provided a nice equilibrium either side of 'the thin blue line', with a veteran star of vaudeville and cinema, Jack

Warner, taking the lead in both films. In each production, as in the thirties documentary films, we are initiated into the work of the public services. First, alongside 'the Borstal boys' we are initiated into a regime remarkably close to that of a public school; second, we experience life in the police force through the eyes of young PC Mitchell, played by James Hanley, the surrogate son of the older Dixon, who is to so violently meet his demise, at the hand of an alarmingly virile young Dirk Bogarde. Fortunately, he is subsequently resurrected in the eponymously named television series, *Dixon of Dock Green*.

As Barr observes in *The Blue Lamp*: 'The film opens with a traditional image of police benevolence, Dixon giving directions in the street to a passer-by and ends with Mitchell doing the same.' Nothing could be more ideo-logically consensualising than the rehearsing of the familiar trope 'ask a policeman', topping and tailing the narrative, a structure which television separates out as a free-standing entity in Dixon's famous address to camera, opening and closing each weekly episode.

Yet *The Blue Lamp* was a ground-breaking film. As Tony Aldgate and Jeffrey Richards have argued, it moved away from the more farcical filmic representation of the police as in George Formby's *Spare A Copper*, in which 'the music hall image of the slow-talking, dull-witted, good-hearted bumbler was transferred to the screen'.[102] These authors further discuss how this film, notably made with the co-operation of the Metropolitan Police and dedicated to the police service, was shot at several police stations, including Paddington Green. They note that actors were coached in police procedure and etiquette by serving officers and were often mistaken for real policemen during filming.[103]

Aldgate and Richards see *The Blue Lamp* as the final endpoint of the Ealing film, combining documentary style 'complete with location shooting' and a very specific view of England and Englishness. They observe that during the post war period:

> the life of service and duty under discipline that had characterized Ealing's wartime films passed in peacetime from the war against the enemy without – the Germans – to the war against the enemy within – the criminal.[104]

Although this is certainly true for the subsequent television series, it is perhaps less so for the *The Blue Lamp*, which, for all its public service references, possesses a renegade quality which sets it apart from the consensus film.[105]

Diana Lewis and Paul Riley, two problem youngsters, are seen as 'extreme cases' who, according to the voice-of-god narrator 'lack the code, experience and self-discipline of the professional thief'. Both stand apart from 'the shared

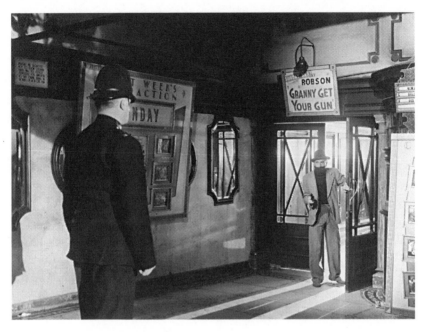

4. PC Dixon confronting Tom Riley, played by Dirk Bogarde, who has just held up
the cinema box-office, in *The Blue Lamp* (1950).

code, the shared idiom' which unifies the police, authorities and the 'underworld'. Lewis's defiant individualism, portrayed by an organisation of looks within the diegesis, and the scene showing her 'striding out' to a jazz music accompaniment – with its connotations of hedonism and sexuality – squares uneasily with the narrator's description of 'a young girl showing the effect of a childhood spent in a home broken and demoralised by war'.

Critics have interpreted Dixon's death not so much as representative of those deviant forces, but more the result of a renegade sexual desire. The *mise-en-scene* of the long shot in which Riley is presented admiring his own reflection in the mirror and brandishing a gun, permits a psycho-sexual reading. As Barr has nicely summed up, he is 'violent, hysterical, irresponsible, and – a significant part of the package – sexy. The way he handles his gun when threatening the girl announces that his violence and sexuality go together'.[106] From this viewpoint, Dixon's death can be read not only as the necessary casualty of a cauldron of unfulfilled desire, but as a symbolic fissure with the social contract of post-war reconstructionism. At the instant of the bullet's impact, the image of a certain kind of consensus politics is

5. Diana Lewis reacts after Dixon is shot down in *The Blue Lamp* (1950).

forever shattered: the moment recalled in an endless 'loop', held in the freeze-frame of the collective, public memory.

Although the documentary film met its demise following the closure of the Central Office of Information (CoI), in 1951 it crossed over to television, which reprised film and radio's public service function during the post-war period as a means of 'documentation, education and instruction'. The series of police films during the 1950s, such as *Street Corner* (1953), *The Long Arm* (1956) and *Gideon's Day* (1958), initiated a genre that was short-lived and did not transfer straightforwardly to television.[107] According to Richards, the genre's short duration was because, following the Conservative election victory in 1951, story narratives concentrated on senior officers rather than – as in *The Blue Lamp* – the ordinary police officer, 'thus reasserting the hierarchy of the culture of individualism'.[108] However, a more cogent reason may well have been that television – as will be seen – was simultaneously developing narratives along very similar lines.

Of the many influences which transmigrated into the new medium during the pre-television era, was that of Ealing's 'sober' narratives and 'green leaf' ideology. Juxtaposed with this predominantly Southern depiction of the nation with its comforting, suburban values, another was about to emerge, one influenced by Northern regions and earlier documentary experiments: that of a critical new realism which would reach its fullest realisation in television in the controversial television police series, *Z Cars* (1962). Meanwhile, as will become evident, the 'celebrated rapprochement' that occurred during the war between documentary and the feature film industry was to be repeated – almost in parallel – by television. In this respect at least, the process of documentary assimilation which occurred across the period represents a first cycle of generic innovation; one that was to be rearticulated by the new medium after the war had ended, in accordance with its own, specific needs.

6. A man under the assumed name of Major Colin Forsythe commits acts of fraud until he meets his come-uppance in 'Phantom Millions', an episode of *I Made News*, the experimental weekly story-documentary series (1951).

2

New forms for old

There was an occasion many years later when Sir Peter Hall
said during a public address that: 'If it had not been for
Look Back In Anger, there could have been no *Z Cars*.' An
assertion to which I replied that, 'If it had not been for the
audiences prepared by the television drama documentaries,
Look Back In Anger would not have found its moment.

Michael Barry[1]

It is the common view that British realist drama, both of stage and television,
began with John Osborne's controversial play, put on at the Royal Court
Theatre in 1956. By claiming that *Look Back in Anger*, rather than being
original in its own right, is indebted to the television drama documentary,
Michael Barry, Head of BBC Television Drama (1952–1961), raises the profile
of a previously unsung form: that of the television drama – or story – documentary.

It is in support of this reassessment, that this chapter argues that television
drama – or story-documentaries – not only prepared the way for new
industrialised forms of series production, including the British television
police series, but were of fundamental importance to the development of
British Drama: of stage and screen, both large and small. As Duncan Ross,
an early television documentary practitioner stated:

the story documentary form with its antecedents in film, radio and theatre
had a new application for television, one which forced a different perception
of the medium from that of 'a window on the world' to the notion that it
might be capable of producing its own dramatised inventions.[2]

Caryl Doncaster, another prominent documentarist, reinforces Barry's
assertion with her statement that television audiences were prepared to watch
and take an interest in subjects which would usually have been unacceptable

but, offered in the new format, proved as popular as 'football or the Sunday night play'.[3] As Doncaster implies, the story-documentary's popularity was that it presented information through dramatisation. In a quasi-Griersonian manner she stipulates that: 'The talk informs. The dramatised story-documentary interprets. One appeals to the intellect, the other to the emotions'.[4] From evidence on file, however, it is evident that this dichotomy was far from straightforward. For, whereas early story-documentaries were news-based and produced by ex news-journalists like Robert Barr, later on, with the arrival of theatre playwrights, like Duncan Ross they became subject to increased dramatisation. This trajectory therefore needs to be contextualised in terms of early perceptions about television. First and foremost, television was considered a *live* mediator, hence the importance of the Outside Broadcast, especially for sport but, increasingly, it began to be evident that the new medium could produce its own, self-originated forms.

It was to be the television story-documentary which pioneered new, institutional narratives, centred upon communitites such as 'the police, welfare workers and neglected children', radical precursors of so-called kitchen-sink realism. Not only was the story-documentary the initiator of a new form of aesthetic, it also negotiated innovative forms of rationalised production, in much the same way as Rank, with its Independent Frame techniques, using back projections, matched film inserts to studio sets. It went even further in terms of increased rationalisation, in experimenting with series formats. A key programme in this connection, was *I Made News* (1951), which both instituted the 'weekly strike' system and introduced a new directorial system to replace the previous writer-producer practice (accepted from sound broadcasting).

All these developments were remarkable, considering they took place within a live, studio environment. It was only during inserted film sequences telecined into the live performance when television became momentarily a recorded medium, that it was possible to juggle with time so that the 'passage of hours, days, months could be represented'.[5] Whereas in film, the narrative can be shot in any order and edited later, live television editing involves a continuous process of shot-selection, cutting from camera to camera: a complex choreography whose order is recorded on a camera script and pre-rehearsed. In technological terms, productions benefited from increased cutting speeds, with the ability to cut from camera to camera and between camera and telecine.

The first half of this chapter sets out the main cultural and institutional contexts of early post-war television, before moving into a discussion of the small Documentary Unit and its key players, including Robert Barr.

The second section moves into a detailed examination of the programmes themselves and their connection to the nascent British television police series. My analysis of key productions in this process commences with the Scotland Yard series *War on Crime* (1950), produced by Robert Barr on a monthly basis; next, it looks at *Course of Justice* (1951), a six part monthly production produced and written by Duncan Ross; third, it discusses *I Made News* (1951), which established the 'weekly strike'; and finally, it traces the development of *Pilgrim Street*, the earliest weekly British television police series, and precursor of *Dixon of Dock Green*.[6]

Here comes television, again!

At the end of the Second World War, the Hankey Committee, which as previously mentioned met to discuss the future of television, suggested it be restored on the pre-war model. The perceived failure in America by sponsored commercial networks to develop television successfully convinced the Committee that the BBC should be entrusted, at least for the immediate future, with providing a public service television system. British television recommenced on 7 June 1946 with the same *Mickey Mouse* cartoon with which it had so abruptly ended. From the start of its restoration, neo-Reithian stalwarts were determined that the new medium should maintain a low profile. Television was kept in line both by being starved of funds and through its institutional set-up. Just as Reith had split the functions of Administration from those of Output in sound broadcasting, the post-war Television Department was divided between the functions of Output, which included planning (and the commissioning and funding of programmes), and Supply, responsible for production (and the production department). Asa Briggs details how, on behalf of the administration and management, a Programmes Board met weekly to discuss programming, reporting to William Haley, newly appointed Director of Television, who made executive decisions. Confusion arose about Haley's responsibility for the rest of BBC management, because television was not yet a separate service – it achieved this status late in 1950 – nor was it integrated with Sound.[7]

Television's continued lowly status was exemplified by the fact that the Beveridge Committee, set up in 1949 to investigate the 'brute force' of the BBC's broadcasting monopoly, devoted only 18 of the 325 pages in its published report to television.[8]

Until the early 1950s, British television was perceived by BBC authorities as radio's junior partner. However, certain enthusiasts were all too aware that the new medium had different needs to those of sound broadcasting and were prepared to say so. Anxious to keep its growing band of vociferous lobbyists in the background, Haley decided to stage a sound broadcasting heist. Radio personnel would take over all the important jobs in the Television Department. Accordingly, Norman Collins was appointed Controller of Television and Cecil McGivern Head of Television Programmes (1947). However, the plan went awry when the marauding generals, to use an appropriately imperialistic phrase, went native.[9] Collins, in particular, spoke out against the restrictions, encouraging officials to recognise that their self-interest was holding back the 'adventurous development of television'.[10] He was precipitately sacked for his pains and replaced by George Barnes, who in 1951 was installed as Director of The Spoken Word, BBC Radio *and* Television, in a self-evident bid by sound broadcasting to re-establish its authority. This incident shows the high degree of tension running between the different levels in the BBC's hierarchy, exacerbated by the split between policy-makers and programme-makers. Whilst BBC senior management shared the metropolitan assumptions and policies of Whitehall and Westminster and of the ministerial and departmental circles in which they moved, producers working out 'in the field' had closer contact with the 'local' public.

During his brief sojourn at the BBC, Norman Collins managed to secure for television a number of significant long-term commitments. These included the acquisition of the 13.5 acre site at White City, eventually to become Television Centre, which was planned to open by 1960. Rank Studios at Lime Grove had been previously been acquired, and the conversion of its five studios was well underway. By the time of Collins' ejection in 1951 there were four separate programme groups. I have set these out schematically below, for easier reference:

1. *Drama* Val Gielgud (1949–1951), Michael Barry (1952–1961)
2. *Light Entertainment* under Ronnie Waldman (1951–1960)
3. *Talk and Talks Features*, headed by Mary Adams (Grace Wyndham Goldie, Assistant Head)
4. *Outside Broadcasts and Films* (the two categories were separated in 1948, headed by Orr-Ewing and Philip Dorte respectively)

As the above chart shows, there was no documentary programme group, as such. Until the small Documentary Unit became the Documentary Department in 1953, it tended to hover precariously between Talks and Talks

Features on the one hand and Drama on the other. According to Elaine Bell, Mary Adams, Head of Talks and Features, was an empire-builder who took advantage, within this vertically integrated hierarchy, of the fact that Cecil McGivern did not appoint a Head of Documentaries until Paul Rotha's late arrival (1953), by suggesting that Documentary be subsumed within her group.[11] It soon became apparent that Robert Barr, unofficial leader of the small documentary department, was unafraid to cross departmental boundaries, which were in any case, far from clear.

Whilst radio retained the effects of its wartime democratisation, reconstituting its output in three channels, Home, Light and Third, there was no intention of allowing single-channel television to become 'a sort of Light Entertainment with pictures'.[12] As John Caughie has observed:

> it was during the immediate post-war period that the BBC's cultural mission was most explicitly undertaken. This was a time when the BBC had ceased to be at the service either of direct national propaganda, or of Reith's own narrower moral and religious imperatives.[13]

During its immediate post-war period, television saw itself projecting and affirming a corporate national life by conveying a 'panorama of actualities' from the outside world into the home, in an unmediated and unproblematic way.[14] After the closure of the Central Office of Information (CoI), which took over briefly from the Crown Film Unit at the end of the war, story-documentaries took over the ideological role performed by the public service documentary film. Titles like *Chorus Girl* (1946), *First Time Ever* (1946, thief caught by radio) and *For the Housewife* (1950, keeping burglars out), give a flavour of the mixed diet on offer.

In terms of the division between the political and the social subject, Scannell distinguishes the former as that which relates to the affairs of government and party politics, as contrasted with the 'social subject', dealing 'with issues of general social concern (housing, unemployment, delinquency, old age, etc.)'.[15] It was for the Talks Department that new kinds of programme were developed (later labelled 'current affairs') to handle political issues. Social issues were supposedly to be separately developed by Barr's small documentary group, operating under the aegis of the Drama Department under Val Gielgud, Head of BBC Drama (1947), until Michael Barry's arrival.

In an article on the television documentary, published in the *BBC Quarterly* in 1950, Duncan Ross, an early practitioner wrote:

> In 29 years the word 'documentary' has spread all over the world to describe almost all films of social significance ... The word has now overflowed its

original intention and is often applied to radio programmes, books, articles and paintings. Indeed, it has been so tortured and transformed even within the limits of cinema that, at times, it must be a wise Grierson who knows his own child. It is however perfectly at home in television. Indeed, so many opportunities occur in television for 'the creative interpretation of reality' through the visual image that Flaherty himself has said that the eventual future of documentary lies there.[16]

As Grierson himself stated, 'all sensible people are taking a close look at the technical possibilities of television, and for the good reason that it is something new – a new box of tricks may I say – which makes our older movie one look clumsy and slow'.[17] Grierson and the documentarists, including Paul Rotha whose subsequent cross-over was some cause for regret, were initially very interested in television.[18] However, the 'documentary idea' as adapted by television was, as we shall see, to develop in a very different way to Grierson's original notion of it.

We bring you live pictures, but are they?

From the earliest, television was celebrated for its capacity as a medium of demonstration, as has been exemplified by John Caughie's example of *The Golden Hind* (1936), a 15-minute programme in which a Mr Stocks, in an address to camera, describes how to make a model of Drake's ship, assisted by close-up shots of the ship itself. A glance at the pre-war *Radio Times* shows many new television programmes influenced by the same factor. Philip Harben's cookery programmes and items on how to lay a carpet, or make a rag doll, are all critically enhanced by vision. What story-documentaries achieved was to shift the notion of television as a medium of demonstration to one of *explication*, in a similar way to that in which the GPO Film Unit operated during the 1930s. The difference between television and radio is most obviously that whereas the listener to 'blind radio' must have every detail verbally described to visualise the scene, this is not necessary when there are images. In the words of Philip Dorte:

> The sound broadcasting commentator has not only to point out what is going on; he has, above everything, to paint a word picture of the general scene. On the other hand, the television commentator can to some extent ignore generalities as the picture makes these largely self-evident.[19]

The small Documentary Department came into being in July 1948, at Cecil

McGivern's behest. Drawing on his wartime work, the newly appointed Director of Television was especially concerned that post-war television broadcasting should focus upon people and personalities, as opposed to professional performances. The result was new magazine programmes like *Picture Page* (1936) and *London Town* (1948). These radio-inherited formats were designed to emphasise television's live capacity whilst remaining non-partisan. As Steve McCormack, *London Town*'s producer, recalls:

> We had no political axe to grind. We didn't give a damn about anything. But we were fascinated by what we were doing ... John Grierson said to me, 'When we made *Drifters*, we were really politicians with cameras. We felt extremely left wing'. But our attitude in BBC television early documentaries was nothing like that at all. You could almost say we were naive.[20]

Just as in sound broadcasting earlier, television producers discovered that series were an ideal way of constructing common points of reference and thereby creating a schedule. *Picture Page* encompassed a weekly quiz show and sports magazine, producing the first television 'personalities', like announcer Jasmine Bligh. Robert Barr, also an occasional producer on *London Town*, stated that his aim was, 'to avoid subjects which can only interest a minority. As far as possible every item will bear on something which each of us knows a little about or wants to know something about'.[21] *Kaleidoscope* (1948), another magazine programme, introduced by McDonald Hobley and produced by Stephen McCormack, went out at 8.45 pm on Fridays and was one of the earliest examples of adherence to a time-slot. Both Barr and an ex-Fleet Street journalist and film-writer, Percy Hoskins, were contributors. In terms of mapping the evolution of the story-documentary, a significant entry in the *Radio Times* lists a separate item within *Kaleidoscope*. It describes itself as 'a story-documentary, written in co-operation with Scotland Yard, to explain some of the new and ingenious frauds that have recently been worked on the unwary'.[22] *It's Your Money They're After* (1948), earlier produced on radio by Barr, was a dramatised reconstruction concerning post-war fraudsters and black-marketeers, featuring Scotland Yard. It is noteworthy on two accounts. First, it demonstrates the way in which the discrete form of the story-documentary emerges from the magazine programme, most likely in order to avoid the animus against series which were not associated to forms previously established by sound broadcasting. Second, Scotland Yard and crime were a prime source for institutional dramatised reconstructions, combining popularity with moral instruction, and from which grew the ordinary, British television police series.

It was from his knowledge of working in radio on magazine programmes that Barr gained the knowledge and expertise to realise that the function magazine formats performed could be imitated by story-documentary forms, thereby building up a regular schedule and economising on sets. Unofficial leader of the documentary group, Barr recognised the potential of the television story-documentary to provide both explanatory and didactic models, as well as opportunities for experimentation, particularly in terms of dramatised and repetitive forms. Prior to the war, Barr had worked in radio, under Lawrence Gilliam, Head of the BBC Features Department. He had also worked overseas as a BBC war correspondent, producing *Germany Under Control* (1946), a post-war documentary film, shown on television.

A traditional writer-producer – the term was carried over from sound broadcasting – Barr wrote and produced every programme item that came along. He went on to produce a television version of an earlier radio production, *I Want to be an Actor* (1946). This guide to the acting profession was followed by Michael Barry's *I Want to be a Doctor* (1947), a series of sorts, albeit on an annual basis. By the early 1950s, recruiting from radio, theatre, films and journalism, a mix of backgrounds which was to benefit the hybridity of the new medium, the small Documentary Unit had made a name for itself.

The move towards dramatisation occurred gradually, and was assisted by the arrival of personnel trained not in journalism, as Barr and McGivern, but in theatre, like Duncan Ross. This founder member of the documentary group had already established his reputation in the film world of docu-mentary. In 1944, Ross became a member of the Screenwriters Association and in 1947 the first scriptwriter for the recently re-opened television service: as Briggs would have it, the first full-time 'Documentary Writer and Script Supervisor' in the world.[23] Barry describes Ross as a 'wild, and sometimes difficult man' who had 'neither the professional workmanlike, staying power of Robert Barr, nor the vision and poetry of the much later Denis Mitchell, but he possessed a craftsman's eye for a subject'.[24] Ross's own 'first' was *London after Dark* (1946), a 'consensus' series to explain court life, and the work of the metropolitan magistrate to a newly en-franchised public. Claud Mullins, an 'actual' magistrate, advised on the programme, instituting a similar practice to that of the public service documentary film during the 1930s.

Mullins actually appeared in person, during *Magistrates Court*, produced in 1948, a programme based on police reports and Ross's own observation and research. A replica of Marlborough Street Court was built in the studio, and film inserts were telecined into the dramatised performance for outdoor scenes. Writing in the *BBC Quarterly* of his experience on the new series, Ross describes his modus operandi, in terms of camera-work:

> The first problem after selection was what angle should be taken for the general 'establishing' shot. That would almost determine the shape of the story. From the public benches, we would not be able to see the defendants' faces. The magistrate's point of view would be interesting but not for the 'key' shots – he was too important to them. Opposite the witness box seemed best.

He goes on to relate how once this decision about point of view was made, 'observation really started'. This mode of 'research' is interesting to follow, since it lays down a specific procedure that was to be fundamentally influential, all the way through to *Z Cars* and beyond. In the same article, Ross describes how, following the compilation of 'facts, figures, stories, data, contacts, cases', his own processes of observation from 'real life' court cases worked to construct the story-documentary narrative:

> Watch expression on a pressman's face – tells you the verdict, almost. That policemen, old RAF type. Officer too – obviously an officer, it's a DFC. Two Bibles, the Koran, a skull-cap; wonder a Quaker takes the oath, or does he. Funny how that spinster in the indecency case reads the oath, saying 'so help me God!'.[25]

Internal correspondence at the BBC from Ross, to Robert Barr and Atkins, points out that despite the fact that 'Probation Officer' was shown on the Friday just before Christmas Day, a time when an audience might not be guaranteed, the viewing figure was extremely favourable. The Audience Research Department, which had expanded from its war-time beginnings in radio, rated it the highest ever recorded for a studio production 'only one point below a cup-tie final' (here again, the OB is used as an index of popularity).[26] When Cecil McGivern decided that only part of the series would be repeated, Ross replied that a bowdlerised version, 'would divorce the theme from its context and spoil its build-up; it would lose the momentum and continuity of interest which is the main value of a series'.[27]

Ross next worked on the five-part *Course of Justice* (1951), which was, like its predecessor, a monthly, dramatised programme. Each *Radio Times* entry is accompanied by a mini-synopsis, usually centred upon a named individual: 'George Bunting, who liked the Remand Home', Henry Green, 'who stole a pigeon', 'the girl who boasted of the Approved School' or the 'sensitive and delicate Timothy Wade'. All these *fictitious* characters incarnate the different problems confronting 'Miss Hemmingway', the Probation Officer of the 'Juvenile Court'.[28]

Despite the previously cited evidence of its dramatisation, 'Probation Officer' was described in the *Radio Times* as the second of 'A series of five documentary programmes dealing with the work of the Juvenile Courts, Magistrates Courts and The Assizes'.[29] Obviously, producers here are capitalising on the known popularity of the form, but at the same time, there is an evident nervousness about misleading viewers, as implied by the *Radio Times* pre-publicity, written by Ross himself:

> Like the others in this series, 'Probation Officer' has virtually been hewn out of life itself. The area scoured in research stretches from Hammersmith to White Chapel and Wood Green to Peckham. The stories you will see have all been founded on fact, but they have been disguised so that no viewer in that area who may know the actual source of the stories will recognise them.[30]

Ross further informs *Radio Times* readers that James Bould and Eddie Wallstab, the designer and film editor respectively on the *Course of Justice* series, are 'working hard in their mission to make sure their work will not be noticed.' This concern for identifying to viewers the constructed nature of these representations sometimes went awry. Critics have cited the way in which Maurice Wiggin praised what he thought was a hospital OB, 'the real thing', as distinct from 'fact cooked up as fiction', when what he was seeing, was in fact a story-documentary.[31] Apart from building sets, it was also necessary for producers to construct relationships with the institutions which provided them with their storylines, a process which was often extremely tedious. A memo, from Ross to McGivern, dated 19 December 1950, states that whilst researching the first programme in the series, *Juvenile Court*, the:

> scripts had to pass five departments of the LCC, six departments of the Home Office, the Magistrates Association (since I had involved two magistrates in the programme, it seemed wise that I should consult the Association), the NSPCC (as I required facilities from them) the Chief Clerk of the Juvenile Court, two magistrates, five probation officers, principals of Goldhawn Remand Home and the resident psychiatrist. Many other organisations could have been consulted: the Civil Service Trade Union, the National Union of Teachers, the Police Federation, the Ministry of Health and several others.

Understandably, Ross saw a need to establish more formal procedures, 'otherwise we can be completely exhausted fighting scripts through the various organisations'.[32] Nonetheless, in press terms, the series was highly regarded. The 'Critic on the Hearth' in the *Listener*, stated that:

> owing to the competence of the writing the *Course of Justice* series has been one of the television successes of recent months ... We were the jury, the witnesses, the public in the gallery, small-part players in the unending drama of the layman v. the law.

The writer further praises the production for making use of 'the biggest composite set ever used in television'.[33] As Atkins observed, programmes of this type presented a challenge. Because of the documentary nature of this new style of drama, producers were anxious to preserve the illusion of reality 'and not to have an East End mother immediately recognised as the eccentric Duchess of last week's drawing-room comedy'.[34] Fearful of such an occurrence, producers sought out as yet unidentified actors. Ironically, as Troy Kennedy Martin, a *Z Cars* writer, discovered to his cost, when it was produced in series, familiarity bred not so much contempt as adulation.

Caryl Doncaster, previously mentioned, was a prominent member of the documentary group, who produced a number of story-documentaries during the 1950s, including *Report on Women* (1951), *The Rising Twenties* (1952) and *The Pattern of Marriage* (1953) – for which Ted Willis, author of *Dixon of Dock Green*, was the co-writer. Doncaster wrote about the nature and construction of the story-documentary form as, 'a method of translating complex social problems into human terms in a way which caught and has continued to hold the average viewer'.[35] She further noted that it was often the most unexpected and 'unrewarding' social problems, like those to do with the rehabilitation of ex-convicts in *Return to Living* which proved highly popular.

In order to trace the development of the British television police series from the dramatised story-documentary form, the final section of this chapter moves into the case studies of the key programmes which collectively map out the trajectory of the nascent British police series, first offering a profile of Robert Barr and his interest in crime and the police as a subject for mediation.

Crimes, Barr-none

Robert Barr's early concern with crime as a subject for the story-documentary is best explained in his own words. As he recollects:

When the war was over I went to TV as a new adventure. So you won't be surprised that in the early days I became interested in producing a police series ... Why police? In the early days of TV when all programmes were live, the 'closed community' was the easiest and neatest story to present on the screen: hospital wards, police stations and so on. And both provided neat and recognisable uniforms, which were, and still are, a bonus.[36]

As a crime reporter, both on Scottish newspapers and later in Fleet Street, Barr had covered both the daily run of crime in the magistrates courts and murder trials in the High Court. He therefore knew about both ends of the spectrum of police work, a knowledge which he was to exploit in his invention of the uniform police series, as well as his numerous productions about Scotland Yard:

in Fleet Street I had covered Scotland Yard, getting to know most of the top brass and especially Bob Fabian who was head of the Flying Squad: the Sweeney.[37]

It was in fact an early weekly story-documentary produced by Barr, *I Made News* (1951), featuring the dramatised true story of a protagonist who had made the news that week, which introduced the Fabian character, leading to the subsequent film series *Fabian of the Yard* (1954), undertaken by an independent film production company.

As stated in the Introduction, the theme of Scotland Yard was introduced early to television by *Telecrimes* (1946), closely followed by *The Murder Rap* (1947): both were reconstructions, done in the studio, of true crimes taken from the case-book, each introduced by a Scotland Yard inspector. On 26 June 1947, Barr produced *Armed Robbery* and *The Case of Helvig Delbo* followed a couple of months later. All these programmes were concerned with violent crime and murder and all cases were based on real-life cases from Scotland Yard. What consituted a constant diet of crime and violence was found by viewers to be somewhat 'lurid'. Jacobs cites correspondence in the *Radio Times* complaining that such fare is not suitable for a family audience, as well as a memo from Norman Collins to Cecil McGivern, which states:

we must be careful that nothing we do could provoke any action by the Lord Chamberlain to assume control of television plays by analogy with the control which he already exercises in the theatre.[38]

Such a statement is revealing of the high regard and nervousness with which the authorities viewed television's independence. Although dramatised reconstructions, or story-documentaries did not, at this time, constitute 'drama' as such, as will shortly become evident, Cecil McGivern was extremely anxious about how they might be perceived. In particular, he was chary of allegations of sleaze and the 'tabloid' references which seemed to confound story-documentaries, especially those connected to crime. Given the current climate, it may well have been that producing a programme accepted as a radio production, in a pre-established magazine format, as in the case of *It's Your Money They're After* was the safer option. Such programmes would be seen to emphasise the importance of post-war television accepting as well as extending radio's role as a means of moral reconstruction. Indeed, in correspondence, Barr stated his reason for wishing to portray crime representations in these terms:

> I believe that demobilisation will bring an increase in crime and that it would be a good idea to:
>
> (1) Persuade the public that crime doesn't pay.
> (2) Put the public wise to the technique likely to be employed by those who believe it does pay.[39]

Of course, this can also be seen as the beginning of the end of a rather thin, double wedge. Barr, as will be demonstrated, was not unaware of the popularity of crime representations which made them such ideal material for experimenting with extended formats. It was often a case of pulling the wool over McGivern's eyes, in terms of pleading the educational value of productions that might otherwise be regarded as too sensationalist in a *News of the World* sense. McGivern, far from blind to such strategies, would only allow him to go so far before engaging in his own rug pulling tactics.

The six-part *War on Crime* (1950) was Barr's earliest post-war television story-documentary series. The idea for the *War on Crime* series was first mooted during a lunch discussion between Barr and Morgan who had been researching a film script, for Twentieth Century Fox, at Scotland Yard. Morgan's copious notes during research for the film, provided a basis for the programme.[40] Hoskins, a well-known ex-crime reporter on the *Daily Express*, had previously acted as collaborator and contact for Barr in his radio series *It's Your Money They're After* (1947) and was on good terms with 'the heads at Scotland Yard'. Barr had himself met all the Scotland Yard Chiefs, from the Commissioner downwards, from the previous radio series, which the Commissioner had himself introduced. Apart from the difficulties of securing institutional cooperation, which I will be discussing further, there were those of finding a mode of expression for the new genre. This is evident in the inconsistencies with which they are publicised.

'Gold Thieves', the first programme in the *War on Crime* series, is cryptically announced, entered in the *Radio Times* in the somewhat ambiguous terms borrowed from radio:

> *War on Crime*
> A feature programme.[41]

There is nothing much here to indicate the programme's documentary nature or the fact that it was to be the first of a six-part series. As Duncan Ross has argued, neither the term 'talks' nor 'features' is appropriate to documentary:

> Indeed, both are peculiarly uninformative in describing their purposes: 'talks' suggests housewives gossiping over the back fence, while 'features' conjures up the image of a face that is interesting but not very handsome.[42]

The *Radio Times* entry for the first episode of the *War on Crime* series indicates that it was to be broadcast during the same week as the documentary film *Target for Tonight* (1941). The juxtaposition of the two productions suggests that despite winning the real war, the reconstructionist ends of winning the peace are still being waged, particularly against crime.

The entry for 'Woman Unknown', the second programme in the series again remains anonymous, but it is a little more expansive in describing itself:

> *War on Crime*
> One of a series of documentary programmes
> which open the casebooks of Scotland Yard and presents
> authentic methods of crime detection [sic].[43]

The emphasis on *authenticity* is similar to the later *Course of Justice* series, articulating the need to inform the public about the practices of organisations which, prior to the war, had hitherto only been superficially portrayed in films.

Juxtaposed with *War on Crime*'s programme entry in the *Radio Times* is a cartoon advertising the Territorial Army. In the second picture of the advertisement a young boy asks, 'What's your Dad joining the territorials for? Doesn't he know the war's over?'[44] It is as if the language of combat, familiar from the war has now been deflected to the civilian interests of reconstructing the nation via a new, home battalion engaged in gaining popular consensus, via the 'War on Crime'.

'Gold Thieves' represents a true event, that of a large-scale gold bullion robbery from London Airport. Internal correspondence describes it as, 'The story of a robbery attempted on a scale unprecedented in British criminal records, and the attempt to steal gold bullion to the value of a quarter of a million pounds from London Airport, July 1948'.[45] Whilst nothing remains of the script or performance of this particular programme, correspondence from Barr to McGivern indicates that television story-documentaries of this kind considerably strained the resources of the producer, actors and technicians. Documentarists were trying not only to satisfy the reconstruction remit, but also, despite being hampered by financial restraints and a lack of technology, to push the form to its limits, experimenting without fear of failure (and despite McGivern's sometimes fussy supervision).

The cast list for the first programme in the *War on Crime* series runs to 18 people. Film details indicate that four pieces of archive footage of London Airport are to be inserted: the initials CFU indicate that this is to be obtained from Crown Film Unit archives. Four separate pieces of original footage are also to be especially shot by the BBC TV Film Unit and six tracks of music are to be incorporated, including Ravel's 'Alborada del Gracioso' and Fagan's 'Motif for Murder'. In addition, nine special effects discs are listed. The supply of especially shot film was an unusual occurrence because of the financial restrictions placed upon the early Documentary Group.[46] Film inserts had been used right from the beginning of television's restart after the war, but only for prestige productions. During the 1950s, with the creation of the BBC Television Film Unit (1955), they become more usual. Prior to that, it was necessary to commission outside companies, an expensive process.

An internal memorandum from McGivern, marked 'private', gives an idea of both the authoritarianism inherent in the BBC's internal organisation and the risks Barr was prepared to take defying it. Commenting about the performance of 'Woman Unknown' McGivern remarks:

> There was fortunately, a very great difference between the transmission and the completely chaotic rehearsal … the show was good, nearly very good. But please Robert, do not do this again. It is so bad to risk a flop, to worry actors and technicians till they do not know whether they are on their head or their heels, to put out an unrehearsed programme with fluffs and prompts and all the rest of it.[47]

He continues, as if berating a tiresome but talented pupil, 'Your programmes are valuable – too valuable to play about with like this. And I mustn't allow it. And I have to point out that Robert Barr now has a reputation for this sort of thing. Can he get rid of it, now?'[48]

Here, McGivern is showing the typically patrician attitude of the more senior member of the BBC hierarchy towards the junior, in an organisation where inter-personnel relationships appear to resemble that of a public school rather than a public service corporation. McGivern's specific complaint here, however, seems to be that of under-rehearsal. A shortage of studio space permitted only one final studio rehearsal before transmission, earlier ones being carried out in schools, pubs, or wherever the BBC could find a suitable space. This inevitably led to near misses which understandably caused some nervousness on the part of senior managers, who ultimately had to carry the can. Undeterred, Barr, the *enfant terrible*, writes back to McGivern by return enclosing a favourable press-cutting – one of many – from the *Daily Mail*:

> It was so well done that even the most fixed anti-documentary critic could have no complaint … It told its story, it put over its little bit of education, and with that combined first class entertainment and genuine artistic merit in its treatment.[49]

Reticent, modest, but quietly confident, Barr, perhaps a touch dis-ingenuously, adds a self-effacing comment: 'All of this baffles me. I feel that it was under-rehearsed, that the clamour of the rushed rehearsal upset my cast, and that the background sounds weren't quite right. This was due to lack of sound rehearsal'. And, arch-Machiavellian that he is, he precipitately takes the opportunity to request an extra day's studio rehearsal for his next show, 'Woman Unknown' (17 April 1950). The camera script for this second programme in the *War on Crime* series fortunately survives. In terms of generic development, it is deserving of some analysis and is therefore worth quoting from in some detail.

From the first, it is evident that the role of the *War on Crime* series is to inform the public as fully as possible about Scotland Yard procedure over serious crime, in this case, that of an unsolved murder, and to use television to its best advantage, combining its demonstrative capacity with its story-telling ability. Despite the public service documentary films, which had penetrated most public institutions, the television camera was regarded with a great deal more suspicion. Representing the inner sanctum of Scotland Yard was a move akin to the later penetration of Westminster Abbey on the occasion of the Queen's Coronation (1953). Nonetheless, since the Met had co-operated earlier with film companies, in terms of allowing them access to film and newspaper personnel and even case files, it felt obliged to co-operate, especially as there might be a fortunate public relations outcome. The storyline of 'Woman Unknown' was based on the real-life Manton Murder, investigated by police between November 1943 and March 1944, a fact not distributed to the general public so as to protect the identities of relations still alive. Correspondence from New Scotland Yard warns producers that if the story is not 'considerably camouflaged' it will be recognised.

The programme's debt to the detective film is most immediately indicated by the opening titles. Following a fade-up on the opening caption '*War on Crime*', a blue lamp rising behind it is seen flashing above a Metropolitan Police box. Both are resonant icons, carried over from the earlier Ealing Studios film production, *The Blue Lamp* (1950). Next, a policeman is seen turning by the box, a sequence which is to be repeated in the later *Dixon of Dock Green* series (1955). As the programme title 'Woman Unknown' comes up, the back projection of a squad car is seen driving into camera, a film noir trope seen in the opening sequence of the later *Fabian of the Yard* (1954). The third establishing shot is set in Scotland Yard's Map Room. A close-shot of a map headed 'Deaths by Violence' is explained by the action of a hand placing a flag on the outskirts of the Metropolitan area. The voice-over supplements the visuals:

> This is the story of a murder – a murder apparently without a clue, unpremeditated and followed by meticulous skill in concealment; the detection of which, for sheer tenacity and perseverance, has few equals in the records of Scotland Yard.[50]

According to the camera script, the next shot, somewhat ironically, shows a map which is coded in rings and flags whose colours indicate the kind of crime committed: Green for murder, Yellow for manslaughter, Red for abortion, and Blue for infanticide. Since the 1951 audience can only view the live studio production in black and white, its full significance can only be made evident by the voiceover. This further explains, that:

> The flag marks the spot, the ring the sequel but between the pinning of a flag and the placing of the coloured ring, weeks, months, years of painstaking investigation may take place, for in Scotland Yard, the file of a murder is never closed until it is solved.[51]

An establishing shot is followed by individual shots of police and detectives filing into a lecture room; the voice-over commentary continues but is subsequently attached to an inspector, lecturing on the homicide tree, showing 14 kinds of homicide. It was subsequently thought by Scotland Yard that graphic representations of the 13 omissions might give too much information away to would-be criminals, as well as place too great an emphasis upon the existence of crime more of a problem post-war than the government cared to admit.

Following its opening titles, the first close-shot in 'A Woman Unknown', taken from above, focuses on 'the disordered body of a woman' lying face-down in rough undergrowth, 'the limbs twisted in the ungainly posture of violent death'. Thankfully, the figure is 'Hettie from Hendon', the police model used for demonstration purposes. The voice-over continues 'unemotionally', as the viewer is shown how to spot clues and take evidence from a corpse, its fictitious nature reassuringly displayed by the hand which comes into shot to unscrew its head. There follow scenes of the CID room and the mortuary, all in the service of explaining just what is involved in the solving of a serious murder, still punishable in 1951 by hanging. The commentator then dis-appears and the action becomes fully dramatised. It is as if once its authority has been established via its little bit of instruction, the story can start to entertain.

Writing in the *Sunday Times*, Maurice Gorham cites 'Woman Unknown' as being both well-written and well-acted: it is 'the best documentary I have seen on television, and it need not fear comparison with its opposite numbers in films ... the chief credit goes to the producer, Robert Barr, who succeeded in breaking away from the confined atmosphere that still cribs and cabins so many television shows'. He comments further that Barr has obviously ben-efited from his 'sojourn' with documentary film-makers, not least in the neat-ness with which he 'covered' his inserts of silent film.[52]

Such an accolade provides good ammunition for the junior producer in his unspoken war of attrition with the Head of Television Programmes. Perhaps, to keep his potentially renegade producer in line, McGivern's praise for this second programme is somewhat qualified. Whilst 'a very much better show from the point of view of scope, casting and production than the first ... Eighty per cent successful', he proceeds to set out his reasons for its ten percent shortfall.[53] Firstly, he claims that the production was exceedingly noisy, so that 'fifty percent of the effect was killed'. Secondly, that it was 'still too slow', alleging that on many occasions an actor only appeared to perform after 'he had been faded in' by the camera. He also notices that some of the camera fades were very late, especially over the captions: 'January, February and March', which he felt were left on the screen a ludicrously long time. Was this, he asks 'simply due to the lack of camera rehearsal time? The point is an extremely serious one'.[54]

McGivern's general complaints about finding the production slow are connected to a more serious one about over-running. For early television, where none of the material was pre-recorded, programme start and finish times were crucial. If the schedule went awry, by even the smallest amount of time, it meant that the subsequent programme was held up. In the case of 'Woman Unknown' which, according to McGivern, overran by four-and-a-half minutes it:

> had a most unfortunate effect on the following programme and both Joy Nichols and Jimmy Edwards had to return to their theatre before they appeared on the programme. This practically ruined the end of the OB from Madame Tussaud's and must have upset Michael Henderson very considerably for he had prepared this OB very carefully indeed.[55]

Undaunted, Barr's reply is quick to refute McGivern's criticism, cheekily commenting, 'I wonder whether your knowledge that this programme was over-running, and what the over-run would mean, made you feel this'. He further points out that McGivern's opinion is contradicted by favourable press reports and that: 'none mentioned studio noise. I am sure they would have referred to it if *fifty per cent* of the effect was killed.'[56] In the same three-page memorandum, Barr is decent enough to take the opportunity of suggesting ways of improving sound technology. Problems with studio noise arise from:

(i)   The design of the studio
(ii) The movement of floor lighting equipment.
(iii) The employment of iron men dollies which trundle across the floorboards.
(iv) The type of unit sets we use.
(v)   The necessary movement of studio staff.[57]

Having got his 'oar' in, he exploits an opportunity to expand upon on the difficult conditions of live production. When McGivern criticises the slowness of the programme's captions. Barr replies that this was due to:

> missing an early chord in the music for a fade-out of the first month, with the result that the second chord became the first, the third the second, and we found ourselves waiting an interminably long time for a point in the music where we could conveniently fade out. This should also have been backed by a loop of film showing some interesting movement such as leaves blowing in the wind etc. but our library could supply only daffodils. This, I refused.[58]

Whilst fully owning up, Barr does not miss the opportunity to draw McGivern's attention to the problems of limited resources in the film library. His memo concludes with waspish thanks, 'for your kind summing-up. I will try to make the next in the series 95% successful. This is a bonus of 5%'.

Not only did Barr have to negotiate complex technical problems, as well as parrying constantly with McGivern, he also had to ensure good relations with the police on whose co-operation these productions were dependent. A letter from the Met congratulates the producer on his success with the *War on Crime* series, but indicates that the police will continue to co-operate with future productions only if they promote good police public relations. In these circumstances, they will:

> give such assistance as we are able, provided that, like the radio series 'It's Your Money They're After', the programmes are designed to warn the public against various types of criminals and to encourage them to co-operate with the police in their efforts to combat crime ... It might also be possible in such a series to urge the need for more recruits to the police if crime is to be kept in check.[59]

Furthermore the letter states that Scotland Yard will in future want to 'see scripts for checking and approval a month in advance of rehearsal'.[60] Subsequent internal correspondence from the Met requests that future episodes in the *War on Crime* series be based 'on the work of experts not directly employed by the Yard, i.e. the ballistic expert, the pathologist, and the work of the International Police'. Barr resolves the problem by agreeing to base the remaining episodes on Scotland Yard's outside work, and to submit a copy of each script to the Yard, welcoming their alterations and advice. However, the matter of including a 'full co-operation' credit in the titles will be deferred until a new series is agreed.

Despite Barr's skilful negotiations with Scotland Yard, their 'full co-operation' was secured with increasing difficulty. Series dramatisations, so far as the Met was concerned, seemed to blur the boundaries between fact and fiction until they were being misrepresented. Documentarists, on the other hand, saw dramatisation and series production as the only way forward for television expansion, in terms of establishing it as a medium capable of producing its own, self-originated forms. Although Barr ensured there would be detailed discussions between the BBC and the Metropolitan Police, the arrangement for the checking of scripts fell down because of the sheer volume of work involved. The resulting delays began to strain not only the internal relationship between programme-makers and the BBC, but the relationship between the BBC and the Met. This tension was not going to disappear, and was to resurface spectacularly in the *Z Cars* series.

Striking it weekly

A typical criticism of the *War on Crime* production from the *Daily Mail* was that 'it was separated by much too long a gap. A month is too long a period to expect anyone to remember the idea behind the series'.[61] In order to achieve maximum effect from a series format in terms of building up a predictable audience, Barr realised the necessity of programmes being produced on a weekly basis.

I Made News was the first story-documentary series produced by Barr, in response to McGivern's request to produce an experimental *weekly* show or 'strike', over a nine-week period. Its production marks a significant point in the growth of the Documentary Unit, whose growth was represented by its removal to new premises in the Marylebone Road, and the setting up of an additional production unit.

Although McGivern was not naturally disposed to series forms, he nonetheless saw the wisdom in establishing more streamlined production method. Following a trip to America, he had been highly impressed by the way producers were managing to do one show a week, 'not one a month, as we were'. At his behest, Barr experimented with setting up a production unit, for which *I Made News* was to be a case study, designed to produce a 30-minute documentary programme each week over 12 weeks. This was to be the first time that directors had been used in television. In both radio and television, writer-producers directed their own shows. The new experiment of separating out the functions of direction and production was set up to see if it was possible for the producer, who had choice of the story, could also supervise casting and rehearsal, whilst at the same time being able to impose a style of production on the series.

A breakdown of the day-to-day work of each programme demonstrated that the minimum time necessary for the preparation of these weekly shows was 14 days. Having tried three units in operation, Barr felt that this would be too costly in terms of personnel and office accommodation, so he decided to try to see if the same output could be achieved by two units. Each unit was to consist of a director, a production secretary and a stage manager. These were to remain constant factors throughout the series, working as a team and in the same rehearsal rooms. A single designer was to be appointed 'giving continuity which was most valuable'. There were three different senior technicians responsible, although in retrospect it was felt that for the sake of continuity 'it would have been smoother all round if one S. Tel E [Senior Television Engineer] had been given this series'.[62] The work of the studio manager was seen to significantly increase throughout the series until he was acting as unit manager. Barr mentions the importance of the script itself: 'The cost of a programme starts with the script and experience of TV saves money'.[63] He notes, without a hint of self-congratulation, that out of nine programmes, the three which rated highest in terms of audience appreciation were written or co-written by himself.

I Made News was controversial from the start, due to its experimental nature. Barr was less concerned with producing a good programme than a vehicle by which to advance series production methods. As he states, 'It was understood that this was an experiment in quantity rather than quality'.[64] Nonetheless, the audience research report named *I Made News* as one of eight programmes out of 29 under survey which had a viewing audience of 'over two million'.[65] The series' narrative interests centred around the exploits of a well-known weekly 'newsmaker'. Some were based in Holland, featuring the exploits of the Dutch police, others involved the FBI. The person who had been 'in the news', for example a detective who had uncovered a smuggling racket, introduced the programme, which then took the form of an acted dramatisation of the event in question. At the end of each programme, the newsmaker in question would appear in person, commenting on the story. However, the 'real' character's appearance following that of the actor, was often a problem which caused a clash of registers, which became particularly evident when they were not natural performers. As Barr discovered, although detectives like Robert Fabian could be highly articulate in 'real life' (especially over a convivial drink in a Soho bar), they found the pressure of television telling. As he told me:

> Now Bob Fabian was a fascinating story teller and very funny with it. When talking about his memoirs he would put one hand to his nose and stretch out the other hand like a tailor measuring cloth and call it Fabian By The Yard. I've seldom heard anyone talk so well or tell a story so well but … BUT … BUT like so many others when faced with a microphone he dried up and then tried to put on a BBC voice.[66]

Critical opinion was divided about the *I Made News* series. The *Listener* complained that 'not the least mystifying part about *I Made News*, has been the necessity for importing American villainy into the programme', further commenting that the most recent of the series 'had little visual interest, let alone dramatic force'. Other critics maintained that 'the two FBI cases supplied tensions that made good viewing if not exemplary television'.[67] The *Listener* berated:

> The compilation of these programmes had better have been handed over to the staff of *The News of the World*. At least we might have been spared the miscellany effect. And the detective inspector who went to spend the night in the home of the parents of the threatened child would have been offered a drink very much sooner. *I Made News* has only occasionally made good television. As the creator of 'Raffles' may not have said, there's no police like Holmes.[68]

From such a perspective, the only legitimate forms of police representation are those drawn from golden age *fiction*, hence the reference to Sir Arthur Conan Doyle. Here, yet again, we see the authorities trying to foist onto television the respectability of literary, derived forms.

The importance of *I Made News* lay in its introduction of a more efficient division of labour and a distinction between producer and director, moving away from the old writer-producer system established by radio. What Barr aimed to establish within the Documentary Unit, by the rationalisation of production techniques, was a more collaborative process, taking away the authority of the writer and delegating it to a team. Seeing a parallel between the teamwork of the television studio and the police, he stated that 'The TV police series is team work even when all of the episodes are by the same writer'.[69] Once more, we are reminded of the Ealing plaque, but now, the 'film studio with the team spirit' has become the television studio. The new methods Barr introduced in *I Made News* both increased production and considerably enhanced the BBC's ability to compete with the arrival of Independent Television (ITV), contributing to productions like *Z Cars* during the early 1960s. This was no mean achievement, because, unlike ITV's series and serial production, expensively shot on film, that of the BBC continued to be produced live.

Barr saw that the first step in the process of rationalisation he wished to introduce was to break the power of the autocratic Producer, sharing the responsibility with these new creatures called 'Directors'.[70] He explained that the word was not in use to start with. The object of the exercise was simply a weekly strike. Series as such simply could not happen in 'live' television until the weekly strike had been perfected. *I Made News* introduced a new unit scheme with a single producer and two directors, each working on two separate, overlapping productions. This system of production worked on the lines of film practice, having a producer in charge of all productions, but with the newly appointed directors, responsible for rehearsal and studio presentation. This system was to remain in place from 1952 onwards and formed the basis of series television production as we know it today.

Barr was very interested to see what kind of attempt a *film* writer would make upon a television show and gave Jack Howells – a feature-film writer – the ninth programme. It turned out to be the most costly of the lot but since he had saved money on his own programmes he reckoned he could afford to 'give the director a "break" … as part of the experiment'. This was to be of crucial importance to series planning. It meant the budget could operate on a flexible basis, spread across the length of the whole series, so that experimentation could take place without undue risk. Barr notes that out of all the writers he tried out on *I Made News*, there isn't one with whom he is satisfied. Despite paying over the odds, at 50 guineas a script and breaking down the process into three phases – story, treatment and scenario, each to be paid separately – scripts were still late, indifferent, and written with little knowledge of television practice.[71] By getting in a script on time and writing it 'with a knowledge of TV studio practice', Barr estimated that he could considerably cut down on *I Made News*. The directorial experiment was an unqualified success. With each programme was learned more and, less supervision was required. Finally, Barr rounds off the *I Made News* experiment to conclude:

> I have now learned enough about this system of production to say that:
>
> (a) A Producer can impose his style on the production
> (b) Obtain a better production by knowing what is wanted, watching and advising.
> (c) Smooth the way for the director provided the producer and director work well together and that their temperaments are suited to this style of work.

In conclusion, although the director was closely connected with the creative work and therefore important he was also, according to Barr's system, expendable. Leonard Brett, an *I Made News* director, looked upon the new scheme, working with one producer and two directors, as groundbreaking. In a short report he wrote under the subheading, 'advantages':

> Some form of this scheme is essential if Television is to expand naturally using its best brains to best advantage. I feel that similar layouts should be tried in other departments (particularly Drama) in view of the considerable measure of success obtained in Documentary. Television must always be in danger of losing its best production brains to better paid jobs inside or outside the Corporation. Robert Barr's great experience in Documentary as

a writer and producer in both films and Television was available to his two directors; personally, I found it invaluable. His responsibility for the series' success meant that the benefit of his advice when needed was freely and immediately available; at the same time he was not bothered with the routine, the trivial or anything that was going well. By this scheme the great technical and practical experience of the best Television producers like George More O'Ferrall, Royston Morley and Michael Barry can be passed on and absorbed, their creative genius imitated, digested and made to stimultate the best in others before they are lost to Television production.

Under 'Disadvantages' Brett clearly feels that any more than six productions begins to strain the system, placing too great a demand on the directors. He states:

> The idea of weekly Documentary seems to me excellent; staff get to anticipate, the viewer remembers easily, difficulties in one production are noted as warnings for the next with less time in between to forget. But it is a very great strain on directors. Nine productions in a row is too many under the 1 producer, 2 directors scheme, and throws too much of a strain on all concerned, but particularly on the director. I am sure that both Kevin Sheldon and myself can take it as well as anyone but I know that we were both finished at the end in a way that is not desirable at any time, but certainly should not happen again if work is to keep the standard that this series held. Six in a row is quite enough for anyone.

Rounding off the report, Brett suggested that the new distribution of roles be publicised in the *Radio Times*, conveying 'a brief idea of what Producer, Director and that unique Bird, John Oxley (the set designer) do respectively for a Documentary'. The new regime introduced by *I Made News* was a milestone in streamlining BBC television practice, enabling the production of popular drama series and introducing the role of Director, a term alien to television and 'not used even in other Documentary programmes'.

Blue Lamp series

Pilgrim Street was a six-part series put out on a weekly basis during 1952 and built out of Barr's experiment with *I Made News*.[72] It contains all the germinal ideas of *Dixon of Dock Green*, as well as those for the later *Z Cars* series. The new series was made 'with the co-operation of New Scotland Yard', an acknowledgement which seemed to guarantee its authenticity. *Pilgrim*

Street, like its immediate long-running successor *Dixon*, has many parallels to the Ealing film, *The Blue Lamp* (1951), not least the fact that Jan Read, who co-wrote the script with Ted Willis, was also the television series' writer.[73]

Pilgrim Street ran from June to July and was produced at the newly acquired Lime Grove television studios. Robert Barr was the series' producer, Kevin Sheldon its director. From internal correspondence, it seems that Scotland Yard were only prepared to give their full co-operation to the series provided Jan Read, with whom they had collaborated on the original treatment of *The Blue Lamp*, as previously discussed, wrote the scripts. This is demonstrative both of the way in which television had to collaborate with film personnel and of the transmigration between film, radio and television. A article, written by Read himself, shows that *Pilgrim Street* was made with an eye to educating the public about the more mundane aspects of policing. Drawing links with Edgar Wallace-style narratives the new programme-type defines itself against the spectacular crimes of stories which:

> generally centre on a murder; a Superintendent ... always a Superintendent ... hurries to the scene from Scotland Yard; after two hundred and fifty pages or eight reels of film, and by dint of superhuman ingenuity, he succeeds in cracking the case and pinning the crime on to the unlikeliest of the suspects.

The piece reminds its audience that so far as the real-life police situation in 1952 is concerned, 'murder is the rarest of crimes'.

Whereas Barr's previous *War on Crime* series had focused on the work of the élite members of Scotland Yard and the most serious crimes, *Pilgrim Street* was a deliberate attempt to represent those incidents which 'never find their way into the pages of the Commissioner's Report and in which the police act as helpers and protectors of the public'.[74]

The new focus on ordinary everyday crime, as well as the ordinary everyday policeman represented a close link with the aims of the early Documentary Movement's discovery of the heroism of the ordinary man. Barr and Read conceived the series around the Pilgrim Street station, which, although linked by modern communication methods with Scotland Yard, 'the most up-to-date police organisation in the world', is nonetheless centred upon the 'few square miles' round the station. It was 'the manor' that was to provide the action, not only for the present series, but for *Dixon of Dock Green* and, years later, the Sun Hill Police Station of *The Bill*. *Pilgrim Street* was supposed to be a spontaneous record of what occurs when 'a fire breaks out, an old lady is taken ill in the street, a child runs away from home ... in the houses, the pubs, the amusement arcades, where police-work begins'.[75]

However, the series almost did not come about. Disturbed by the negative reception to *I Made News*, a supposed experiment in rationalising production methods, McGivern yet again felt Barr had slipped past another traduced variety of television. His fears are raised in an internal memo, dated 18 February 1952, expressing a 'profound dissatisfaction at the new series':

> I do not like these at all and the series is heading for trouble – or postponement ... Perhaps I expected the wrong thing but these stories are pretty sordid without doing any good at all, in my opinion. They are 'News of the World' and not, as they are, worth the expense bother etc. of a television series.

McGivern's sleaze allegations echo those of the *Listener*, cited previously. In his estimation *Pilgrim Street*'s stories are 'ordinary to the point of dullness'.[76] Such condemnation hardly seems to square with his other allegations. It is illustrative of the nervousness with which these new, dramatised forms, produced in series, were negotiated, as senior BBC authorities struggled against their own residual Reithianism and producers like Barr, pioneers of television.

In terms of marking a departure towards more narrativised modes, *Pilgrim Street* was important. Once again, the new series deliberately set out to define itself as a *fictitious* location. As the *Radio Times* entry states, 'You will not find *Pilgrim Street* listed in the telephone directory'. Previously, story-documentaries authenticated their veracity by using real locations and true stories – although in the case of serious crimes these were sometimes disguised (as in 'Woman Unknown') so as to protect its victims. Nonetheless, its presentation belies a certain confusion, evidenced by the contradictory roller title which describes the establishing programme as 'The first of a series of six documentary stories about a London police station, written with the co-operation of New Scotland Yard.'[77] Nothing here to indicate its fictive nature, bar the word 'story'. *Pilgrim Street* is a hybrid of styles. It continues the use of the authoritative voice-over of the *War on Crime* series. As the roller title-wording clears the screen, we see the title displaying the words: 'No. l: 'On Our Manor'. As it changes, the background slowly dissolves to a map on which a thick black line shows the boundary of the 'manor':

> *Voice (Overscene)* Our manor – our ground. It's as varied as anything in London. The railway station is in the centre there, and around it are the cinemas, the shopping streets, the warehouses, the pubs, the pawnbrokers, and the little streets. Up here, luxury flats, spacious squares and gardens, and the embassies. Skirting it all, the Embankment and the river. That's our ground – our manor. And right here is our station – Pilgrim Street.

According to the script, the series' opening titles, similar to those of *EastEnders* today, map out the terrain in which the dramatic action is to take place, but with the addition of a documentary-style voice-over. Behind the opening titles, the first shot shows the doorway of the station: off-centre, a lamp bears the inscription 'Police'. Like the later *Dixon* series, *Pilgrim Street* closes with an identical shot to the first establishing one. In this way, it invents the device of framing the narrative which was to become a distinctive feature of the uniformed police genre. The inscribed lamp would have had resonance for those who had seen *The Blue Lamp* (1950) and it was no accident that one of *Pilgrim Street*'s working titles was the same as that of the film, as picked up by pre-publicity in the *Evening Standard*:

> Inside Job: TV is also to have its Blue Lamp series. Once again this will be a Barr project. In May six programmes will start on life in an ordinary police station – reconstructed in the studio and with actors in uniform.[78]

Again, it is noteworthy that the programme's truth status is made as clear as possible, lest there be any misunderstanding. Lessons have also been learned from the experience of *I Made News* and only six programmes are to be broadcast so as to lessen the strain on the directors. A memo from Barr to Cecil Madden expresses nervousness about the *Blue Lamp* name, 'because of fears it might cause offence in celluloid circles'.[79] This refers to the problematic relationship between the television service and the cinema industry during the post-war period: as a consequence, the programme name was changed to *Pilgrim Street*.

'On Our Manor' was the first episode in the *Pilgrim Street* series. It established its location in, and is full of the small events which occur at, a police station: missing children; lost visitors from abroad; a girl who has taken a fall down some steps; and a bag-snatcher. The police are seen out on the beat around their 'manor' giving directions, discovering stolen fur coats in the back of a car and drinking endless cups of tea. As Chris, one of the police constables, says, 'a lot of small stuff'. However, he is reprimanded by 'Taff', older and wiser, who speaks for the series as a whole: 'Take it from an old gravel-cruncher, the CID isn't so different. More spectacular maybe, but what is it in the end – lost property too – main difference, it's more expensive'.[80] When Chris, undeterred by such home truths, replies that at least at the CID there are murders to investigate, Taff replies that lives also: 'were somebody's property too, once. And when do we come across a murder, except in the papers?'[81]

And this was to become the common discourse of the uniformed police show, as it developed within the documentary tradition in British television.

Its main concern being not so much with the larger crimes but the smaller everyday concerns which affect people and their property. These programmes, the very opposite of the whodunnits inherited from golden-age detective fiction, do not present great mysteries which have to be solved. Instead, they provided people with a sense of reassurance and comfort that their ordinary, everyday concerns are being met.

'On Our Manor' gives a good indication of *Pilgrim Street's* content. The police are shown dealing with several situations. The first involves a problem to do with 'aliens'. Two Italian women turn up at the station, after failing to meet their daughter's fiancé at a railway station. They speak little English, and are represented as dazed and thoroughly bewildered. A WPC named Miss Kelly is despatched to administer comforting cups of tea. Meanwhile, an ambulance is on its way to Pilgrim Street with a pregnant girl who has fallen from a pavement. Plenty of procedure is shown, including a police parade of men lined up for night duty. A note on the script for the next scene states: 'There should be about a dozen PCs on parade. If necessary the longer shots can be pre-filmed, the action being covered in two-shot'.

In the scene that follows, we see the different 'beats' taking over:

SERGEANT   One-o-five?

PC 46   Sergeant.

SERGEANT   Nine beat, taking over 12 beat between one and two fifteen.
                  819? *(there is no reply)*
                  819?

CHRIS HAYNES, a tall, well-favoured young P/C of about twenty-three, answers up from the ranks.

CHRIS   PC Davis is playing the match against the Railway Police, Sergeant. They should be just about finishing.

SERGEANT   *(with a twinkle)* Don't put him off his game.

CHRIS   *(loudly)* Sergeant!

SERGEANT   And that's the lot. Anyone not called?

There is no reply, and Inspector Cove now enters and goes over to the sergeant.

COVE   'Evening sergeant. Anything for me tonight?
                  The sergeant hands over various lists of lost cars, etc.

All this is far more reminiscent of the *Dixon of Dock Green* series than the *Blue Lamp* film, with an extra emphasis on the dramatisation of a particular kind of beat-policing. Leisure activities such as the darts match are seen as an important part of engendering a team spirit, in a similar way to that involved in making the production itself. Characters are typologies: Welshmen say 'bach', and gentry are given bad names like 'Lady Smithers'. A central incident occurs when this last particularly tiresome individual rushes into the police station having lost her furs and jewels which she has somewhat carelessly – not to say improbably – left lying around in her large American car. Luckily for her, Chris (PC Davies) has earlier spotted the boot of her large American car. 'You'll get a letter of thanks and a packet of moth balls', he is told upon their recovery. The Italian girl's fiancé finally turns-up; the police constable's missing son is found at a station 'up North'; the two suspicious rat-catchers are discovered to be bona fide after all, and the action closes with the – somewhat ironic – comment that, 'It's been a very quiet night'.

Despite McGivern's initial antipathy towards the *Pilgrim Street* series, it was obvious by the second transmission that it was popular. The Viewer Research Report for the second programme 'The Runaway' considered it 'admirably effective both as instruction and entertainment'. However, this public service discourse is tempered by criticism. Far from finding the series 'sensationalist' some viewers found it dull, 'because it was still an account of normal police station events with no major crime in the offing.' One viewer quoted his wife, 'an ex-policewoman of six years standing', as finding 'the whole ... completely true to life and just as things happen. It "spotlighted" the everyday escapades as well as the non-stop life and patience of the police'.[82] Others referred to the cast as 'inclined ... to make the policemen and policewomen they portrayed seem rather more polite and patient than is normal'.[83] Such conflicting attitudes anticipate the reception of *Z Cars*.

By 1953 there were many changes; not least was the arrival of Paul Rotha to head the Documentary Group, which, as a result of its previous activities, had been raised to departmental status. Although members of the staff wanted Robert Barr, appointed Acting Head, to take on the position, he refused to comply because he felt that had McGivern felt satisfied at the way the unit was being run, he would not have seen the need for appointing a head. Always at the more radical edge of the Documentary Movement, Rotha may well have hoped that in television he would be able to continue the Griersonian tradition, especially since he had worked previously with Duncan Ross at Strand Films. However, whilst Barr was well aware of the importance of exploiting the exciting qualities of television in its own right, Rotha only saw this in terms of film. He was, as Norman Swallow, who instituted *Special Enquiry* (1951), the current affairs programme that Rotha took over, stated, little interested in the drama documentary. What he *could* not come to terms with was the mixture of studio-reconstruction and film inserts which constituted documentary television realism. As he later said, on taking up his new position, 'I came across almost immediately what Cecil McGivern had never warned me about, that I had to use a minimum of film and a maximum of live in-the-studio'.[84] It was this institutional requirement, to do that which so strongly ran against his preference which led to the circumstances of Rotha's resignation. Although he had been approached by the then head of television George Barnes to practice his film expertise within the BBC Television Documentary Department, when he arrived he found that there were no facilities for processing film. After he left, due to mutual unhappiness on each side, Barnes told him, 'The trouble with you Rotha, you know too much about film'![85] The incident neatly summarises the way in which television required radical, innovative practitioners like Robert Barr, if it was to develop in its own terms. Just over a decade after Rotha's departure, Norman Swallow wrote of *Special Enquiry*, on which both were occupied throughout the period:

> what was missing was, simply, people. The men and women who appeared in our programmes were used merely as statistical evidence, and hardly ever did we try to discover what they were really like. The only occasions when people appeared 'in the round', with recognisable personalities and emotions and hopes, were ironically in dramatised documentaries, and then they were not real people at all, but the creations – based on facts no doubt – of a script-writer, a producer, a director, and a group of actors.[86]

The reminiscence is similar to Pat Jackson's comments about the British documentary film. The solution then, as we saw, was found in the arrival of the film story-documentary and it was to be exactly the same in television. But in addition, the threat of the break-up of 'the Brute force of monopoly' meant that what may be regarded as a second phase of documentary assimilation into the mainstream, crucially involved mass-production. That these changes were effected, through the small Documentary Department, within the exigencies of 'live television', on a limited budget and often in the face of reluctant authorities is, surely, truly remarkable.

Following Rotha's resignation, 1955 was a watershed generally for television. The BBC's monopoly was broken and with it the assumed dominance of radio over television. At the time, there was something of a diaspora within the Documentary Department. Members were shifted to Talks or Drama or moved to one or other of the new commercial companies. Accompanying an increase in story-documentary series production was an even greater move towards increased dramatisation. The shift towards fiction was partly technologically determined. Elaine Bell states that one of the reasons was that the old forms of story-documentary 'began to look increasingly unwieldy as soon as lightweight equipment allowed programmes to be recorded free from the confines of the studio'.[87] Programmes like *Special Enquiry* could now be shot on location, leaving the 'strange hybrid' story-documentaries to take on a new lease of life, building on the narrative experiments and series production of these formative years.[88]

Robert Barr's move towards establishing a new format of stock characters and a repeating format during the 1950s was fundamental to the development of the dramatised police series and its move into mainstream popular television where the actors built up their parts until writers wrote to suit the characters they had created. What he began to establish was that the format of the series was to take away the authority of the writer as auteur, delegating it not only to the actors, but to the team. As Barr himself has said, 'The TV police series is team work even when all of the episodes are by the same writer'.[89] Barr meanwhile had exiled himself from the BBC for a couple of years, until, after Rotha's 'resignation', he was asked back to head a reconstituted Documentary Unit (as will subsequently be discussed). In his absence, the achievements of the small documentary group were capitalised upon, and even appropriated by BBC Light Entertainment, as will be seen in the next chapter.

7. The debonair Bruce Seton, who plays the eponymous hero in
Fabian of the Yard (1954).

3

Entertaining Lightly: *Fabian of the Yard* to *Dixon of Dock Green*

> There are two main strands to the British police series
> which can be seen as characteristic of two kinds of realism.
> One strand derives from American films and TV series ...
> The other derives from the realism of Ealing and, in a
> distant sense, from Thirties documentary: a care for
> authenticity of location, an interest in working-class themes
> and setting ... *The Blue Lamp*, and Ted Willis' 1955 revival
> of the Jack Warner character in *Dixon of Dock Green*
> belongs to this tradition.
>
> Cary Bazalgette, *Crime Writers*[1]

As this book has already demonstrated, there is no straightforward ancestry to the realism of the British uniform police series. Whilst Bazalgette correctly implies that it derives from American films and TV series, 1930s documentary (if indirectly) and the realism of Ealing, this statement needs qualifying, for it omits the genre's central connection to the television story-documentary. Further, Bazalgette's implication of a shared tradition of authenticity, whilst qualified by the caveat of 'distance', tends to conflate Ealing's realism with that of 1930s documentary.

It is important to make the point, for the purpose of my argument, that whilst the Ealing film later assimilated to documentary realism, it nonetheless emerged from the *commercial* sector of the film industry, rather than that of state sponsorship. As has been well documented, the cosy, benevolent realism of Balcon's films with their poverty of desire, is different from the more stringent social critique of 1930s documentaries. Not until after the Second World War did the Ealing comedy inflect the different values and more considered analysis of the so-called problem film, exemplified by *The Blue*

Lamp.[2] Further, Bazalgette's juxtaposition of this Ealing production with the *Dixon of Dock Green* television series, implies a direct transference from film into television. As I demonstrated in the previous chapter, this is an ellipsis which avoids the complex negotiation which first takes place within the small Documentary Department. It was, above all, the earlier *Pilgrim Street* series, produced and directed by Robert Barr, that completed the story-documentary's trajectory towards full dramatisation, thereby providing the prototype for the metropolitan-centred British television police series from *Dixon of Dock Green*, up to today's *The Bill*.[3]

During the mid-1950s, due to the arrival of the Competitor, there was in all departments an urgent quest for new forms. The magazine format, derived from radio, as we saw in the previous chapter, provided the first repetitive forms and a popular, tabloid, news journalism that was to prove foundational. As one critic observes:

> the breakthrough in the BBC came not from the conservative news division but from the new 'Current Affairs' complex, with the launching in 1957 of *Tonight*, a typical daily programme with a magazine format, descended from both *In Town Tonight* and *Picture Page*, which won great popularity, and whose format was instrumental in shaping a whole new range of news and current affairs programmes.[4]

In terms of generic *fiction*, the breakthrough came, not, as might be expected, from Drama, but from Light Entertainment, in its production of new serial and series-forms which aimed to attract viewers in terms of their entertainment values, in order to educate them. First, there was *The Grove Family* (1954), British television's earliest soap opera (unlike in America where *The Guiding Light* transferred from radio to television in 1952, the British radio soap opera has never crossed over). Next came *Dixon of Dock Green* (1955), whose format was 'hatched' within the story-documentary department. Whilst fictional series forms (as I shall demonstrate) were earlier established by radio broadcasting, the Reithian attitudes which prevailed in post-war television, despite the absence of Reith himself, dictated a far stricter policy. With the 'threat' of competition, a change in attitude began to filter into BBC discourse, resulting in a reconfiguration of the terms of the public service remit, exemplified by Grace Wyndham Goldie's retrospective observation that, after all:

> it is enjoyment which enables television to enter the homes of individuals and, by doing so, offers to those interested in power a chance of influencing

the attitudes of millions and persuading them to courses of action – whether of buying specific goods or supporting specific policies – which, without that influence, they might not even consider.[5]

Just as the GPO, later the Crown Film Unit, realised that public service narratives must entertain to become popular, in order to instruct, so, too, the BBC was finally forced to recognise the power of the previously neglected third term of its remit: entertainment. *The Groves* and *Dixon of Dock Green* put BBC popular series fiction on the broadcasting map.

It is possible to compare television's collaborative methods during the 1950s both in terms of the previously mentioned team spirit, epitomised by the Ealing Studio plaque, and those of amateur theatricals. John Caughie rather nicely sums up this latter view of early television as:

> still driven by the enthusiasm of the amateur inherited from the pre-war pioneers. The whole discourse of production, the celebration of disaster, the informal working relations, the try-outs, carried something of the 'wizard prang' about it, an extension of church hall dramatics.[6]

As we have seen, this pioneering spirit is fully illustrated by the BBC television Drama-Documentary Department, particularly in Robert Barr's live series experiments. However, by the mid-1950s, the television medium significantly shifts away from its early period of amateurism. Tied in with a move towards a more professional production practice, are important cultural, social and institutional shifts, in particular the creation of the new Light Entertainment Department (1951).

This chapter tracks the process whereby BBC Light Entertainment (LE), in parallel with the small television Documentary Department, begins to produce its own self-originated narratives. It looks at the way in which LE reinterprets the BBC's public service remit, its policy-making decisions, and the new generic forms which arise. In this context, the influence of radio is further assessed in relation to the television police series. Examples for discussion include radio favourites like *Up the Pole* and *PC 49*. The chapter also discusses the importance of audience research, in connection with the increased awareness of television's potential as a product of exchange. *Fabian of the Yard*, a filmed series, produced both for home consumption and US export, will be discussed in this respect. Finally, it moves into a discussion of *Dixon of Dock Green*, looking at its strategies of address.

Towards professionalism

Commentators cite the coronation of Queen Elizabeth in 1953 as a developmental milestone in television's history.[7] Twenty million people are alleged to have watched this public event, over ten million outside their own homes. For the first time, cameras were allowed into Westminster Abbey. The thrill of 'being there', whilst nonetheless remaining 'at home', at so spectacular an occasion, converted many agnostics to television's attractions.[8] In addition, an expansionary but welfarist Conservatism, newly arrived in 1951, which had earlier begun its project for a New Britain, promoted the concept of rising affluence, famously encapsulated in Macmillan's phrase 'You've never had it so good'.[9] In January 1951, the Beveridge Committee, with the Charter shortly to expire, met to determine the future of television and, with the negative American sponsorship model in mind, rejected the idea of a commercial channel; a view accepted by the Labour government. However, Selwyn Lloyd, a Committee participant, felt that competition, paid for by advertising, or in the last resort by public funding, could be beneficial, hence his minority report.[10] Campaigns were mounted, each side of the divide.[11][12] For the anti-lobby, the National Television Council against Commercial TV cited the negative example of America. Pro-lobbyists constituted the Popular Television Association (PTA), backed by set manufacturers, the advertising industry and Tory MPs, who all vigorously campaigned for a 'peoples' television'. Before the Labour government, to which it fell, was able to deal with the Beveridge Report, the party was toppled and the Conservatives – dedicated to competitive enterprise – returned to power.

Commercial television opened on 22 September 1955. It unsettled the hegemonic practices of the BBC, forcing the institution to define a new set of cultural relations between the people and the media, one crucially, where audiences could no longer be ignored. When the 1954 Television Bill became law, it required that a public authority, the Independent Television Authority (ITA), be set in place, acting as ombudsman and overseer and owning the transmitters, as well as appointing and supervising programme companies and controlling advertising. This early quango was directly responsible to parliament. In effect, many of its features were similar to those of the BBC. It should be emphasised that rather than ITV heralding a new pluralist era of broadcasting, what was ushered into place was a *duopoly*: a modified form of what had previously existed.[13]

As early as 1949, Norman Collins, then Controller of Television, had sought to increase the proportion and quality of light entertainment within the BBC, but neo-Reithian attitudes created an animus against it.[14] The process of the BBC's shift towards a more mature television broadcasting practice was discernible during the early 1950s, characterised by both an increasing media cross-fertilisation and a closer dialogue with America, whose industrialised methods had previously been held in scant regard. Following a two-month visit to America in 1953, Ronnie Waldman, the new Head of Light Entertainment, described how he 'hated the jungle atmosphere of commercial television', in particular the power of the sponsors. Nonetheless, he was 'bowled over by the intoxicating discovery that the Americans accepted as perfectly natural that television was *entertainment*'.[15] Inspired by this discovery, Waldman wrote a report saying that by comparison with US television, 'British TV was small, dull, slow, poor, starved and amateurish'.[16] Such sorties discovered what American broadcasting had always known, the value of entertainment, regarding the term 'Light Entertainment' itself as a highly amusing tautology. Writing about a similar fact-finding trip to America during the late 1950s, Eric Maschwitz, who was to take over from Ronnie Waldman as Head of Light Entertainment in 1960, recalled the amazement of an American TV executive upon hearing of his title, 'What do the rest of 'em provide, *Heavy Entertainment?*'

Taking up his appointment as Head of the new Television Light Entertainment Department, Waldman circulated an internal memo (6 April 1951) to all producers concerning what he perceived should be its policy goals. First and foremost he observes, 'we must create something that has never existed before the invention of television – something that we call Television Light Entertainment'.[17]

Waldman acknowledged, however, that such a development would not be achieved immediately. To illustrate the point, he described how it took sound broadcasting 15 years to reach *Band Waggon*, the first 'pure radio' comedy format. Nonetheless, he singled out the Terry-Thomas television comedy series *How Do You View* (BBC 1950–1953) as an encouraging sign. Waldman believed there were three main criteria that Light Entertainment should satisfy:

(1) The ideal and perfect Light Entertainment programme is one which satisfies three different sets of standards:

    (a) The standards of popularity as judged by the Appreciation Index of the Audience Research Department.

    (b) The aesthetic standards of style and taste which should be observed by a Service such as the BBC's Television Service.

    (c) The standards of 'pure Television' which we have set ourselves to

> achieve and to maintain. (These standards are our own in this country – the Americans, as we know, have an entirely different set of 'T.V. standards').

The final comment in parentheses is telling. 'Standards' here are seen to be integrally bound-up with local conditions of production, including taste-markers of style and aesthetics. Waldman revealingly emphasises that whilst the three imperatives listed are not in any order of importance, 'it must be realised that it is the job of Light Entertainment to observe (a) infinitely more than, say, Talks or Music need to do'. This is the first time there had been a positive affirmation of the work of the Audience Research Department, as installed by Stephen Tallents in 1936. Next, Waldman ventures an interpretation of Light Entertainment:

> We do not pretend that Television Light Entertainment is a complete art-form in itself and we realise that its material and its approach must be based on general ideas of Light Entertainment familiar to the public ... too close an adherence to the forms of Sound Radio, the theatre, or the cinema will prevent the growth of TV as such and although most of the authoritative and experienced comedians in this country have had considerable experience of Sound Radio, we should be careful to avoid using the methods of Sound Radio when employing them. Similarly, a purely 'theatre' technique, e.g. 'Music Hall'.[18]

Here, Television Light Entertainment is being viewed – rather as television itself, previously – as a hybrid product of all other forms. Those variety acts inherited from radio shows – themselves derived from music hall – were grist to the early Light Entertainment mill. In production terms, Waldman's group of Light Entertainment personnel included Bill Ward, Brian Tesler (Creator of *Ask Pickles*, a well-known request programme), Francis Essex and Bill Lyon Shaw, all of whom went on to become programme controllers for ITV companies.[19] By 1954, they were producing up to nine variety shows a week.[20] As Waldman punningly put it, 'there was no lack of variety in Television Variety'.[21]

Whilst the BBC Documentary Department had no need of attracting stars, precisely because of its collective ethos, BBC Light Entertainment relied for its ratings on 'personalities'. Indeed, many of its early formats were vehicles for people like Terry-Thomas and Norman Wisdom. However, the BBC's rates of pay were so poor that not only did it fail to attract calibre artists, but once established, television actors often took their craft elsewhere. As producer and critic Peter Black argues, 'Television made stars of Terry-Thomas and

Norman Wisdom and priced them out of its market'. The toughest opposition Waldman had to fight came not from the Competitor, therefore, but the contractual practices of sound radio holding personalities to restrictive, inclusive, contract clauses.[22]

Waldman soon realised the necessity for discovering new forms *outside* those of show business in order to articulate the concept of Light Entertainment. The early series sitcom accepted from music hall and vaudeville was considered a suitable form. However, the new writers seen as crucial to this enterprise, once again, cost money. The BBC got precisely what it paid for. It is hardly surprising, therefore, that commentators describe early situation comedy as 'rudimentary' and highly predictable.[23] Of four short comedy-series made during the early 1950s, Peter Black recalls *Friends and Neighbours* (BBC, 1954) and *Dear Dotty* (BBC, 1954) as 'terrible, but an improvement on the ghastly'.[24] But despite its early gaucherie, sitcom was seen to be a step in the right direction, creating new opportunities for writers.

Until 1955, according to Arthur Swinson, the television writer was 'employed on sufferance'.[25] Goddard cites topical satire as being moderately successful in *The Erik Barker Half Hour* (BBC, 1951–53), seen as the forerunner of more successful shows, including the infamous *That Was The Week That Was* (*TW3*). Ray Galton and Harry Simpson's *Hancock's Half Hour* began on 6 July 1956 and followed the American practice of crossing over directly from radio (almost the only British generic form to do so). The show was innovative in using a sitcom format with episode length narratives, moving it beyond the 'turns' of the variety show. As Neale and Krutnik discuss, it showed a new sort of lower middle-class realism which diverged from the bourgeois family norm of domestic sitcom. Hancock was an outsider.[26]

Apart from these newly-devised comedic forms, the Light Entertainment Department possessed little in the way of scripted series or serials. As we have seen, in the Documentary Department early 'producer-writers' took on the combined function of producing and writing their own programmes, a practice inherited from radio. The arrival of a centralised Script Department, during the early 1950s, together with the innovative production methods pioneered in *I Made News*, resulted in the function of writer and producer becoming separated out into discrete functions. In addition, there were for the first time in television, 'directors' who could alternate within a series to speed up production. In contrast to Cecil McGivern's pronouncement that the BBC had reached 'a limit of series', during a Programme Board Meeting of 14 May 1953, Waldman stipulated that 'series were the best way of building Light Entertainment'.[27] By now, with the Competitor visible on the horizon, the need for building up the schedule was self-evident. Once again, the BBC tended to look toward pre-legitimated forms, in particular that of the radio-derived soap opera.

Soaps, Slapstick and Boys Own

As early as the 1930s, BBC sound radio had instituted series and soap opera forms, both of which had originated in America.[28] The term soap opera was an indicator of the form's genesis as a commercial product, sponsored by the soap-company Proctor and Gamble. By contrast, the British soap opera was articulated within the public service environment of the BBC. The earliest British radio soap opera to reside in the popular memory was *Mrs Dale's Diary*, broadcast in 1948. This replaced the previously popular *Robinson Family* (1936), which had run over from the Forces Programme during the war (now transformed into the Light Programme). *The Archers*, Britain's longest-running soap opera, and its nearest equivalent to the American *Guiding Light* (1937), was first produced in the Midland Region in 1950, as a service to farmers, but shifted to the Light Programme in 1951.[29] Conceived as a sort of 'farming Dick Barton', according to Briggs, the idea behind this 'tale of everyday folk' was devised to inform and entertain, in prescribed proportions: 60 per cent entertainment; 30 per cent information; and ten per cent education.[30] The bucolic accuracy of Borchester's farming community and propagandist implants (that vital ten percent) were supplied by the Ministry of Agriculture (MAG). The programme had attracted audience figures of 9.5 million by the beginning of 1953. Grace Archer's tragic death in a fire was spectacularly staged in order to eclipse press coverage of Independent Television's opening in 1955.

A series which owed something in terms of its slapstick humour to Will Hay's Gainsborough comedy *Ask A Policeman* (1939) was Archibald Berkeley-Willoughby, alias *PC 49* (1947), a radio original.[31] The show was characterised by villains with names like: 'Knocker Dawson', 'Slim Jiggs' and 'The Shadow'. *PC 49*'s frequent use of catch-phrases was a device carried over from music hall and early radio programmes. 'Good morning all!', 'Yes Sarge!', if not the eponymous protagonist's famous response to Detective Sergeant Wright, 'Out you go forty-nine!', subsequently became absorbed into the *Dixon of Dock Green* series. *PC 49* went on to become translated into two movies, *The Adventures of PC 49* (1949) and *A Case for PC 49* (1951); advertisements; a board game; a jigsaw puzzle; several books; and, most notably, a strip cartoon in the pages of *Eagle* (1950).

Eagle was a boys' comic published by Chad Varah, evangelical Christian and press baron. It brought together an educational design, highly praised by teachers, whose format and content in many ways resembled the 'mixed programming' ethos of the BBC's Light Programme.[32] Its historical 'Great Men' series included Winston Churchill and Lord Baden Powell amongst other national heroes and upholders of empire.

Concurrent with *PC 49*, and also produced by Vernon Harris, *Up the Pole* starred Jimmy Jewel and Ben Warris, cross-talking proprietors of a trading post in the Arctic, with Claude Dampier as Horace Hotplate, Mayor of the North Pole. *Up the Pole*'s supporting cast included Jon Pertwee (later to star in *Doctor Who*) as Mr Burp and Betty Paul as his girlfriend. The programme ran from 1947 to 1952. The third series was relocated to a rural police station, with Hotplate reassigned to Chief Superintendent. An article in the *Radio Times*, replying to those mystified by the programme's success, contended that *Up the Pole* was identifiable with that breed of humour which has flourished since Shakespeare wrote in situations and gags for his clowns:

> It is not too much to say that the four principals of *Up the Pole* could be transported in a body to that memorable wood near Athens where certain other craftsmen rehearsed 'the most lamentable comedy and most cruel death of Pyramus and Thisbe'. On the contrary, it would be admirable casting.[33]

Here we see Great Auntie Beeb resorting to Shakespeare in order to gain legitimation for the production's dubious cultural values. George Inns, the series' producer, argues more accurately that the programme had roots in the music-hall sketch with its knockabout humour, 'in point of fact, "Up the Pole" is an old friend cut to a modern pattern and adapted to the techniques of radio'.[34]

Once again, this alerts us to the fact that generic forms do not just appear as fully-fledged entities but are derived from other formations, adapted to new circumstances. Raymond Williams is useful in this respect, when he argues that:

> certain meanings, experiences and values which cannot be expressed or substantially verified in terms of the dominant culture are nevertheless lived and practised on the basis of the residue – cultural as well as social – of some previous social and cultural institution or formation.[35]

It was, above all, radio's soap opera and series formats which established the pattern for routinised 'listening in,' thereby securing for it a ready-made audience. Just as the weekly comic was eagerly awaited, so too could radio programmes command the same sense of anticipation. *Up the Pole* regulars waited with all the impatience of the comic-strip addict to know what new embarrassment would confront our friends. What new villainies would Mr Burp be up to? In what astonishing capacity would Mr Hotplate ('You'll never guess') appear? Similarly, in the same way that the *Dan Dare* comic-strip in the *Eagle* acted as a weekly hook which might lead its readers to looking at its more serious educational stories, so too *Up the Pole* could guide young listeners to the more middle-brow Home Service 'listened in to' by their parents.[36]

Dick Barton, Special Agent (1946) was an overnight success with the junior audience.[37] Starring Noël Johnson and broadcast in more than 400 episodes, the stories centred upon the exploits of a clean-living detective who never drinks or uses 'even slightly profane language': he fights clean and never lies. The programme far outstripped *The Archers* in terms of popularity. After 1950, amid fears that the programme might be *encouraging* juvenile delinquency rather than the opposite, a codicil was added to each episode. It took the form of an extra-diegetic voice-over which deliberated over the moral rights and wrongs of the episode in question. As we will see, this tailpiece was to be incorporated in the *Dixon of Dock Green* address to camera and is illustrative of the nervousness with which producers regarded the 'effects' of the mass media.

BBC television's first ever television soap opera, *The Grove Family*, went out on Friday 2 April 1954 at 7.40pm, from Lime Grove Studios. Rather than the bourgeois middle-class families depicted in *The Dales* and *The Archers*, the self-reflexively named 'Grove' family portrayed a lower middle-class family who were just beginning to feel comfortable after years of hardship. It was one of the first British television serials depicting working-class characters which, in the words of Andy Medhurst 'did not have to be funny all the time.' Unfortunately, a disagreement arose between its two chief scriptwriters, each of whom failed to distinguish either its narrative direction or characters' development; as a result the serial only lasted until 1957. One of the main reasons both for the show's lack of advancement and for its producers' disagreement was the fact that its range of characters was too limited to allow sufficient development within what critics have identified as the soap opera's paradigmatic axis: that is, the relationships between characters.[38] Once these began to grow up, there was nothing to replace them. This structural difficulty did not occur so easily with the series form, because of the way in which it returned its characters to the same starting point each week.

In just the same way that *The Grove Family* features a working-class family which viewers were encouraged to take seriously, *Dixon of Dock Green* was the first police series that extended a non-risible depiction of the work of a uniformed police officer. However, as with television generally, the programme had problems being taken seriously within the departmental hierarchy of BBC Television. As a result of its radio ancestry in slapstick audio-representations including *PC 49* and *Up the Pole*, the uniformed figure of the copper on the beat was more inclined to inspire feelings of ridicule than respect. As early as March 1948, Donald Stephenson, the Head of General Overseas Television Programmes, had written, 'the Police are either painted as ludicrous music hall caricatures or else reflected as having no common humane principles or scruples'.[39]

Even as late as the early 1960s, after the arrival of Sir Hugh Carleton Greene as Director General and subsequent departmental reorganisation, Ray Galton, producer of *Steptoe and Son* was to state:

> It is very difficult, no matter what prestige one attains in a good Light Entertainment show, to realise that prestige in comparison to other parts of the BBC output. The cachet is not there.[40]

Eventually, however, *Dixon of Dock Green* – at this stage the BBC's only series – started to change such perceptions, as will become evident. In so doing, it brought the relatively unknown quantity of popular drama into the forefront of mainstream television production.

Television as commodity

Although I have not been able to trace its precise source, correspondence on file at the BBC Written Archive demonstrates an early interest in British television series – especially those featuring Scotland Yard – as important export commodities. According to written correspondence, Robert Barr was asked by Associated British Pathe Ltd during 1950 to undertake a synopsis of a series of 30-minute *films* suitable for US television, featuring Scotland Yard. The outcome of this request is not on record. However, another letter, dated 26 July of the same year, confirms that Pathe were prepared to jointly commission Barr and Percy Hoskins, his old Fleet Street colleague, to prepare a shooting script for a 28-minute television film based on an actual crime in the Scotland Yard 'series'. An exclusivity clause was proposed, whereby the entire copyright was to be assigned to Pathe and neither Barr nor Hoskins were to be concerned with any similar series for US television for 'a reasonable period of at least six months'.[41] By the mid-1950s, there was the beginning of a two-way process of exchange. *The Cisco Kid* (1954) and *I am the Law* (1953), starring George Raft as Lieutenant George Kirkby, were shown on BBC Television.[42] Significantly, *Dragnet* (CBS, 1951–1970) was given its British preview in London on 23 September 1955, the day after Independent Television went on air. Arguably, such infiltrations and exchanges were as important as the Competitor in breaking down the BBC's monolithic material and institutional practices. Indeed, as we have seen, it became increasingly evident that British television could learn much from Hollywood series production.

Fabian of the Yard (1954) was the first specially filmed Scotland Yard series, co-produced and directed by Anthony Beauchamp of Trinity Productions, Great Britain, and as such is deserving of closer attention.[43] Significantly, both *I'm the Law* and *Fabian of the Yard* were transmitted in the popular Saturday night slot just after the so-called Toddler's Truce break.[44] *Fabian* was later moved to Wednesday evenings. In both cases, the fact that these programmes were originated on film obviously allowed them a greater flexibility in terms of organising the schedule and repeats. On the other hand, *Dixon of Dock Green*, being live, was not, in programming terms, a moveable feast.

Between the *Dixon of Dock Green* television series and the *Blue Lamp* film runs a common thread of characterisation aside from George Dixon. According to Robert Barr:

> It is quite likely that *The Blue Lamp* was also a Fabian story since Bob (Fabian) as head of the Sweeney had a hand in most of the London crime at that time.[45]

In correspondence, Jan Read confirms this theory:

> What gave me the idea for the 'Blue Lamp' was the Antiquis case, I forget the details after all this time, but I was given a summary by Scotland Yard and it was investigated by the famous Fabian (I don't know whether he was a Detective Chief Inspector or Superintendent at the time).[46]

Several critics mention that *The Blue Lamp*'s plot derived from the famous Alex d'Antiquis case, a murder trial which took place in the 1950s and was solved by real life Robert Fabian.[47] The *Fabian of the Yard* filmed television series was, in effect, a spin-off from the story-documentary *I Made News*, made in the Documentary Unit, and produced by Robert Barr. Interestingly, in terms of the subject of the Scotland Yard genre as exchange commodity, this series featured not only the famous Fabian but also the American FBI. There was also a 'Fabian' radio programme, which Jack Warner compered. To add further to the cross-over confusion, this series was also known as 'The Blue Lamp' series.[48]

As we will see, *Fabian of the Yard* was an interesting hybrid of fact and fiction. By calling upon the character of a real-life detective, Robert Barr had earlier managed to establish a fertile new ground for the kind of television programmes which brought real-life *living* history in front of the camera. Because Fabian was a detective rather than an ordinary policeman, he had 'clout'. During an era when people were defined by their work, that of the Scotland Yard detective would have been seen as infinitely superior to the ordinary, everyday tasks of the beat policeman. What was essentially a class attitude was inherited from literary precedents whereby 'golden-age' detective narratives eschewed crime in favour of solving the puzzle of serious crime, usually murder. For, as Sherlock Holmes put it:

> The cases which come to light in the papers are, as a rule, bad enough, and vulgar enough. We have in our police reports realism pushed to its extreme limits and yet the result is, it must be confessed, neither fascinating nor artistic.[49]

To begin with, the uniform police series was far from aesthetically 'fascinating'. Nonetheless, it was to break new generic ground.

The filmed-for-TV *Fabian of the Yard* series provides an interesting generic crossover point in metafictional terms. For the first time on television, a living character was played by an actor: Bruce Seton, who took the part of the illustrious detective. The production's status was, therefore, similar to that of the previously discussed film, *In Which We Serve*, in which Noël Coward played the character of Lord Louis Mountbatten. The producers' concern to demonstrate the programme's 'authenticity' led to the inclusion of an end-sequence to camera, featuring the real Bob Fabian. The moment of his appearance was one of extreme bathos, caused by a clash of registers. Such a confusion of the 'codes' of representation, resulting in an identificatory problem in which both the real-life detective, 'Bob' Fabian himself, and the actor, Bruce Seton, lost out, each proving the other false.

That *Fabian of the Yard* was a series made for export is clearly shown in an early episode, concerning a suspected terrorist attack. 'Bombs in Piccadilly' tells a story of suspected terrorism when bombs are found planted in the vicinity. Whilst offering an 'inside Scotland Yard' portrait, it is clear that the series was not solely for home consumption. Its opening car-chase scene, camera editing and clipped voice-over of the 'I' protagonist presented a noirist aesthetic, indebted to Raymond Chandler:

> an informer took me to Pepper's Bottle Room in Soho. It was more than I could bargain for. I could kick myself for walking into a trap. I couldn't figure it out. I'd helped a lot of these men.

Although the detective thinks he has been double-crossed, he is in fact walking into his own, highly unofficial, 'award ceremony', one whose ideological purpose is to dramatise the consensus – just as in the *Blue Lamp* film – that exists either side of the law. The medal's inscription, 'To Bob Fabian from the Boys', is a carnivalesque inversion (these are *not* 'the boys in Blue') and emblematic token of respect from the underworld.

Moreover, the promotion of the British nation as one large family is good British public relations. Engendering the sense of a United Nation, seamlessly attached to a unified past, the heritage discourse is reinforced by the travelogue-style narrative voice-over. This takes us past some of London's tourist sights including, 'the tower of London, started by William the Conqueror in 1078'.

'The Executioner' (1955) is a tale about a psychopathic middle-class killer, who, deranged by the loss of his son Bobby, dissolves five victims in bath-tubs filled with acid, until discovered by the intrepid Fabian. Once again, the 'tour of London sights' act as a strong location of British national identity for an anglophile US audience:

> Somerset House, built beside the Thames on the site of an old Royal Palace is the resting place for all records of births, marriages and deaths registered in England. Somehow in its vast filing system I hoped to find a connection between the five murdered people, but my sergeant got no place fast.

In this connection too the series departs from fictional representations of Scotland Yard in its concern to show television (despite the fact that this is filmed) to be a medium of demonstration, hence 'The Executioner's graphic and attentuated forensic scenes.

In 'Bombs in Piccadilly', Scotland Yard is described by the Voice-of-God narrator as:

> the brain of Great Britain's man-hunting machine. Routine, detail science

and tenacity is used by squads of highly trained men. Men like Robert Fabian, hailed by the press as one of England's greatest detectives.

The episode dramatises Scotland Yard's Special Branch as a modernist 'man-hunting machine.' Its contact network is demonstratively seen to include the underworld, informers, customs and immigration officials, all co-operating as a reassuringly unified body in the fight against crime.

Fabian is not strictly 'television' in the 1950s sense of live production in the studio. Produced more with an eye to its commodity exchange value than usual, it is shot by an outside film company. The series nonetheless represents an interesting crossover point in terms of the generic development of the television series' truth status in terms of its progressive narrativisation, from fact to fiction: whilst the story is true, the characters are fictitious in that they are played by actors. At the same time, the production is concerned to produce 'evidence' of its authenticity.

Together 'Fabian' and 'Dixon' represent a bifurcation in early television police representations between the detective and the uniform police series. As Robert Murphy states, in the tradition of crime-writing policemen played second fiddle, first to gifted amateur detectives, and, by the late 1940s, to real-life Scotland Yard detectives.[50] A late example of this, in view of the arrival one year earlier of 'Dixon', can be seen in the previously mentioned 'The Executioner', whose opening scene features two subordinate looking PCs on their beat. They do not look at the camera and are shown only in profile as they lope away, almost comically, out of shot.

Representations of crime achieve an interesting class-based realism during this period, over more tabloid forms of populism. Moving away from 'Fabian's' elevated Yard, 'Dixon's' locus within Dock Green establishes him as a populist hero.

Scheduling Dock Green

In order to situate *Dixon of Dock Green* within a viewing context, it is useful to analyse the schedule surrounding its first ever episode, as featured by the *Radio Times*, and to compare it with those of subsequent years. A brief scan of the edition dated 3 January 1955 reveals a typical BBC Saturday's television viewing during the 1950s. Apart from a children's literary adaptation there are no other television-originated popular drama series being broadcast.

The viewing schedule begins at 3.00pm with Percy Thrower's *In the Garden*, followed by Children's Television (4.00pm) featuring Billy Bunter, adapted from the novels by Frank Richards (another 'first' episode). Cricket follows between 4.30 and 6.30pm. From 6.30 to 6.40pm is a Commentary (a form of early television 'editorial', on the previous match). There is then a break (the 'toddler's truce') until 7.25pm, when a weather chart is shown. This is followed by *In Town Tonight*, the magazine feature about 'Interesting people who are in town tonight', interviewed by John Ellison. The news has moved from its previous 7.30pm position to 8.00pm and at 8.15pm the first episode of *Dixon of Dock Green*, 'PC Crawford's First Pinch', is billed.

The second *Dixon of Dock Green* series commences with 'Ladies of the Manor' (9 June 1956), also on a Saturday but not transmitted until 10.00pm. Throughout the third, fourth, fifth and sixth series, *Dixon of Dock Green* occupies the 7.30pm slot, until the 17th episode of the sixth series (1960), when, following the end of the toddler's truce (1957), it moves back to a regular 6.30pm position. *Dixon of Dock Green*'s early peripatetic status shows that it took time for television producers to become aware of the benefit of retaining specific points with which the audience would identify and locate their evening's activities.

To return to the original 1955 schedule, at 8.45pm, *Saturday-Night Date with YANA* features a song-and-dance show, followed by *Secombe Here*, a variety show but with a comic turn, starring the eponymous Harry Secombe. The final programme on air is at 10.00pm and features wildlife experts Armand and Michaela Denis on *Filming in Africa*, a repeat from 28 May of the same year. Finally, at 10.30pm, the News is broadcast but on sound only.[51] What is immediately observable from the schedule is that apart from the *Billy Bunter* series – a literary adaptation – the magazine features and nature programmes are all established, non-fiction forms. Because the break from 6.40pm to 7.25pm is a sort of cut-back toddler's truce, the first episode of *Dixon of Dock Green* at 8.15pm is comparatively late: it is usually remembered as being put out at 6.30pm, making it viewable by children as well as adults.[52]

After a few years, *Dixon of Dock Green* became the visual equivalent to radio's *The Archers* and introduced the terminology whereby a single series run is known as 'a season'. As the series became established, season in and season out, it fulfilled a similar calendrical role, reminding citizens of the month and time of year. In terms of its popularity, by the first quarter of 1961 Dixon was the second most popular programme in the whole of the BBC schedules, with a viewing average of 13.85 million. *Dixon of Dock Green* ran for 21 years. It consisted of 464 episodes and 22 seasons. Jan Read, who had worked on the scripts, had also collaborated with Ted Willis earlier on the *Blue Lamp* film, creating the characters for the subsequent stage play. Correspondence indicates that he handed them over to Willis at his request, including the eponymous Dixon himself. Douglas Moodie was the series' chief producer, and Willis its main writer, until the mid-1960s, when a stable of writers and producers expanded to include, amongst others, Arthur Swinson, Gerald Kelsey, David Ellis and Eric Paice. Eric Paice became *Dixon of Dock Green's* first *series* Script Editor in 1965. There were three main producers: Douglas Moodie (1955–1963); Barry Lupino (1963–4); and Ronald Marsh (1963–1968).

Dixon of Dock Green introduced new, increasingly rationalised methods of working. Ted Willis wrote the scripts from 1955 until 1976, although the practice of using an Assistant Scriptwriter began during the mid-1950s.[53] The George Dixon character was assigned to Jack Warner from the *Blue Lamp* film and, at this time, of radio and Huggett fame. The story, somewhat confusingly called 'The Blue Lamp' as a working title, was supposedly based on that of a real policeman once stationed at Leman Street in the East End of London.

Dixon was supposed to be the friendly, local bobby with a kind word for everyone. He started off as a Constable, but on 19 September 1964 was promoted to Sergeant at the ripe old age of 63. Although the actor grew past the age where he was able to pound the beat, he circumvented the Met's retirement rules by continuing to work behind the desk at Dock Green, thus allowing the CID, headed by his son-in-law Andy Crawford, to take the lion's share of the action. Andy was married to George's daughter Mary (she made George a grandfather by having twins) which permitted the occasional family scene away from the station. Other characters at Dock Green police station were PC (later Detective Constable) Lauderdale, known as Laudy, and Desk Sergeant Flint, played by Arthur Rigby.

Not until Jack Warner was 80 years old did the Dixon character finally retire. Warner died five years later. At the funeral his coffin was borne by officers from the real Paddington Green, where Ted Willis and Jan Read had conducted their original research. On top was a wreath in the shape of a blue lamp, whilst over the public address system, 'An Ordinary Copper', was played. A tribute from Scotland Yard described him as:

> a charming character who served the Metropolitan Police and public so well. His warmth and understanding of the problems of London PCs will long be remembered with affection.[54]

From art into life, rather than the reverse, as in the case of *Fabian of the Yard*. Dixon still survives in the collective memory as the incarnation of a certain type of policeman, despite the fact that he originated, not in the Met, but BBC broadcast television. However, for all the central *character's* eventual mythologising power, in terms of its reception, the *Dixon of Dock Green* series got off to a somewhat inauspicious beginning.

Reception matters

According to the Audience Research Report for the first episode of the *Dixon of Dock Green* series, 'PC Crawford's First Pinch', the public found it somewhat anodyne, as the following general comment, taken from the Report, makes clear:

> Although this first edition of *Dixon of Dock Green* was seldom if ever actively disliked, a fair number of viewers supplying evidence were by no means very enthusiastic. It was, they thought, altogether a very 'tame' affair with little action and no excitement. 'Dixon' himself was 'just too good to be true' – the actual story was, to say the least, very thin and the whole programme seemed 'humdrum' and slow in the extreme. It follows that most of these viewers were not particularly keen on seeing the rest of the series; most, in fact, were inclined to agree with the wife of an Accountant who wrote 'I must confess I like my crime to be more spectacular so although this will not be a "must at any cost" for me I shall probably be pleasantly entertained any time I happen to look.'[55]

Technically, too, there was criticism: in particular, it was noted that, 'One or two people thought the change over to film inserts might have been smoother'. According to the shooting-scripts on file there were around five film inserts per half-hour episode.

The size of the audience for 'PC Crawford's First Pinch' was reckoned to be 13 per cent of the adult population of the UK, equivalent to 38 per cent of the adult TV public. The Audience Reaction Index (ARI), which was worked out on an average percentage collated from five grades of response, was 75, considered a good figure: an official states 'There is no strictly comparable programme but the average for the last ten films of the 'Fabian of Scotland Yard' series is 69'.[56] By the sixth programme, entitled 'London Pride', the audience reaction had improved and included such comments as 'a simple human story which could really have happened'. The ARI had gone up to 80 and the audience itself increased to 49 per cent of the potential viewing public. Although there are still some adverse comments most members of the sample audience thought the stories to be sufficiently factual and down to earth 'to be educational as well as entertaining'.

Such an improvement in reception figures may be put down to the repeat factor of the series, as well as a continued need by the public for more information about professional and legal institutions. A methods engineer for instance, remarked of the series that, 'more could and should be done on these lines for bringing the public services to our notice'.[57] *Dixon of Dock Green*'s producers came to realise that the series could fulfil the goal of providing competitive popular entertainment compared to Independent Television. It could also provide similar satisfactions to the earlier story-documentaries, whilst putting them across fictionally.

That the *Dixon* series had to struggle to gain legitimacy in the Light Entertainment Department is aptly illustrated by an incident which occurred in the second episode, 'Needle in a Haystack'. This programme required the use of an infant in order to illustrate its drugs safety message. A memo from the Head of Programme Planning implies that although the use of children in fictional representations was at the time not permissible, there were certain extenuating circumstances. However, as the advice of Mr Bush Bailey, legal adviser to the series makes plain, these were not available to the *Dixon* series:

> if we seriously think a Saturday night serial play – he says 'this isn't even a documentary' – a placing which will of course give maximum publicity to our breaking the law is justifiable, I suggest that if the primary object of the programme is entertainment, rather than moral lessons to the public about leaving dangerous drugs about, to break the law is not justifiable.[58]

The instance is demonstrative of television's uncertainty as to the programme's precise ontological status. Was *Dixon of Dock Green* entertainment or education, or, was it a fulfilment of Grace Wyndham Goldie's theory of television's power as a hidden persuader? Throughout its long life the series successfully hedged its bets, thus proving that it was perfectly possible to both 'entertain' and 'educate' at one and the same time. It was simply a case, in the words of Mary Poppins's inimitable song, of 'a spoonful of sugar makes the medicine go down'. Nonetheless, despite the odd music-hall moment, as in Warner's memorably adroit shoe-shuffling performance at his daughter's wedding in 'Father-in-Law' (1955), nothing else showing on early television was more culturally respectable.

As it matured *Dixon of Dock Green*, like its soap twin *The Archers*, took on the role of seasonal commentator and unofficial 'adviser' of the public interest.

An internal memo from the Assistant Head of Children's Programmes to the Head of Entertainment (Ronnie Waldman), dated 5 November, thanks him for the way in which he 'plugged the fireworks warning to great effect'. Similarly, a letter on file from Eric Maschwitz, who took over from Ronnie Waldman as Head of Light Entertainment in 1958, to the National Society for the Prevention of Cruelty to Children, set out the agreed dialogue to be spoken by Dixon on the telephone, in a forthcoming episode: 'have a word with the local inspector of the NSPCC ... He may know something about the family ... oh, yes, they do a wonderful job ... yes of course. Thank you for ringing'.[59] Dixon was not only the policeman's PRO, he was also that of the 'Nanny state'. It is therefore no wonder that 'Auntie Beeb' became an affectionate soubriquet for the BBC at around this time.

Relations with the Met itself were never to be so cordial as during the early *Dixon* days. According to internal correspondence the series had a number of police consultants on its books. A memo from Waldman, dated 31 December 1957 states:

> There is indeed a very considerable volume of police correspondence and comment reaching Jack Warner and Ted Willis about this series. This is due partly to the very lively appreciation of the Commissioner downwards and partly to a shrewd move made a little time ago by Ted Willis. He advertised in the *Police Gazette* etc. asking for members of the Force, anywhere, to submit story-lines for the programme (in return for payment, of course). The response has been very great and has improved the already excellent relations between the programme and the Force.[60]

In 1957, after the series had run for a hundred episodes, a *Radio Times* feature stated that not only was *Dixon of Dock Green* mentioned in the House of Commons, but the police service could trace an increase in recruitment due to the series; both facts were strongly applauded.

The benevolent aspect of *Dixon of Dock Green* was arguably achieved by *de-politicising* the image of the police so as to conceal any political affiliation, however, and whenever it might arise. A small incident which occurred following a 1957 transmission, entitled 'Presented in Court', is illustrative of the way in which this strategy operated. Following the programme's transmission there were complaints about a 'Vote Labour' slogan which appeared on a wall during a particular sequence. An internal memo, once again from Waldman, hastens to explain that the implied political position was not representative either of his own, or the programme's affiliations:

The words 'Vote Labour' – obviously very old – were found to be whitewashed on the wall when the Producer arrived for shooting and he felt that they created excellent local colour for a district such as Dock Green and it did not occur to him in any way that they were capable of causing offence more especially since there was no likelihood of a General Election for several years. According to the producer's own statement, he was thinking purely in 'aesthetic relations'.

Waldman goes on to state further in his defence, that 'he points out that his own politics are strongly right wing'.[61] From the start of its post-war re-transmission, the BBC was determined not to engage in controversy or debate regarding politics.

Although no single generic influence can be identified, in ideological terms the *Dixon of Dock Green* series continued to extend the public service ethos of the war films. It also consolidated the strategies of address already developed in programmes like *I Made News* and *Fabian of the Yard*. Dixon's direct address to camera, with its topping and tailing of the narrative, interpellates the viewing subject; by identifying with the paternalist figure of Dixon she or he is enjoined to take care of her or his own family, in the interests of state and country.

The opening, freestanding filmed sequence, begins with a close-up shot of the highly motivated 'Blue Lamp', its metonymic status reinforced by the tune whistled on the soundtrack by Warner himself ('Maybe because I'm a Londoner', later changed to 'An Ordinary Copper'). The camera then tracks down the Dixon protagonist, moving into extreme close up (ECU) for his address to camera. Often, this address took the form of a mild 'teaser' concerning some aspect of the narrative, but the common assumption that each episode commences with 'Evenin' all' is a misapprehension. Evidence on file suggests that there was a wide range of different salutations. At the end of the story, the final address to camera served to tie up any loose threads of the action whilst also ending on a more personal note. This constitutes a more distanced 'documentary' style of public address and a more private, or personal appeal: 'Keep in touch won't you … drop me a line … always glad to hear from you. God bless … See you around again soon … Cheers!' The audience here is being reminded that Dixon is as friendly and familiar as part of the furniture – just like the television in the sitting room.

These addresses to camera have become part of Dixon folklore, with their variable greetings and homilising end-notes, and constitute self-contained mini-narratives. What amounts to a double articulation serves to give the

Dixon character extra credibility. Inside the narrative the audience is aware of the character's fiction. Outside of it – in the address to camera – the actor appears as a real-life policeman. This strategy of introjecting the public into the private signifies an instrumental use of television which serves to continue the consensus politics of the public service war film. Despite being devised with an eye to the competition, *Dixon of Dock Green* was a fiction series made very much with a traditional interpretation of the BBC public service remit in mind. We saw Jack Warner, incarnated as the original 'Dixon' in the *Blue Lamp* film, and his embodiment in the role of the older, wiser counsellor to the new recruit, played by Jimmy Handley. This was, of course, a role overlaid by several others, including those of the 'Huggett' films. Dixon is a father in several senses, both literal and symbolic: he *fathers* the format of the uniformed police procedural and he is father-in-law to Andy. Dixon represents the law and is strongly identified in that capacity with the figure of the father as bearer of prohibition: 'thou shalt not'. *Dixon of Dock Green*, more than any other police series, frames a patriarchal ideology.

Patriarchal strategies

Horace Newcomb suggests that in television as in film, there is 'the presence of an older father figure, often dealing with the problems encountered by a young surrogate, or actual, son'.[62] This observation is deeply inscribed into the British police series. Its lineage can be traced from the PC Mitchell figure in the *Blue Lamp*, through Andy Crawford, Dixon's son-in-law, to the young *Z Cars* patrol men, through to PC Digby, of *Softly, Softly*.

'Father in Law', the appropriately named fifth episode of the *Dixon of Dock Green* series, does more, therefore, than just tell the story of Mary's marriage to the young Andy Crawford. Its ideological function is to re-position the feminine at the heart of the domestic sphere. The episode blatantly promotes marriage as the desirable norm for all women. This 'message' is illustrated by the story-line featuring Pam who has, we learn through the diegesis, allegedly been jilted at the altar by her fiancé. Following this desertion she turns to thieving for attention. After establishing her culpability in stealing a purse at the wedding reception, the message seems to be that women who are let-down by men become neurotic or delinquent, or both. Even worse, they may even become a surrogate man: this is surely the case with 'Frankie', alias Grace Millard, a WPC whose gender is ambiguously represented. Not only is Frankie never the object of the camera's gaze, but in many shots her image could be substituted by that of a man.

8. Jack Warner as PC George Dixon, in *Dixon of Dock Green* (1955).

Mary and Andy's white wedding ritualistically establishes the process whereby daughter is passed from father to son-in-law. The dialogue between the two demonstrates the system of reciprocity in action:

Andy   You took me in here as a raw young copper.

Dixon   Well you've taken my daughter off my hands and any man would be grateful for that.

Andy   I'll look after her George.

Dixon   I know you will.

Andy Crawford thanks George Dixon for taking him in whilst his 'father-in-law' thanks Andy for taking his daughter off his hands, the implication being that in doing so, he has more than adequately repaid the debt. The quid pro quo stands as a metaphor for female subordination. If Pam's neurosis about being unable to participate in such normative transactions seems exaggerated, the feelings of the bartered bride are just as extreme. Mary's sense of fulfilment at achieving the pinnacle of feminine ambition – her wedding to Andy – is tinged by a sense of foreboding. As she tells Frankie, her tears of happiness are because she cannot 'believe it will last'.

Episodes such as 'Father in Law' overtly posit an ideology that a female's biology is her destiny. To contravene this natural law results in deviancy and marginalisation. By contrast, marriage brings about beatification. In her wedding dress, Mary is seen by Billy the tramp as appearing 'like a white angel with a smile as warm as a pile of fire'. Such rhetoric idealises Mary; she is simultaneously transcendent, and domesticated. On entering Dixon's house on the morning of the wedding, Billy comments upon its cosy domesticity. It reminds him of 'kippers and crumpets spread with hot butter and crusts of bread with heavy gravy dripping on 'em. Sort of comfy'.

Mary's symbolic beatification is in marked opposition to Pam's demonisation, and calls to mind the Madonna/whore double-bind common to constructions of female identity.

So far as the social context of such a representation is concerned, it is worth recalling that the post-war, newly demobilised woman was encouraged into believing the importance of her role as homemaker. Publications such as John Bowlby's *Child Care and the Growth of Love* (1953) stressed the importance of mothering and the danger of maternal deprivation. Motherhood was represented as a valuable craft and those who practised efficient housewifery and domestic economy were considered intelligent and creative. Richard Hoggart, author of *Uses of Literacy* (1957), who went on to serve on the Pilkington Committee, noted that women's popular literature:

> accepts completely, [and] has as its main point of reference, the notion that marriage and a home, founded on love, fidelity and cheerfulness are the right purpose of a woman's life.[63]

Hoggart's influential enquiry on working-class life further stated that what women wanted from men was a 'good steady provider, one who is not violent'.

Although many new jobs had been opened up to women during the war, these disappeared soon after it ended. During the subsequent bid to re-feminise the private sphere, the status of masculinity remained uncertain. The production of macho genres like the uniform police series can be seen as offering not only a substitute for the disappearance of masculine war narratives (in the same way as the 1950s resurgence of

9. Taking a break during rehearsals for *Dixon of Dock Green*.

Second World War films in the cinema) but also a return to gender roles of the pre-war period.

Unlike the 1950s 'problem films', which mediate a collective ideology, or the products of the television Documentary Unit, *Dixon of Dock Green* retrieved an individualist discourse. It displayed a conservative attitude to crime, viewing the criminal not as a product of poor social conditions, but one endemic to all classes. Such value assumptions were represented in an early episode, entitled 'The Rotten Apple' (1955), whose robber antagonist is, in his own words, a man of class and education with no need to thieve except 'just for the hell of it'. This ideological framework portrays the criminal as pathologically evil: apart from, rather than a part of, society.

In this respect, the ideological values of the *Dixon of Dock Green* series are strongly differentiated from the Ealing production of *The Blue Lamp*. In 'The Rotten Apple' story, crime is portrayed as a disruptive force rather than – as in the film – something that is perpetual and inevitable. Yet is has its own codes – of honour amongst thieves – and practices. In 'The Rotten Apple' we are given the time-honoured 'message' in George Dixon's address to camera:

> You know when you're a cop you get a bird's eye view of people in all walks of life. The criminal population is not confined to one section of the population, not by a long chalk.

The narrative bears out this 'truth' concerning a series of burglaries where the prime suspect is a somewhat unlikely toff. According to the victim who 'came up the hard school', he should know better. But whilst the perpetrator, a captain no less, seems to act outside his social character, he does so less than the individual who is eventually revealed as the true culprit. When young PC Tom Carr is identified as the true guilty party, he is ritualistically unfrocked. Held in shot whilst he removes his uniform, the camera moves across to linger in close-up on the fallen jacket. 'There's nothing worse than a rotten copper', Dixon tells the disgraced former recruit. The disrobing of the policeman mimetically reproduces the very processes of the law, 'exposing' corruption. This is made evident by the character stepping out of his part in the address to camera, as if taking up his 'real-life' identity in similar fashion to *Fabian of the Yard*. Only this time, it is for 'pretend' rather than real. Yet, as Dixon homilises direct to camera – as a 'real-life' policeman – it is easy to forget the impersonation, especially when he seems to be acting as a mouthpiece for Her Majesty's police force.

> Well … that was the only bad copper I ever met. They say you get a bad apple in every barrel, the police have to build on trust and the papers will print a page about one bad policeman and never mention the thousands who do their job properly … When we find a bad one we're down on him like a ton of bricks. Well I'd better be on my way …

As we are fully aware, PC Dixon, too, is part of the masquerade. The episode works as television spectacle by showing what happens when the binary 'heroes' and 'villains' terms are reversed. The de-frocking comes to signify a ritual aimed at placating any fears the viewer may have of the police organisation itself becoming a rotting barrel. Such representations are the very stuff of *Dixon of Dock Green*. The broadcasting institution is aligned directly with the Met, acting almost on its behalf, in terms of public relations. These values were to remain largely unchanged during its 20-year period of broadcasting.

'The Rotten Apple', like many of the documentary feature films of the war, featured the radio set as a piece of essential domestic furniture. Its function conveys a metadiscourse which implies that post-war reconstruction owes much to the tireless work of the police, particularly that of the ordinary copper. One early scene shows Andy Crawford adjusting Dixon's wireless as he tunes into a programme which announces itself as 'Focus on Crime', about turning 'the spotlight on the modern police and their daily warfare against the criminal population'. Having adjusted the set, Andy makes as if to turn it off:

Andy   It works all right.

Mary   Leave it on Andy, I want to hear that programme.

Andy   Don't you hear enough about the cops?

Mary   I want to find out what you really do with your time: after all, I'm one of your employers don't forget! I pay taxes to support the likes of you!

Grace   How much tax do you pay Mary?

Mary   Income tax, about ten pounds a week. *(laughter)*

Carr   You know what they are always telling us the public's the boss!

Grace   You work for an ordinary boss, you do your eight hours a day, then you've finished, but not us. The policeman's lot is never off duty. An ordinary boss gives you the week-end off.

Mary   Oh! You'll have me crying in a moment, you poor policemen you're so hard done by!

Carr   A copper's work is much the same anywhere.

The public relations discourse explains why George Dixon is famously known as 'the policeman's PRO'(Public Relations Officer). But such a self-serving discourse was to alter radically. Those consensus values which were promoted by the public service culture during the period between the two great wars were further consolidated by the events of the Second World War and went on to reach their zenith during the 1950s. At the same time, the demands of a rising market economy was generically reflected in the uniform police series by a shift to a less nostalgic, symbolic type of realism, of the kind found in *Z Cars*. Thereafter, the neat, suburban landscapes envisaged in *Dixon of Dock Green*'s Hoggartesque reminiscence of working-class life give way to a depiction of 'life as it is messily lived'.

To return to the question of influence it would obviously be incorrect, given the Dixon character's immediate identification with the *Blue Lamp* film, to disavow its importance. The point I want to register is simply that we should not let this *obvious* connection entirely rule out other trajectories. Although these may be less immediately visible (in a very real sense) they are nonetheless of equal value. In his seminal study on the Ealing film, Charles Barr suggests that the famous studio was made obsolete, 'primarily because television was taking away its audience: the regular, respectable audience for modest British films on which Ealing relied'. He sees the BBC's purchase of Ealing Studios in 1955 as symbolic and postulates that despite being taken over by the new medium, Ealing had, at the last, 'infiltrated its conqueror'.[64] Indeed, at first sight, both *The Grove Family* and *Dixon of Dock Green* display Green Leaf values in their very titles. *The Grove Family* (1954) is self-evidently named after Lime Grove Film Studios, whilst a pastoral resonance that is 'very Ealing' resides in the connotations of Dock Green. However, whereas the *Blue Lamp* film contains an almost carnivalesque, anti-hegemonic strand, as we have seen, the iterative format of the subsequent television series makes such a counter-hegemonic strategy much less likely. In any case, in the *Dixon of Dock Green* series, other significant determinations – none more so than its public relations role – came into play. In terms of finding an aesthetic style and thematic, the Light Entertainment Department inevitably came to focus upon the same popular tradition that Ealing offered. Within this re-oriented context, Charles Barr's suggestion, that we should perceive one of the last Ealing productions, *The Long Arm* (1956), as a television police series pilot-feature is slightly misleading in that it once again sees television as dependent upon film.[65] Given its early date, it is more the case that television series like *War on Crime* (1951) actually influenced these productions. This is especially so as both series and film were written and produced by Robert Barr. In addition, *Gideon's Day* (1958), starring Jack Hawkins and based on a novel by JJ Marric, is of particular interest, because it is something of a hybrid, made with an eye to the American market, by John Ford (British Columbia). Because of this, it is not afraid to sacrifice 'authenticity'.[66] In doing so, it anticipates an important theme which occurs in the television police series, that of mixing the CID and the uniformed branch, a departure which was to be requested by the real-life 'Met' during the 1960s and is taken up most noticeably by *Z Cars*, as we shall see in the chapter after next.

Whilst it is important to note television's *continuities* with film, it is also necessary to be aware of the way in which it *adapts* – at the same time as it adopts – to its very different mode of transmission. As Martin McLoone states, in the 'essential' differences between film and television, 'the crucial point is that the economic and strategic imperatives of the institutions will dictate how each is used and developed. It is the confusion over them that gives rise to much of the false essentialism'.[67]

The realism present in the BBC television police series, therefore, has at least as much to do with the distinctive cultural and material practices of the BBC, such as favouring live over recorded production, as it has with those iconographic and thematic influences from other media, film and radio included. Meanwhile, the canonisation of Jack Warner as the Dixon persona began to obscure the fact that he had ever played any parts that were not entirely exemplary: proof that he had finally crossed over into the 'never-never land' of television mythology.

10. Behind the headlines: Bill Prendergast, Colin Morris and Harold Welsh, during rehearsals for *Tearaway* (1956).

4

Jacks, Knaves and the 'other' North

Cinema and latterly television, as the pre-eminent mass
entertainment media of the twentieth century, have
functioned as propagators of the national image, both in
reflecting widely held views and constructing, extending,
interrogating and perpetuating dominant national myths.

Jeffrey Richards[1]

Where's the justice? It's enough to break a writer's heart.
Chaps unaccountable are slogging away in attic and
penthouse, bedsitter and semi-detached; some trying to
write documentaries that are not actually dead boring, some
sweating on comedy scripts that are half-way risible, some
fabricating crime stories which may establish a faint claim
on the grown man's attention. And up pops Colin Morris
with a crime series that is rooted in reality, funnier than any
of the funnies, and fascinating on a deeper level than either
crime or comedy normally explores.

Maurice Wiggin, *Sunday Times*, 1961[2]

During the 1950s, British police series became more socially inclusive,
featuring the ordinary copper, as well as the élite Scotland Yard officer.
By the late 1960s 'television had definitively taken over from the cinema as
the mass medium and it is to television thenceforth that we must look for
projections of the national image'.[3] With both these trends in mind, this
chapter represents both a geographic and generic departure, in its articulation
of a critical new realism with Northern associations. In these interests, it
analyses an innovative trilogy of story-documentaries written by Colin Morris
and directed by Gilchrist Calder, including the singly produced *Tearaway*
(1956) and *Who, Me?* (1959), followed by the four-part *Jacks and Knaves*

(1961), all of which appeared at the end of the 1950s, and were set in the Liverpool vicinity. As such, this chapter illustrates how they constitute the nascent form of what may be regarded as the British Northern policier, of which *Z Cars* (1962) is perhaps the most exemplary. Not only are these story-documentaries innovative in terms of their regional and social geography, in generic terms they add an important additional ingredient to the police-series genre: humour.

At this time, television producers had moved away from the London metropolis to the North-West in search of new territory in which to locate the television police series. In general terms this move was a wise one since, by this time, the capital was somewhat over-represented, not only in the previously mentioned BBC-produced programmes that we have looked at so far, but increasingly those of the Competitor as well. ITV had recently produced the highly popular trilogy featuring Chief Detective Superintendent Lockhart of Scotland Yard and starring Raymond Francis: *Murder Bag* (1957); *Crime Sheet* (1959); and *No Hiding Place* (1959). The regions too, it seems, deserved their turn. In fact, BBC television dramatists – Morris himself was from Liverpool – must be seen as responding to and participating in the Northern Resurgence already occurring in plays and films (despite Michael Barry's remarks cited ealier). This chapter first examines the influence of the British North within the wider cultural framework, including the issues of de-industrialisation and imperial loss. It next looks at how the nascent Northern policier begins to articulate the critical new realism traditionally associated with the North, and its strong associations with documentary. In particular, the emergence of a strong Northern 'personality' will be examined, as well as the practical considerations which led the remnants of the Documentary Department to leave London, in particular, an increasing strain in their relationship with the real life 'Met'. As previously, the second half of the chapter comprises an analysis of the programmes themselves. Following the Morris and Calder trilogy, *Tearaway*, *Who, Me?* and *Jacks and Knaves*, Robert Barr's *Scotland Yard* (1960) series will be discussed, in order to provide a point of comparison from a Southern perspective.

Northern negotiations

At the end of the 1950s, what amounts to a hegemonic negotiation between North and South occurred, both in the wider cultural framework and within broadcasting itself. This was articulated by a double context of imperial decline and de-industrialisation. The first has been traced in relation to BBC

North and those documentarists working at the Empire Marketing Board (EMB) Film Unit. Here, the projection of far-flung dependencies to the nation soon became substituted by the inner workings of the state or nation. These were eventually taken on board by television which accepted the public service film's brief as a means of 'documentation, education and instruction'. During the post-war period, the gradual decline of Empire, exacerbated by the 1956 Suez Crisis, meant that Britain was no longer confident of its place in the world.

In terms of de-industrialisation, during the 1920s and 1930s radio broadcasters wished to observe the effects upon working-class life of those areas badly affected by the slump in the major industries. Television during the 1950s seems to have been engaged in a similar pursuit. But such initiatives tended to elide the fact that regions such as Lancashire already had a distinct tradition of their own of strong women, stand-up comics and above all the existence of a supremely democratic Northern 'personality'. As Jeffrey Richards comments:

> the great Victorian towns and cities of the North had their hearts ripped out in the redevelopment schemes of the 1960s and the tightly-knit communities were broken up and scattered. Cultural and technological change, centred on the growth of television, motor cars and private housing, promoted a more privatised society in place of the bustling communality of the nineteenth century. All of this had a profound impact on projections of Lancashire and Lancashireness.[4]

Writers too – as earlier – focused on these concerns, not only in the North and West, but also in the Midlands and the South. In the latter, clustered around newer light industries, where workers were largely protected from the ravages of unemployment, pockets of affluence – as early as the late 1930s – reflect the 'soapflake Arcadia' of the 1950s. This aligns with JB Priestley's 'first' post-war England described in *English Journey* (1933):

> an England of arterial and by-pass roads, of filling stations and factories that look like exhibition buildings, of giant cinemas and dance-halls and cafes, bungalows with tiny garages, cocktail bars, Woolworth's, motor-coaches, wireless, hiking, factory girls looking like actresses, greyhound racing and dirt tracks, swimming pools and everything given away for cigarette coupons.[5]

Whereas previously the working classes had been described in terms of their relations to production or as a threat to social order, here they are defined primarily in terms of their leisure activities. With the arrival of the relatively affluent 1950s came a belief that real poverty was at an end. Harold Macmillan's well known speech epitomised the period:

> Most of our people have never had it so good. Go round the country, go to the industrial towns, and you will see a state of prosperity such as we have never had in my lifetime – nor indeed ever in the history of this country.[6]

But, some asked, at what price? Several critics echoed a tradition which stretched back to FR Leavis, up to the contemporary Frankfurt School of philosophers. They saw this apparent affluence as false and corrupting, viewing the social meaning of cultural products under capitalism as determined solely by their commodity status.[7] Similar concerns were expressed by Richard Hoggart in his book, *The Uses of Literacy* (1957), in which he contrasts what he sees as the rich authenticity of an organic, pre-war working-class culture with that of 'the juke box boys'. These spectral beings were viewed as living in a twilight world, subsisting on a diet consisting of 'a peculiarly thin and pallid form of dissipation, a sort of spiritual dry-rot amid the odour of boiled milk starved of all nutrients'.[8]

Television, in Hoggart's view, was an integral part of this pessimistic perspective on popular culture, it was 'sensation without commitment', a 'phantasmagoria of passing shows and vicarious simulations.' Furthermore, its duplicitous nature aligned it to the devil's work, for, whilst it might seem to create its own cultural group, 'as large as the sum of all other groups':

> it would be a group only in the sense that its members shared a passivity. For the majority of them work would be dull and ambition out of place: nightly dead from the eyes downwards, they would be able to link on to the Great Mother.[9]

By the telling construction 'to link', television is discursively construed not only as a bad object, but a bad Mother: a sort of feminised Dracula.[10] Such opinions are part and parcel of the two traditions which have dominated work on the meaning of popular cultural forms.[11] The first of these, we can call the Marxist School of Pessimists. As we have seen already, they posit that the world of capitalism is irredeemably fallen. The second one we can call the Marxist School of Optimists. This includes contemporary critics like Jon Fiske, who believe that the technology of the mass media make possible 'resistant readings', even within the framework of capitalism.

On a less stringent note, the Granada television series *Coronation Street* (1960) has frequently been seen by critics as a dramatisation of *The Uses of Literacy*, with Hoggart's 'Our Mam' incarnated in the Ena Sharples character.[12] WJ Weatherby, writing in the short-lived *Contrast* magazine during the 1960s, described the new series as one which 'is at some pains to keep authority at bay', by which he means the masculine authority of the law or the trades unions.[13]

If it is at all possible to see the Hoggartian representation of the North as a feminisation, this perspective was more than offset by a counterblast from another quarter: that of the 'Angry Young Men'. These individuals quickly transformed the sympathetic, if stereotyped, feminine portrayal in *Uses* to misogyny.[14] Dramatists and novelists, like John Osborne in *Look Back in Anger* (1956) and John Braine in *Room at the Top* (1957), depict the upward mobility of the working class in terms of an emasculation. As a consequence, the regions, in particular the North, are presented as a more ruggedly physical locale than the South. As the novelist David Storey stated:

> It was in order, so it seemed, to accommodate the two extremes of this Northern physical world and its Southern, spiritual counterpart that I started making notes which two years later, while I was still at the Slade, resulted in the writing of a novel which I called *This Sporting Life*.[15]

In terms of gender, the North become associated with a remasculinisation. Troy Kennedy Martin, talking about researching the Lancashire locale prior to the making of *Z Cars*, wrote: 'it's a man's country alright'. As John Hill, seeking to explain the gender issue seeks to explain:

> What these writers really attack is effeminacy ... the sum of those qualities which are supposed traditionally ... to exude from the worst in women: pettiness, snobbery, flippancy, voluptuousness, superficiality, materialism.[16]

Here we have an instance of writers, dramatists and film critics projecting their own prejudices of gender and ethnicity onto the North. That they often did so from a Southern point of view resulted in an uncomfortable double perspective. Nonetheless, the cultural context affords an explanation of why the British television police series was to gain added currency during the 1960s. Its image of the male collective, comparable to that of the 1930s documentary, identified the North with rugged, physical work, although the task is never complete. The effect, of 'endless work' is of course reinforced by the repetitive nature of the series form itself.

Production contexts

Just as 'real-life' *contemporary* characters from the regions – like Bill Blewitt – had inspired the increased dramatisation of the pre-war GPO public service film, so the same process was repeated in television. Recently retired Detective Inspector William Prendergast – something of an iconic Northern policeman – was the inspiration for the leading protagonist in two case studies of the earliest television Northerns: *Who, Me?* and *Jacks and Knaves*. This represents a shift back to individualism and lends the regional forces some of the 'character' previously reserved for the more élite, metropolitan police detectives of Scotland Yard, in productions such as *Fabian of the Yard*. The existence, noted by Jeffrey Richards, of a recognisable Northern 'personality' was a tradition which Morris, himself a Liverpudlian, drew on. Indeed, this phenomenon, with its roots in the comedy of Lancashire greats such as George Formby and the inimitable Frank Randle, were an important shaping force in terms of constructing the Northern policier.[17] In terms of class, the Lancashire character shared with Mancunian Man, a:

> strenuousness and determination, directness and independence of judgement, intense civic pride and a belief in 'that fundamental and cheering principle: namely that every man is as good as his neighbour'.[18]

At a micro-level, the move away from narratives based upon the metropolis was influenced by more pragmatic concerns. As we have seen from the trials and tribulations which beset Robert Barr, delays in production were frequently incurred when scripts, especially those featuring Scotland Yard, were endlessly held up by 'the Met'. There was, in addition, the problem of ident-ifiable metropolitan locations in productions emanating both from the Documentary Department and Light Entertainment. With an increased use of film to expand the diegetic space beyond the studio, producers became increasingly frustrated by the restrictions placed upon them by Central London police. These became most apparent in the production of *Scotland Yard* (1960), the 13-part series written and produced by Robert Barr and the newly recruited David Rose.

Scotland Yard, with its 'action' scenes (car chases for example), crystallised the problems the Documentary Group were facing as they strained against generic restrictions brought about by institutional censorship. Although both *Pilgrim Street* and *Dixon of Dock Green* had, to a certain extent, circum-navigated the problem of 'authenticity' by becoming fictionalised, they nonetheless still needed to use London as a location backdrop. Barr began to see that whilst there was still room for narratives about Scotland Yard, as well as *Dixon of Dock Green*, whom by now there was no stopping, there was a value in introducing new dramatised forms set in the regions.

Tearaway, *Who, Me?* and *Jacks and Knaves* were written by the previously mentioned Morris and Calder, working together in the traditional writer-producer mode. However, they differed in that they were not ex-radio personnel like Robert Barr, newspaper journalists like Guy Morgan and Percy Hoskins or film-writers like Jan Read, but dramatists. Their programmes shifted away from the earlier journalist-based productions of *I Made News* to a new dramatic field of social problems, in which individualism and intersubjectivity represented vital ingredients. *Tearaway*, the first of the trilogy, was innovative in its depiction of the bleak conditions of the North and anticipated the drama of Ken Loach in productions like *Cathy Come Home* (1966). By contrast, *Who, Me?* and *Jacks and Knaves* incorporated an important humorous strand, centred on the figure of the policeman as a distinctive, fully-rounded *character*, one set apart from the increasingly benign and somewhat elderly 'Dixon' incarnation.

Prior to a more focused approach to these particular programmes, this chapter now picks up and advances the narrative concerning the Documentary Department's development between 1955 and 1961, so as to lay the ground for my subsequent analysis.

Institutional texts

During the mid-1950s, the relatively small BBC Television Documentary Department was in a state of organisational flux. Following Rotha's resignation in 1955, Robert Barr went over to the competition, and worked under contract to ABC TV and ITN until 1958.[19] Duncan Ross also left to work for an outside film company. Any remaining members went over to Talks, Drama or Light Entertainment. Ian Atkins, an active member of the documentary unit during the early 1950s, became Liaison Officer between the technical and planning staff. His deep involvement in complex discussions over the BBC's new studios at White City meant that he had little time for production work.

Although the Documentary Department was disbanded following Rotha's brief sojourn, so far as story-documentarists were concerned its institutional demise did not dissolve its influence. Far from it. Whilst Robert Barr and his band of fellow documentarists had previously survived, Robin Hood-like, in the spaces in between departments, they eventually found not only accommodation but also *legitimation* within the newly organised BBC Drama

Department. BBC Drama became reorganised under Plays, Serials and Series and it was this latter category which was to provide a home for documentarists. Meanwhile, the 'gap' before Sydney Newman's appointment in 1961, provided the most fertile space yet for documentary innovation.

The figure of Elwyn Jones was also important during this period because of his role in reconstituting what was left of the Documentary Department. He was recruited from the position of Television Editor on the *Radio Times* to become Organiser of Drama. Jones's official working title was Administrator to the Head of Drama. His mission, to re-establish the old Documentary Group, was initially made more difficult by practices introduced by the BBC during 1955 to streamline production practice. A centralised Script Department, under a new Group Production scheme was introduced. Independent script editors, under a Group Producer, were responsible for the day-to-day script planning and discussions with authors. This presented problems of divided authority and differences of opinion on both matters of policy and the actual quality of material, as well as with commissioning material. As Deputy Head of Documentary Drama, Jones was engaged in a persistent battle to ensure that he, rather than the official script editor, commissioned scripts: in order to do so, he had to bend the rule-book:

> Whilst I was all for having a Department who could advise me and to whom I could go and say 'Who do you have on your books, who can you recommend?' … it is my department's money and I should be able to spend it my way. So we played a nice sort of political trick. We had some staff posts we never filled and used the money to get a whole string of writers… You would hire them for three months and give them enough to pay the rent, you didn't really expect any work out of them though you might ask them to look hard at a script.[20]

By enticing Barr back to BBC Drama as a Group Producer in 1958, Jones effected a major coup and was able to build up once more the structure of what had previously constituted the Documentary Department. Morris and Calder, both of whom Jones had known previously, worked in a writer-producer partnership in a manner similar to that of their predecessors Ross and Atkins. The small size of the group meant that it had unusual autonomy, especially after Michael Barry resigned as Head of Drama in 1961. Barry was not re-placed, but Norman Rutherford (existing Assistant Head of Drama) became Acting Head of Drama. Jones acted as his deputy. It was both the hiatus at the top and Barr's brief absence, until his return in the late 1950s, that facili-tated another 'turn' in the story-documentary trajectory. Morris and Calder's dramatisations not only brought a sympathetic approach to social problems which the BBC had previously categorised as 'sordid subjects', thereby widening the remit of what could be shown on the small screen, they also introduced a sense of humour.

Born in Liverpool, Morris's theatrical background was highly influential. His first London stage production, *Desert Rats* (1945), which he also directed, had drawn on his wartime experiences in North Africa. The second, *Reluctant Heroes* (1951), an army farce, was popular as both a play and a film (the latter produced by Gaumont British).[21] Gilchrist Calder was to go on to direct Dennis Potter's first play, *The Confidence Course*.[22] Potter himself notably moved from documentary to drama. Calder and Morris's first jointly produced television drama documentary, *The Unloved* (1955), was about a delinquent boy and examined the long term effects of a deprived childhood. *A Woman Alone* (August 1956) dealt with unmarried mothers. In shifting the object of dramatisation from the institution to the social subject, documentarists met with criticism. William Salter of the *New Statesman* complained that Morris's *A Woman Alone* was 'neither a documentary in the genuine sense nor a work of fiction'. What seemed to worry him most was the persona of the actress. He felt it diverted the audience's attention away from the programme's documentary message which was consequentially 'forced to make some judgement about her performance as an actress'.[23]

However, as we have seen, story-documentaries were able to dramatise issues which would have been unacceptable to the authorities if presented in other forms, a fact of which practitioners 'on the ground' were all too aware. Writing in *The Times* of his significant preference for dramatisation over documentary, Morris revealingly stated that whereas:

> The documentary camera can only record what is at once visible, it cannot explain what brought the situation about. I approach a subject not with any social conscience, but simply with curiosity ... What I want to know is why and how. What makes this woman a prostitute and that not.[24]

In this analysis dramatisation gives a narrative explanation for social conditions, one which documentary treatment, in its observational, overlooking mode, cannot. Since the Aristotelian definition of drama is that it presents conflict between individuals, it became necessary to incarnate the narrative themes – in this case, intimidation of witnesses, crime, poverty, bullying policemen – within *characters*. Dramatisation creates an ambivalent space, one which can avoid the necessity for complete authenticity whilst conveying a different kind of truth. It can, therefore, avoid the difficulties, inherent in factual accounts, of having to be accountable.

It was Morris's interest in police procedures which set him investigating police interrogation methods: first in *Tearaway*, about the problem of witness intimidation; second, in a programme called *Who, Me?*, a result of a night spent in the company of Detective Sergeant Bill Prendergast of the Liverpool Police. He was to be publicised in the *Radio Times* as:

> a man with a talent for acting and more than a touch of psychology of whom it was said that when he had interrogated a thief, the prisoner would leap into the dock and shout: 'GUILTY'.[25]

Prendergast may be read as part of the plain-speaking, independent-spirited set of characters which emerged out of the industrial landscape of Lancashire. Jeffrey Richards states that in his *English Journey* JB Priestley observed that being in Lancashire was like landing among a million music-hall comedians and that 'the Lancashire accent, flat and broad vowelled, lent itself to ironic understatement and was admirable for comic effect, being able to suggest either shrewdness or simplicity, or … more likely a humorous mixture of both'.[26]

Prendergast possessed both qualities in abundance. He was shrewd and humorous, whilst the other characterisations, especially in *Jacks and Knaves*, were full-on slapstick comedians.

Jacks and Knaves, which followed on directly from *Who, Me?*, was based upon four more Prendergast cases. It was this series which won Morris a Screenwriters' Guild award for the best script of 1961 and, in terms of presenting a non-eulogistic portrait of the police, paved the way for *Z Cars*.[27] Sequentially, the triad of programmes describes the process of a trajectory, moving out from the one-off story-documentary form of the first two programmes, towards the four-part series production of *Jacks and Knaves*. All three productions by the Calder/Morris team were created under the documentary department's new regime, to which Barr had returned by the time *Tearaway* was produced.

William Prendergast was not only the inspiration for the burly chief character of Detective Sergeant Hitchins, he was a key figure in supplying the story material for all three productions. According to internal correspondence, *Who, Me?* comes directly out of the experience of researching *Tearaway*. *Jacks and Knaves*, the third four-part programme, builds out from *Who, Me?* in terms of its *mise-en-scene* and thematic interests. The chief protagonist, Detective Sergeant Hitchins, anticipates aspects of the Barlow persona in *Z Cars* and is exemplary of a new way of creating character in using a little-known stage actor to play a living personality. This method of creating character contrasts strongly with that of the *Blue Lamp* film or even the subsequent *Dixon of Dock Green* television series, where the police character is based upon that of a well-known actor.

Seen as a collective, the sequence of programmes both significantly shifts the geographical and social ground of the dramatised story-documentary and contains many of the seeds which come to germination in the *Z Cars* series (1962). As no recording survives, I shall once more be quoting from the surviving scripts of *Tearaway*, *Who, Me?* and *Jacks and Knaves* in as much detail as is required, looking consecutively at each production. *Tearaway* (1956) is perhaps the fullest realisation of Michael Barry's comment cited earlier, that the television drama or story-documentary was a fundamental influence, not only upon *Z Cars*, but also on the work of dramatists, film-makers and novelists.

Tearaway, first of three

Responding to those current literary and dramatic concerns referred to earlier, it is notable that all three productions were set in the North of England. The attention to a specific locale, in *Tearaway*, the first of the Calder and Morris trilogy, demonstrates how the region may be treated as both *sui generis* and in national terms. This reverses the way in which the regional is usually subsumed under the national. In the first scene Chief Inspector Hall, Head of an unnamed Liverpool police division, implies that the eponymous '*Tearaway*', like that of the muscleman or spiv of the 1930s and 1940s (or even the mugger during the 1970s), is a national incarnation:

> Get the suit off, cut the leash, and you can't tell the difference between him
> and the tearaways in Manchester, Birmingham or Wigan, which is probably
> where he started from. They're the same. The products of bad homes, lousy
> parents, war, greed and bone idleness ... [28]

Unlike *Dixon of Dock Green*, where crime is seen as the responsibility of the individual, *Tearaway* dramatises the social conditions which breed such a phenomenon. Its fully fictional narrative allowed it much greater freedom from police scrutiny than if it had been based on real-life case-histories. Police co-operation was sought – as it would be later for *Z Cars* – in a very different way: for atmosphere, procedure and character, rather than, as in the past, for procedural exactitude.

Tearaway continues to dramatise the shift from an examination of the public work of institutions, pioneered by Robert Barr in the early 1950s, towards a new focus on individuals who are at their receiving end.[29] Of the numerous claims made for its direct antecedents, Gilchrist Calder states that *Tearaway* was the genesis of *Z Cars*:

> If you read it, [*Tearaway*] is the exact formula for the later *Z Cars*. *Who, Me?* was an interrogation piece on three planes but *Tearaway* has the chase, the clip of the film, the coppers here and the crooks there, patrol cars and everything ...

But, on reading the script, it is in its presentation of a critical new social realism, as much as in terms of its iconography, that *Tearaway* most closely anticipates *Z Cars*.

Radio Times publicity describes *Tearaway* in a significant reversal of terms as 'A documentary drama showing how certain people remain silent when threatened with violence'. Basically, the plot concerns what happens when two 'tearaways' decide to pick a victim named Tommy Baxter, beat him up, and the witnesses – Tam, Mrs Molden, and First Neighbour – are too scared to come forward. The narrative is concerned to explore this problem as much from the witnesses' point of view as that of the police. Detective Sergeant Bulliver, the main investigative detective, is seen as utterly ruthless in his use of a bullying psychology. 'Before the night is over', he tells Harry Shelton, when they finally get him in for questioning, 'we'll be close as brothers'.

The production's locale offers a genuinely different semiotics. It portrays the grimness of life in the Victorian slum setting and an authentic roughness of language with its use of regional and vernacular expressions. Tommy Baxter is referred to as 'a bastard' and 'Bleedin' Tommy Baxter'. Such a new variety of realism is very different to *Dixon of Dock Green*'s benign presentation. Thematically, Morris's dramatisation focuses upon the socially constructed nature of crime and its crucial link to poverty. He does not shy away from depicting the 1950s underclass whose existence was obscured by *Dixon*'s somewhat bland suburban portrayal of society where working-class characters and racial minorities were represented as stereotypes.

The protagonists in *Tearaway*, from Stella, Tam's wife – and witness to the assault – to the elder Baxter, father of Tommy, are working class and articulate the new 'gritty' social realism that will be taken up later in the 1960s by exponents such as Ken Loach. Stage directions on the *Tearaway* script precisely detail the poverty of Tommy Baxter's sparse yet 'neat' house.

11. Doreen Andrews as Mrs Gorman and Stuart Saunders as
Bulliver in *Tearaway* (1956).

Stella's living room is even 'more sparsely furnished, and untidy with
children's clothes'. By contrast to the 'respectable' poverty of each of these,
Joe Gorman's room, is 'sordid'. The mise-en-scene characterises the
difference that Jeffrey Richards has noted between 'the rough' and 'the
respectable' working class, in depictions of the North West. Whereas
'respectability' connoted a belief in 'education, self-advancement,
domesticity, thrift, restraint and good manners', 'roughness' meant living for
the moment 'rejecting authority, education and thrift, drinking to excess,
fighting, swearing and fornicating without restraint'.[30]

Dispensing with the central narrator device, the drama opens with an ex-
pository scene, one which replaces the narrative voice-over of *Fabian of the
Yard* and the *Blue Lamp* film, whilst demonstrating some continuity with it.
The script details read:

Night. Late autumn evening in a slum street in a Northern City. Near a
newspaper stand on a street corner, a little off the main street, two men are

struggling with a third. Newspapers are strewn all over the pavement. The two men overthrow the news seller.[31]

SUPERIMPOSE CAPTION: "TEARAWAY"

FADE OUT CAPTION

The script continues with a description of how this establishing scene is to be dramatised. As the news seller goes down, the two men start to kick him, he struggles for a while, then lies still:

> One of the men JOE goes to collect the money from the tin box near the news stand. The other HARRY continues kicking. Then both run away from the camera. Track in to show man silent lying on his face, a dark trickle running towards the gutter. It runs across a newspaper opened, crumpled, foot marks on it, but one can read the feature article heading: "GANGS STALK THE CITY".

From the script directions we see here what amounts to a familiar filmic trope. Indeed, *The Blue Lamp* features a similar newspaper stand and headlines. In this television production however, it is incorporated into the main diegesis, so that the newspaper headline forms a wry metafictional comment upon the narrative action. What we see up close on the small silver screen projected into the privacy of our living rooms is not what the newspapers are representing. This brings home the programme's ideological aim, which is to problematise the way in which crime is reported. In the next scene, set in daylight, Hall is shown arguing over the same headlines with a newspaper reporter:

> HALL: *(Thumping newspaper)* What gangs? One night Paddy's drinking with Alf and that's another gang. Another night Len's having a mojo, drunk with Billy and that's another gang. *(Taps paper)* This sort of journalism makes the subject more important than it really is. It's not bad because it gives the muscle men ideas – They don't read anyhow! It's bad because it tends to make the public nervous.

Whereas today it is television which is seen as distorting fears of crime in proportion to its actual risk, during the 1950s, it was self-evidently the press. Morris's script rams home the message with some bolstering – if by now rather familiar – public relations spiel:

> You're making people nervous. The one thing this country's got left – and it hasn't got much – is its justice. And the police are part of British justice.

12. Lily and Chief Inspector Hall in *Tearaway* (1956).
The black eye motif will be repeated in *Z Cars*.

Their reputation grew up over many years on the good temper, the integrity and the fairness of the man on the beat.

Here, once again, the discourse is *sui generis*, rather than local. The problem of media distortion with regard to crime is seen as a national one.

Although *Tearaway* obviously displays its little bit of propaganda, to satisfy the Lancashire police force (without whose co-operation the programme could not, at the time, have been made), the action quickly moves into a close up of 'the living scene'. The urban-based ambience conveys a sense of poverty and brutality and is inhabited by a highly mistrustful working-class milieu, one that is no longer orderly or co-operative.

The second scene depicts the exterior of a public house which cuts to inside, where we meet Harry Shelton, the eponymous tearaway, and his accomplice Joe Gorman. These then are the perpetrators of the petty pilfering, hardly constitutive of a 'gang'. Elsewhere, Harry is described as 'strong, yet stunted, unshaven and, like Joe, uncared for'. Harry is a born bully, with no motive but boredom. Tommy Baxter is a born victim whose unfortunate barrow is the cause of his taking the kind of beating that could not possibly have been shown on the 'Dixon' family slot. The putative 'gang' consisting of the evil duo kick him in the face four times. When Stella, one of six witnesses tries to pull Shelton away, he tells her husband Tam, 'Call this bitch off, Tam, or you'll be next … *(for the benefit of the watching people)* It serves 'im right. He knows what he did!'

The language of street fear and intimidation offers a clear explanation as to why the onlookers keep silent. Even when Tom's own father, Baxter, asks what happened they are evasive. Tam, a primary witness, claims not to have been present. Baxter himself is far too scared to reveal Harry and Joe's identity in a complaint to the police for fear of their reprisals, despite the victim being his own flesh and blood. The task is left to an unseen witness 'standing in the shadows'. There is a strong implication that he is known to the police as a professional informer. This depiction of the police portrays a new, shady side of the law in which 'deals' are made by those who inhabit the margins.

Upon being questioned by Detective Inspector Hall, the unfortunate Tommy, laid-up in a hospital ward and terrified witless of reprisals, chooses not to remember. 'I fell over sir,' he says. It is left to Detective Sergeant Bulliver – as his name connotes, a bullying sort but with the law behind him – to take up the questioning of the previously silent witnesses. But to no avail. When Bulliver asks 'Anyone likely to talk?' Pete replies, 'Not while they're out'. If they are terrified by tearaways on the loose, the victims are equally mistrustful of the police. In this harsh environment, British policemen are no longer presented as benevolent sergeants on bicycles, issuing road directions. Mrs Molden sums up the attitude: 'Best keep quiet I say. You never know with the police.' This is a view reinforced by the First Neighbour, who further elaborates, 'Police are devils'. This is, once again, a far remove from the Dixon-based drama of law and order, public trust and easy solutions.

When, in the next scene, the local police appear on scene and the women try to leave they are physically prevented:

Bulliver   *(Blocking the door)* What's the bloomin' rush? You were all havin' a nice little tate ah tate. Don't let me disturb you.

Neighbour I was just going Mr. Bulliver.

Bulliver   No you weren't. You were set to gab till cockcrow.

The problems of being a responsible citizen in this hinterland of poverty are vividly conveyed in the debate between Stella, who says she wouldn't mind being a witness, and Tam who cogently puts the case for keeping quiet: 'Say two words and pencil and paper's out. A month later you're up before the man with the shawl on.' As a father, he is terrified of 'grassing up' because of future reprisals upon his young son, 'we're marked as having grassed – It might be years, two weeks, or only two minutes. You never know when its coming. *(nodding upstairs)* They might fix Tony for the rest of his life.'

Up North, crime and poverty are depicted as walking the streets hand in hand. Both are endemic, moving through the generations. Harry Shelton's father, a former muscleman or tearaway, is depicted as an old dog who has had his day, his son Sid serving an apprenticeship in crime. From the point of view of the police, the likes of Harry Shelton and Joe Gorman: 'just impress your own kind. The rest of you, reared in slums by fathers who taught you the rule of life by knocking the daylights out of you'. This kind of apprenticeship is an ironic counterpoint to that of the ordered hierarchy of the police station itself. Stella articulates the thoughts of the whole community when she says:

Wouldn't it be nice to have a decent flat, with a bit of light, where we could see there was a decent way of livin' instead of dirt, an' crazy fellers, an' neighbours getting kicked in the face four times.

Hers is a far cry from the plea of Eliza Doolittle in *My Fair Lady*, the sentimental Edwardian hit musical from the 1950s, whose eponymous protagonist also wanted 'a room somewhere, far away from the cold night air'. *Tearaway*'s new realism presents a searingly contemporary portrait of 1950s poverty in an innovative dramatic form that permits different points of view and subjectivities. For the first time, we see the public set against the police.

Who, Me?

The next production in the sequence, *Who, Me?*, departs from *Tearaway* in that it is not centred upon those at the receiving end of a rough form of justice, but upon its administration. The publicity on file describes *Who, Me?* as 'not only an exceptional production in its own right but ... one of the seeds from which sprang that outstanding success *Z Cars*'.[32] The narrative action of *Who, Me?* is, for the first time since *Pilgrim Street*, set entirely in a police station, where three men are held for questioning in connection with a shop theft. It is centred around the activities of another incarnation of Prendergast, the persona of Detective Inspector Hitchins. The reason for the subterfuge may well have been due to the fact of the real-life Prendergast's recent retirement from the police service. In similar vein to Bulliver in *Tearaway*, Hitchins is representative of a new, tough, policeman whose methods are more authentic than those represented by *Dixon of Dock Green*.

In terms of the national public, however, and in spite of *Who, Me?* achieving excellent ratings, local viewers found it disturbing. They were particularly concerned with the fact that the police were shown using what they considered unfair interview methods. An attempt by Gilchrist Calder to counter such accusations, was hardly reassuring. A letter from him stated, 'the people being interrogated in the programme were, if you remember, already criminals with bad records. The methods used would obviously not be used in normal circumstances'.[33]

Such a comment is hardly consonant with the 'innocent until proven guilty' edict of the law, but the unpalatable fact that unorthodox methods of interrogation were regularly practised, is verified by the comments of an acting Metropolitan CID Inspector:

> As I watched the story unfold I found myself reliving again similar situations in which I have played a part, and the authenticity of the whole production was amazing. So many programmes on police work present a totally inaccurate picture. Some people may object to what they saw and deprecate the subterfuge used but they must realise that in dealing with a criminal successfully it is unavoidable.

Moreover, a congratulatory letter from the former CID Training Officer of Cornwall County Constabulary states there is 'a paucity of films to instruct experienced officers in the Police Force', and yet 'this documentary is really live education by any standards'.[34] Here we can see *Who, Me?* being used to show the work of the regional police service in a very similar way to the GPO films that sought to 'bring alive' the Post Office. Not only were later police programmes used as education for training officers, in the case of *Z Cars* they were also used in schools as examples of quality popular drama. Through its appeal to the public service brief to entertain, educate and inform, the police series seems to have achieved its ultimate legitimation. It more than satisfied both its economic and ideological imperatives.

The Audience Reaction Index for the programme, as presented in the Audience Weekly Report, worked out an average percentage as high as that 'for the more sensational crime story documentary of *Tearaway*' at 71, yet the Report does admit to the very mixed reception at a local level. Some viewers said it did not appeal to them because the story was slow and un-interesting, 'dreary, dull and long drawn out'. Others considered it 'very sordid' and complained of the use of 'far too much bad language'. Several hoped it was fiction and not fact, including a nurse who emphatically stated 'if our police really act and speak like this then we should be ashamed and disgusted'.[35]

Jacks and Knaves and the carnivalesque

Jacks and Knaves (1961) was described by the *Radio Times* as 'four self-contained 45-minute programmes which spring directly from the experience and the success of *Who, Me?*' The term 'Jack' is a traditional Liverpool name for a policeman: 'In Liverpool they call a detective a "Jack" – and one of the most colourful Jacks who ever nobbled a knave in that windy city was Detective Sergeant William Prendergast ... Liverpudlians, who nicknamed him "Ace", still swap stories about his exploits'.[36]

The programmes, again based in Liverpool, are about the work of the same uninhibited detective sergeant, 'who doesn't so much break the rules as bend them'. Bill Prendergast himself supplied the storylines and, as correspondence details, was paid 100 guineas for each story, with repeats carrying 'the usual two-thirds fee'.[37] Once more, *Jacks and Knaves*'s storylines are centred on the Detective Sergeant Hitchins character, although this time around he is played by John Barrie, who crossed over from the *Scotland Yard* series. Unlike Lee Montague, who played the part previously but was not credited in the *Radio Times*, Barrie's name appears beside his role. This is a significant move, for it acknowledges, for the first time, the production's dramatic status. However, switching the lead must have been confusing for an audience who had come to identify with Lee Montague in the DS Hitchins role. Fuelling further confusion is the fact that *Radio Times* pre-publicity, describing 'the beefy, granite-faced detective', alludes to neither Barrie or the Hitchins characterisation but to that of real-life Detective William Prendergast. The three-way identification demanded from the audience is the ultimate in the story-documentary's endeavour to prove its authenticity. It is not until *Z Cars*, one year later, that this need to acknowledge the factual basis of dramatic presentations is relinquished: a development which causes problems of a slightly different nature. Meanwhile, advance publicity on file, possibly for use in the *Radio Times*, describes the *Jacks and Knaves* series as 'Four stories concerning the lighter side of CID work in the North of England'.[38] 'The Master Mind', 'The Interrogation', 'The Great Art Robbery' and 'It was Doing Nothing' were transmitted at weekly intervals from mid-November to early December 1961. According to advance publicity, they:

> involve the theft of a church gate and a church wall [this is not a mistake – some splendid demolition characters are careering around the city knocking down anything they think looks useless]; the theft – accidental for the most part – of a painting, the value of which is not even suspected by the thieves who are really after lead; a case of shop-lifting which gets very complicated indeed because it leads to the recovery of other goods stolen more belligerently; and a robbery from a warehouse with the problem of finding out just what was stolen, since the owner says one thing and the actual thieves quite another.[39]

What emerged from *Tearaway* was a sense of irony on the part of the police, that accepts the persistence of criminality. In *Who, Me?*, however, it was nuanced by a more humorous approach. By the time the producer-writer team arrive at *Jacks and Knaves*, irony gives way to a rather gauche *PC 49* version of slapstick comedy. It may well have been that the humour acted as a foil for censorship, for the series' innovation lay in showing the work of villains, a subject strictly censored by the British Board of Film Censors before the war. It also seems to tap into local traditions of music hall. The opening of 'The Great Art Robbery' begins with an especially filmed song sequence, accompanied by mouth organ. The words of the Frankie and Johnny ballad are worth setting out, because they indicate the Northern humour that is to follow:

Frankie/Johnny	Frankie and Johnny were totters
	Golly, and how they did tot!
Johnny	They swore they would have their own scrap yard
Frankie	But a handcart was all they got

Frankie/Johnny	Oh, they didn't see
	That they were were doing wrong
	They went after all kinds of metal
	Wherever it was to be found

Johnny   If they could have climbed Blackpool Tower

Frankie   They'd have had it cut up on the ground

Frankie/Johnny	Oh, they didn't see
	That they were doing wrong
	No place was safe from their prowling
	No matter wher'er it might be

Johnny   They'd cut a lead pipe from a cistern

Frankie   So the water came out floodingly!

DUB WILDTRACK – *Woman screaming and lavatory flushing.*

Frankie/Johnny   Oh, they didn't see

That they were doing wrong![40]

According to the script extracts on file, the *Jacks and Knaves* stories represent a move away from the previous police station location of *Who, Me?* and are concerned with the lighter side of criminal life, of which the first of the quartet – 'Master Mind' – is exemplary. It is a story about a young man named Ron who bails out an old burglar to assist him in 'a brilliantly planned robbery'. The job is cased, prepared and executed correctly, but, 'It's the proceeds which present problems'. Martin and another young accomplice are seen breaking into the premises shortly after cutting the wires of the burglar alarm, whilst Ron drives the Lorry.

TIGHT 2-SHOT: MARTIN/CHARLIE

MARTIN *makes a back for* CHARLIE.

CHARLIE *gets on back, puts his head through window.* MARTIN *slowly straightens up.*

CUT TO REVERSE SIDE OF WINDOW

CS CHARLIE *and cistern.*

He is being eased in too quickly. He reaches out for cistern to support himself.

CUT TO …

REVERSE ANGLE (*outside* WINDOW)

MARTIN, *impatient, gives an extra shove (Sound effect). Yell from* CHARLIE. *Chain being pulled.*

CUT TO …

CU MARTIN's *face. He looks desperate.*

CUT TO …

MS MARTIN *as he pushes legs through window.*

(Pause)

MARTIN   Are you all right?

CHARLIE's VOICE   You nearly broke me neck!

And so it goes on, with realism giving way to knockabout farce. The two men collect the parcels in the lorry, take them to an accomplice's house and carry them to the shed. The accomplice, who is named Ava, comes out to check:

2-SHOT RON/AVA *with* MARTIN *in background taking parcels from* LORRY *to* SHED.

RON   Come on a Martin job an' never get knocked.

AVA   Where're the furs?

RON   In the shed. There's about fifty boxes of 'em.

AVA   You don't keep furs in boxes!

RON   They're ladies gowns, then. At ten bob a time we're all right. We've cleared the ladies department.

The unfortunate pair are left with the problem of ten thousand grey jumpers to get rid of, at least until they are arrested and charged, Ron's father having refused to hide him.

The frantic action in the *Jacks and Knaves* series is made possible because it has a higher than usual ratio of filmed sequences, including exterior shots. The above scene, if transmitted live would have been fraught with difficulties, both in terms of timing and the acrobatics involved in negotiating the window (let alone pulling the chain and synchronising the sound effects of the flushing lavatory). Another new development, in production terms, is that for the first time, the whole of this series was telerecorded. The programme was therefore performed *as if* rather than actually live (as explained in the Introduction). The filmed sequences were then telecined into the performance. It was then recorded on video tape.

Jacks and Knaves's production schedule shows an increased professionalism in terms of scheduling. A memo from Michael Barry to the Head of Programme Planning states that the new series was to fill the gap between the end of *Maigret* (Week 2) and the beginning of *The Adventures of a Black Bag* (Week 7). The memo then goes on to outline the production schedule, allowing three to four weeks for each programme and consisting, roughly, of one day's filming during the first week, half a day's dubbing during the second with a three-day period given over to camera rehearsal and recording of the whole performance. The production sequence, which took place over a 16-week period, did not follow the same order in which the programmes were transmitted.

The Audience Research Report for 'Master Mind' showed some discomfort at the addition of humour to the story-documentary format, as the following excerpt shows:

> no more original than many another 'cops and robbers' story, its comedy angle not very different from that in say, 'Dixon of Dock Green' and the documentary slant not emphasised at all.

Other participants thought the Liverpool accents were poorly done; there was reference to police officers being portrayed with an unlikely casualness and to those of the two thieves as poorly characterised. In general it was found that the documentary slant was not 'emphasised too well'; 'the point of the programme – the nature of the interrogation by the Detective Sergeant' occupied, it was felt, too little time. There were also complaints about production points. One viewer wrote that during the theft scene, 'there seemed to be far too many packages in the warehouse – that a small ex-WD utility could have shifted the lot was impossible.'[41] However, there were some favourable comments. In particular, there was praise for 'getting a good insight into the methods of a famous and human detective', while learning at the same time 'all about the ruses and red herrings used by the thieves'. Largely because of its new subject matter and regional milieu, the programme won the British Television and Screenwriters Guild Award for the best dramatic series seen on British Television in 1961.[42]

From the police themselves, there was qualified praise. Correspondence on file, which is worth quoting at length, cites 'an ex-Metropolitan policeman' as stating that 'Master Mind' was an 'excellent production marred by a jarring note in the concluding scene':

> no self respecting CID Officer, even in Liverpool, would caution a person he was about to charge with the words '… anything you say will be given in evidence against you …' I cannot see that dramatic licence calls for the use of this formula … the words 'against you' have been omitted from the caution at least since 1912 when the first of the Judges' Rules were formulated. Rule 4 says, inter alia, 'It is desirable that the last two words of the usual caution should be omitted and that the caution should end with the words 'to be given in evidence … You are not obliged to say anything but anything you say may be given in evidence'. It is therefore incomprehensible to me as an ex CID officer, that an antiquated formula, abolished as long ago as 1912 should be used in a 1961 play. It is almost on a par with the cartoons which appear from time to time depicting convicts with broad arrows on their clothing.

Such a comment is demonstrative of an increasingly discriminating audience, sensitive to regional mis-representation. Correspondence on file from the then Conservative MP Nicholas Ridley complains that one of his constituents, a Major Neal, thought *Jacks and Knaves* 'showed the police in an unfortunate light, making them out to be fools lacking in discipline'. Replying for the BBC, RD Pendlebury of the Secretariat carefully explained that Colin Morris had achieved a high reputation for serious documentary but that on this present occasion 'he was aiming at a lighter and more humorous effect'. He concedes that his policemen 'though very much closer to the real thing than to the Keystone Cops were perhaps drawn a fraction larger than life'. Another letter to a Dr Bradshaw reads:

> I wish to assure you that it was not the intention of the corporation when presenting the programme … to portray or to imply any of the actions of which you complain, or to suggest that such actions are commonplace to English policemen. The greatest care is taken to ensure that the sources from which material is drawn for drama-documentary programmes are reliable and acceptable … The programme to which you refer, which was pre-recorded, was shown to a group of North Country police officers some weeks ago and … they found no fault in it.[43]

This burgeoning discontent was to burst into full flood with the production of *Z Cars* in 1962.

Jacks and Knaves's experimental nature, particularly its use of comedy, demonstrates the fecundity of new police series dramatisations set in the North. Its innovative 'waggish' brand of humour was to be carried over into *Z Cars*. However, after the fracas caused by problems over the programmes' truth status, Calder and Morris decided to quit. As Calder himself stated, 'Later I was asked if I would do *Z Cars* but after *Jacks and Knaves* I'd had enough'.[44]

Back at the Met

By the mid-1960s, the Scotland Yard series constituted a television genre in its own terms. It was closely associated to, and can be seen as taking over from, the Scotland Yard 3-reeler 'B' Movies, particularly those made by Merton Park and narrated by the British journalist Edgar Lustgarten, who had written many books on famous crimes and trials. The Lustgarten series produced by Montgomery Tully between 1954 and 1957 included titles such as *Murder Anonymous* (1955) and *Wall of Death* (1956), which were often the most exciting aspect of these unremittingly middle-class productions.

A continuation of both the film version and the genre begun in Robert Barr's successful *War on Crime* series, the BBC's *Scotland Yard* (1960) series was committed to educating the public about their responsibilities as citizens, with particular regard to specific forms of legislation. Transmitted just a year before *Jacks and Knaves* and also starring John Barrie, the series was the result of ongoing discussions following on from the earlier *War on Crime*. Late in 1959, Hugh Carleton Greene, the then Director of News and Current Affairs, and Michael Barry were summoned to the Met for 'light refreshments and a general discussion', 'following the facilities given by us during the summer to Mr. Robert Barr.' An unattributed report held at the BBC written archive, dated the same year and entitled 'Interview with the Commissioner' indicates that this social event had been preceded by a long interview with the Commissioner of 'the Met', Sir Joseph Simpson. It is worth quoting from to emphasise the importance placed upon the authentic representation of the police on television, by the police themselves:

> The Commissioner showed very soon that his major concern ... is with the current public attitude towards the Police ... We discussed allegations of violence made against the Police, and the Commissioner had no doubts at all that on occasion a great deal of violence was exerted, and certainly made no bones about the fact that his Flying Squad consisted of some of the

toughest Policemen in the world … he went on to say that it was his considered opinion that there was … far less violence exerted by the Police these days than had been in his young days on the beat. He was more than prepared to have allegations of violence made during our programmes. He even actively wanted some picture given of what happened to such allegations both of violence, corruption or what you will. He said he was not in any sense afraid of our showing a corrupt policeman, because he said corruption in any Police Force is exposed by policemen, and that I think, is something of which we can well be proud.

Here, then, is a carte blanche to show the activities of the police in a newly realistic light. Elsewhere, the Report offers fascinating insights into the thinking behind the programmes. Its writer – in all likelihood Elwyn Jones – begins by stating that the Commissioner was concerned about public attitudes to the police, in particular over the new Street Offences Bill, the gaming laws and the licensing laws. Motoring offences were another a subject for complaint.

The Commissioner agreed that any prolonged television series would have to include some account of spectacular crime, such as the sort of heavy raid on a bank lorry which falls directly into the province of the Flying Squad. But whilst the series might feature 'the Glamour Boys' of Scotland Yard, the Report goes on to state that:

> while the degree of specialisation which exists in the Police Force should certainly be revealed … major attention should be focused on the non-specialist, on the Policeman who whether he stayed in uniform or went into plain clothes, is the actual backbone of the Force.[45]

Conspicuous by its very absence, is any mention of George Dixon of the *Dixon of Dock Green* series. Although *today* he performs a valuable, public relations function for the police – as we saw in the case of the Sheehey Report (1993) – back in the 1960s, before the advent of *Z Cars*, this role had yet to be fully constituted. For the time being, it appears, he was beneath 'the Met's' consideration.

In sum, the Commissioner's report is proof of a certain pressure being applied. A move towards a similar sort of generic portrayal of the ordinary police force to that of *War on Crime* or *Pilgrim Street*, is suggested, but with a 'warts and all' emphasis on realism. The Interview Report terminates with Robert Barr agreeing to show that 'London was well policed, that such policing had its problems and that such policing had its *costs*'. Just as it was for the

13. Detective Sergeant Turner outside Scotland Yard in the
eponymous series (1960).

real-life police-force, so it was for television. What was costly was the holding
up of scripts by the Met, who became ever fussier about checking police
procedure. In addition, finding street locations in London became increasingly
difficult because of traffic problems.

Scotland Yard began broadcasting on 12 April, 1960. It starred John Barrie as Detective Inspector Marshall of 'F Division'. The 13-part series aimed to show the different tasks faced by police across the full range, from uniformed to plain-clothes policemen. Each programme dealt with different aspects of policing. Information was given about the victims and perpetrators of 'Robbery with Violence' (No. 4); international police liaison ('Interpol', No. 8); and what happens in a court of law when the police bring forward a prosecution ('Reasonable Doubt', No. 9). 'Used in Evidence' (No. 11), was written to demonstrate the work of the ballistics department; this was in line with Percy Fearnley's previous request to Barr after the *War on Crime* series, that he should concentrate on the work of individual organisations which interfaced with Scotland Yard rather than purely on their own criminal investigations.

Like its predecessors, *Scotland Yard* pursued a documentary approach. This meant using little-known actors and employing the same mode of production introduced in *I Made News*. The series was made at Riverside Studios and telerecorded, possibly with a view to export, which is suggested but not confirmed in correspondence. *Scotland Yard*'s production practice was very similar to what was to come in *Z Cars*, the reason why, perhaps, Robert Barr saw it as a direct precursor. All the exteriors, for instance, were shot on 35 mm black and white film, together with a number of interiors at Ealing Studios on the large stage, so as to save space in the transmitting studios at Riverside.

It is worth looking briefly at the first episode, 'Nightbeat', to show how its narrative interest is continuous with Barr's earlier *War on Crime*, in terms of utilising television as a medium for *demonstration* and instruction. The production directly contrasts with the Morris and Calder trilogy in this respect. Police techniques such as fingerprinting are shown in great detail, as are their radio control methods. In these two aspects, its documentary tendencies subordinate those of any attempt to portray dramatic realism: it is not until the fifth episode, that the police are portrayed in a more critical light.

'Nightbeat' (12 April 1960) opens with a telecined credit caption to Scotland Yard (faded in) preceding that of the series title, *Scotland Yard* – on film – telecined in and synchronised with a voice-over which indicates further, that this programme is either for export, or training purposes, as follows:

Scotland Yard is the headquarters of the Metropolitan Police … regulating and policing 700 square miles of London … and 8 million people … by day and by night. They say it's a good life … an active life.

The 'Nightbeat' caption is followed by an establishing shot which visually depicts that which has previously only been verbally described – noticeably

14. Detective Sergeant Turner with a colleague in the Map Room,
Scotland Yard (1960).

in the *Blue Lamp* film and *Fabian* series – by an omniscient (Voice-of-God) voice over.[46] Now, instead of being written into the dialogue, extra script comments, obviously directed at the Met, indicate the author's intentions. The film insert after the titles is detailed in the script as portraying the night scene of 'a deserted London street about 2am. A dull street of homes and shops and basement steps'. Next, a cut to an archway is indicated, showing a mews 'of little workshops and garages, dustbins and parked cars'. The written instructions following describe how people complain they 'never see a police-man'. Details given for the next shot read:

> After a moment we see a CONSTABLE … move in and out of the shadows inspecting the lock up workshops, pressing on the garage doors, briefly flashing his torch. His demeanour, is that of the professional policeman; experienced, casual, unobtrusive – the experience of long hours on the beat.[47]

The attention given to presenting an authentic portrait of the British Bobby here is self-evident. Immediately following the opening sequence, showing the constable 'on the beat', a police car is seen approaching and the sequence then moves into a demonstration of how the radio-control system works. The script indicates the presence of three men in the car, two uniformed men in front and a plain-clothes man in the back seat. The uniformed man by the radio set has a clipboard and message pad on his knee. Radio 'Talk' on the car radio is indicated by the script and the 'Radio Man' is making notes of the messages:

> RADIO   Hello all cars, hello all cars. From M.P. Lost or stolen ELP.899. E-echo, L-Lima; P-Papa 899. Gray Austin saloon from Park Crescent, Richmond, since 2230/13. Message No. 12 ends. Origin VR.0223. M.P. out.

From the first, we see the new 1960s interest in hardware and technology. These are to underwrite the ethos of the British television police series during the 1960s, epitomised by *Z Cars*, whose narrative interests are centred upon the new, radio-controlled police-cars. The plot of 'Nightbeat' concerns the theft from a factory warehouse of a stolen safe, whose recovery is largely made possible by the advanced radio-communications system within the patrol cars. The narrative interest lies in the demonstration of police procedure in identifying and finding the culprits, who turn out to be a couple of spivs, and in using television as a medium of explication, in terms of police forensics. The culprits are traced through the technique of checking unidentified fingerprints, known as 'unidents'. A fingerprint taken from the scene of the crime is found to be identical with a print found in Birmingham one year earlier, after a robbery at a local cinema. When Chubby Dawson and his accomplice are 'nailed', his alibi is finally broken by the copper on the night beat who has spotted him. Thus, the ordinary policeman is still seen to have a function. As Marshall states, possibly for the benefit of potential recruits: 'You know, some of them are quite good'.

Don Taylor was a documentary practitioner who crossed over to television and, like Paul Rotha, found great difficulties working in the medium. In his autobiographical account, he recounts his experience of working on the *Scotland Yard* series, of which he was allocated two episodes: 'Interpol' (31 May 1960) and 'Used in Evidence' (21 June 1960).[48] His experience of directing these offers an interesting insight into the process, as well as a graphic description of how little new recruits from the six-week training programme for television producers were prepared:[49]

> David Rose found ... a simple script for me that required only the most standard two-shot and close up shooting ... You entered the studio for the first time at 10am, carefully rehearsed each scene shot by shot, rehearsed the moments when the pre-filmed telecine would be slotted live into the show, and made sure you were finished in time for a run-through at about five. After the run-through, you had a session with the camera-man, then went for a meal at six. At about half seven you returned to the studio, where the cameras were all standing in a troup round the test card, being technically 'lined up' ... at about a quarter to eight everyone went to their places, and the camera and booms moved into their opening positions. The second hand moved inexorably round the dial, the continuity announcer introduced your programme, the red lights came on, and you were on the air. From then on, whatever happened was the director's responsibility. If an actor dried he had to give the instruction to prompt him. If a camera missed a shot, he had to be able to be able to guide the cameras back onto the script without taking his eyes from the six screens.[50][51]

Taylor was interested neither in film-making nor 'naturalism', he was, rather, a natural born dramatist:

> I didn't have the slightest interest in film making as a profession, or as an art, and never had done. I was a poetry man through and through. I directed plays because I had a passion for dramatic poetry, for writers who used language imaginatively, rather than the grainy realists who imitated the incoherence of speech.[52]

Taylor's remarks anticipate attitudes which Troy Kennedy Martin and other television dramatists were later to subscribe to, vis-a-vis the so-called Naturalist debate – these will be discussed in the following chapter. They also reveal how television directing involved a very different practice to film or theatrical representation. Taylor realised 'instinctively that in a TV play the cameras had to be inside the story, not merely watching it. The cameras were the story, they were the expressive instrument, as words were for the poet'.[53]

His statement points to an innate understanding of the way in which television drama possessed its own aesthetic, based upon the television camera's ability to shift the viewer through space in a way that stage drama, with its single viewpoint, could not. In contradistinction to film, where the cuts are made after the film has been shot in television, the cut is made by the camera itself.

Although *Scotland Yard* got a good reception on the whole, episode five, 'Complaints against the Police', anticipated the furore caused by *Z Cars*. It portrayed detectives from a special department of Scotland Yard searching a young constable's home, without a warrant, and interrogating his family. This was a common enough practice, but one rarely admitted to by the police. Following the programme's transmission there were strong complaints. 'It was enough to make any potential recruit tear up his application', stated a Police Federation spokesman; 'the only thing proved against him was that he was so keen he went to undesirable places to try to track down the thieves. What rankles with the police is the stupidity and arrogance with which the constable was depicted as being treated'.[54]

Such a negative reception elicited a Police Federation meeting. Although its outcome is not on file, press cuttings indicate that Barr was not in the least perturbed by criticism. Replying to accusations he told *Television Today*:

> I have been writing the series with the full co-operation of Scotland Yard and I've discussed the scripts with senior police officers ... How on earth can I be painting a black picture when I take typical cases and portray them as true-to-life as possible? ... Authenticity counts a lot with me. The public already has a very good choice of hero detectives to choose from. Nobody has bothered much about stories based on fact. This field is still very wide.[55]

As the above correspondence testifies, Barr had skilfully ensured that, in this instance, he was well covered. However, the experience provided a foretaste of unpleasant things to come. From the mid-1950s onwards, there is a general feeling on file that as soon as *series* production began – in contradistinction to the single dramatised documentary – the police felt they were losing control of their image. To the chief officers in charge of public relations, men like Percy Fearnley, programmes seemed almost to be broadcast before they had time to properly check them. From Barr's point of view, the difficulties after producing the *Scotland Yard* series were such that he sought a break. Although *Z Cars* (1962) provided a necessary geographical and generic diversion, it did not represent a final solution to the problem.

Alongside Scotland Yard, during the 1960s came the addition of a new product – the international spy drama. This was born out of the conditions of the Cold War and the arrival of Interpol, whose organised agreement between participating countries meant that legal borders no longer existed. A villain fleeing from Britain now found that the tentacles of the law stretched right across Europe to as far afield as Africa and beyond. *International Detective* (1959), an ABC production, was a deliberate attempt to appeal to the US market. The 39-episode series featured William J Burns, chief of the 'WJB International Detective Agency' based in New York, although the series was actually filmed in Britain. Such productions anticipate international co-productions, like *Van Der Valk*, the Detective with the Amsterdam CID Division. In response to other cultural influences, the increasingly prolific Robert Barr himself began another genre, that of the war narrative. *Spycatcher* (1961), for instance, was a highly popular series set during the Second World War, featuring the real-life exploits of Colonel Oreste Pinto. Such a proliferation of new generic diversifications was created not only by the variety of different themes, but by the cross-fertilisation between film and television, as well as an increasing internationalism, as we saw in the case of *Fabian of the Yard*, a filmed series made for US export. But whilst anything to do with Scotland Yard, or the figure of the International Spy, immediately found an overseas market, the more 'local' variants of the British television police series never made the grade. Meanwhile, the new regional direction in which *Z Cars* led was to solidify the distinctive genre which today constitutes the Northern policer.

15. Detective Chief Inspector Charlie Barlow played by
Stratford Johns in *Z Cars* (1962).

5

Calling 'Z Vctr 1' and 'Z Vctr 2'

Before *Z Cars* there were three types of phoney policemen –
either comic YOKELS on bikes, touching their forelocks
and calling everyone sir; Scotland Yard GLAMOUR BOYS,
or kindly old father figures like DIXON OF DOCK GREEN.
Z Cars does not claim to be documentary. We don't pretend
it is the truth. What we do say is: IT IS A SIGHT MORE
TRUE TO LIFE THAN ANYTHING ELSE SO FAR.

Daily Sketch, 1 May 1962[1]

In the context of tracing the development of the British television police
series, John McGrath's tongue-in-cheek statement, cited above, suggests
that *Z Cars* (1962) arrived like a vanquishing knight of verisimilitude 'out of
the blue'.[2] From this cartoon-like perspective, pre-*Z Cars* television police
representations are seen as mere typologies – 'comic yokels', 'glamour boys'
and 'kindly old father figures'. All trace of their generic ancestry is obliterated.

Whilst there is no doubt that *Z Cars* was as innovative as critics have
suggested, its production must be seen within a wider context. As McGrath
himself was perfectly aware, the new series was both a continuation and a
re-articulation of what had gone before.[3] The programme's greatest influence
was its institutional and generic origins within the BBC Documentary
Department. What was new, as will later be discussed, was its articulation
around an increasingly reflexive critical discourse about realism. This tended
to mask an important generic innovation: its lightness of touch. In *Z Cars*, a
dash of Northern humour had been added to the 'grittier' realism of 1950s
television dramatists, such as Colin Morris. Both popular *and* educational –
or 'serious' – the series negotiated its way across the public service versus
commercial television divide, in the backwash of the Pilkington Committee
(1960). By 1963, after making a highly controversial entrance, *Z Cars* had
arrived as one of the Corporation's flagship programmes. In technological

terms, the production betokens the end of a certain era, that of live television. *Z Cars'* spin-off, *Softly, Softly* (1966), recorded on video-tape soon after its inauguration, marks a new threshold of fully pre-recorded, industrialised production.

This penultimate chapter begins with some important contextual information surrounding *Z Cars'* production. It discusses the implications of the Pilkington Committee, the subsequent appointment of Hugh Carleton Greene to the Director Generalship (January 1960) and the way in which his leadership endorsed many of the changes that were already being set into train by television departments, especially the Documentary Department. Sydney Newman's arrival as Head of Drama (he was appointed during 1961, although he did not take up the appointment until December 1962), provided a catalyst for a multiplicity of generic innovations in much television production. This period is one characterised by increasing confidence and growth in television, as symbolised by the opening of Television Centre at White City in 1960. The net result is a proliferation of popular new generic television forms, and a marked shift away from the old version of public service culture towards a new, more pluralistic definition. By comparing it to *Dixon* and other precedents, I will demonstrate how, under the aegis of the Drama Department, *Z Cars* achieved a new level of cultural legitimation for the series format.

Pilkington pieties

1961 was not only a cultural watershed, it was also a decisive year for television in general. On 1 January a specially made film, *This is the BBC*, was premiered at the Odeon Leicester Square before an invited audience and released by the Central Film Library. It celebrated the year of the opening of Television Centre at White City. The film continued the Public Relations tradition first inaugurated by the documentary film *BBC Voice of Britain* (EMB 1932) and followed 24 hours in the life of 'the rambling, indefinable multitude of activities' that made up its work.[4] It was televised on 29 June 1960, to coincide with the actual opening of Television Centre and was undoubtedly influenced by an imminent and very important Special Committee Report, which set out to consider the future of broadcasting.

The Pilkington Committee was set up under the chairmanship of glass manufacturer Sir Harry Pilkington and first met informally on 25 August 1960, reporting to Parliament in 1962. Collectively, its members came to outline what Asa Briggs appropriately terms a Pilkington 'philosophy'.[5] This largely stemmed from one particular member, Richard Hoggart, whose previously discussed book, *The Uses of Literacy* (1957), inveighs so heavily against television. As Charles Barr has argued, there are connections 'in language, tone and opinion' between the Report and the book, especially concerning the perceived 'triviality' of the media.[6] For Hoggart, television's 'natural' propensity to spin off a 'candy floss world' implicitly threatened the notion of practices based upon a culture of literacy.[7]

Prior to the Report's publication, Hoggart presented the Harvey Memorial lecture in Birmingham. Defensively entitled *The Uses of Television*, Hoggart's lecture discusses his favourite theme of the breakdown of the community, in which he saw television as centrally implicated. In it he asks, 'What has happened to the old BBC ideal that the invention of television would make it possible to reunite our splintered modern society by giving it a common cultural background?' Indeed, the lecture's very title is indicative of Hoggart's belief that a culture of *literacy* would save television. But his evocation of an Arnoldian precept of culture as 'the best', which tended to centre on the study of the English language and literacy, was somewhat anachronistic by the 1960s. So far as the terms of the BBC's public service remit were concerned, the Report now viewed 'entertainment', the previously disregarded third term, of primary import with 'education' and 'information' no longer seen as incompatible qualities.

As is well known, Independent Television's commercial philosophy brought it into disrepute with the Pilkington Committee. Its attitude is best summed up by the first issue of the original ITV programme journal *TV Times*, which declared: 'The new Independent Television programme planners aim at giving viewers what viewers want – at the times viewers want it'.[8] Although the BBC emerged from the Pilkington Report with flying colours and ITV was 'delivered a magisterial rebuke', the Committee nonetheless criticised the notion of two different ideologies operating in broadcasting. To 'give the public what they want' and 'give the public what the broadcaster thinks is good for it' – were, they claimed, 'falsely contrasted' propositions.[9] Instead of proceeding from such a polarised position, the Report suggested that the broadcaster should explore new means and forms which would both appeal to the public and at the same time, inform it.[10] Such a major shift flew in the face of a residual Reithianism and forced the terms of public service culture, which had long been polarised against commerce to become more integrated. The new Independent Television Authority (ITA), was initially set up as a watchdog committee with a public service remit similar to that of the BBC. Maurice Wiggin, in an article entitled 'Going the Whole Hoggart', stated there indeed seemed a desire 'To make the ITA into another BBC; a move he saw as 'the hopeless last resort of men who fundamentally fear the operation of a free society'.[11] However, the Pilkington Report notwithstanding, enlightened BBC broadcasters in the small Documentary Department, had long been conscious of a fresh breeze blowing from independent quarters. They did not find this a cause for perturbation, since they had all along been pursuing their own experiments to advance television technology. So such experimentation was not solely confined to the Documentary Department. In Light Entertainment, Eric Maschwitz was also interested in, and had identified a need for, developing new generic forms. A memorandum on file, dated 1961 and entitled 'Notes on the Future of BBC Light Entertainment', compares the output of the BBC network and that of ITV programming. It shows that ITV was producing 24 hours more output per week than the BBC. Furthermore 'Light Entertainment', in ITV terms, consisted largely of popular drama series: 'At the moment BBC Light Entertainment is responsible for a single dramatic programme *Dixon of Dock Green* whereas ITV boasts *Emergency Ward Ten, Coronation Street, No Hiding Place, Danger Man, Probation Officer* etc. all of which attracts a vast and extremely loyal following'. A further plea is made for the kind of original 'dramatic writing', at present undertaken by the Documentary Department, over and above other forms of 'light entertainment':

> A compulsive musical show is hard to contrive, situation comedy series not easy to come by; dramatic writing on the other hand is, and should continue to be in good supply ... To strengthen our line for the battle we must eliminate the weaker musical and comedy programmes, replacing them with story-shows. From the purely financial angle popular drama costs less to produce than 'variety', at the same time calling in general for no greater production facilities.[12]

At this time the *Dixon of Dock Green* series was attracting an audience 'of over fourteen million viewers, a figure only equalled by *The Black and White Minstrel Show* and the Saturday "spectaculars", *Juke Box Jury* and *This is your Life*'.[13]

In a memorandum in the *Observer*, which publicised the TAM's 'top ten programmes' for one week in September 1960, not a single BBC programme was mentioned. Of the three top ITV programmes viewed in more than 6 million homes an imported detective series, *No Hiding Place* (1959), came first; *The Arthur Haynes Show* (a variety show) came second; and the quiz show *Take Your Pick*, compared by Michael Miles – somewhat symbolically, in view of a new dawn of popular materialism – came third.[14]

Z Cars was to provide an answer to the BBC's prayers, at the same time allowing the 'evergreen' *Dixon* series to continue. However, just as *Dixon of Dock Green* had not been dreamed up as 'a first wave response' to 'the competitor' but was the result of a gradual evolution of a process begun in the story-documentary department, so *Z Cars* too was the result of a particular historical and institutional conjuncture: one which endeavoured to speak to Hoggart's prayer for the reunification of a disunited society.

Fresh air

At the beginning of the new decade, Greene had taken over as BBC Director General stating that he would 'throw open the windows and let in a breath of fresh air'.[15] The invigorating new climate nurtured a renewal and reinvention of previous popular entertainment forms from revue and radio. In 1962, one of Greene's first moves was to approve the new television satirical series *That Was the Week That Was*. Devised by former *Tonight* producers, including Donald Baverstock, Ned Sherrin, Alasdair Milne and Antony Jay, *TW3*, as it soon became known, mediated the new, more permissive image of the BBC. It was made in the Current Affairs Department and not by Light Entertainment, in case the latter played too safe. This represents another indication of the way in which popular forms were being brought into the forefront of television broadcasting. David Frost was a new type of television interviewer characterised by a sharp wit and nasal delivery. Lance Percival was a contributor, as were Peter Cook and Willie Rushton, both involved in the magazine *Private Eye*.[16]

The importance of the programme was its revival of the acting/review tradition assimilated into a new satirical form of television. This, in its turn, initiated other forms of equally subversive cultural practice, for example in *Private Eye* and subsequent satirical magazines, including the infamous *Oz*. Such *subversion* in 1960s cultural practices began to reveal a break with the values of the post-war consensus.

The grimacing humour of Galton and Simpson's *Steptoe and Son* (1962) initiated a further development of the sitcom form, and followed on directly from the milder comedy of *Hancock's Half Hour* (1956), itself transferred from radio. Both programme formats were derived from the old 'stand up' comic forms. But *Steptoe and Son* was a new departure, featuring the – at times – disgustingly reprehensible 'Dirty Old Man' persona of an old rag-and-bone merchant and his son, played by Messrs Wilfred Brambell and Harry H Corbett. Although the authors signed a contract for a US version of the show, this failed, according to Galton and Simpson, because Americans preferred success to failure and the series was about two significantly un-successful people. US sponsors wanted TV series to be about 'affluent people living in nice homes', an apt indicator not only of cultural difference but of the way in which British documentary realism, as articulated by series like *Z Cars*, had begun to be assimilated into mainstream entertainment.[17]

Newman on board

In another Pilkington pre-emptive move, Sydney Newman was hired to replace Michael Barry as Head of Drama (Greene was directly involved in Newman's appointment). Newman had joined the National Film Board of Canada in his mid-twenties, when John Grierson was Television Director of Features and Outside Broadcasts, a post to which he had himself risen by the time he left to join ABC in Britain. Here, he achieved distinction as creator and producer of *Armchair Theatre* (between 1958 and 1962), whose dramatic practices chimed with those experiments being carried out by the BBC's small Docu-mentary Department. Doubtless influenced earlier by Grierson's democratic principles, Newman later said of his arrival, 'I came to Britain at a crucial time in 1958, when the seeds of *Look Back in Anger* were beginning to flower. I am proud that I played some part in the recognition that the working man was a fit subject for drama, and not just a comic foil in middle-class manners'.[18]

Under Newman's direction, *The Wednesday Play* offered competition to *Armchair Theatre*. In a retrospective after Newman had left the BBC in 1967, *The Times* described *The Wednesday Play* as his greatest achievement: 'Five years ago the single play was a sickly child, a pallid brother to the stage production. Today it has become (in his words) anti-theatre'.[19] Subsequent to joining the BBC (he did not officially begin until December 1961), Newman reorganised the structure of television drama, relocating series drama under a Drama Department, itself organised into separate Plays, Serials and Series sections, each with its own head and small staff.[20] The three main output departments – Drama, Light Entertainment and Talks – were now to be known as Groups. Each Group was to be divided into separate departments under a Head, each with its own area of output for both BBC1 and BBC2. These were to be as independent as possible, working directly to the Group Head, each managing its own programmes and with its own budget, producers and directors and other production staff. They would be responsible for finding their own material which meant they would also need to find their own script editors and staff writers as required. It was therefore decided to remove the editorial function from the central script department and release the responsibility for commissioning writers from its control, in so far as the three major output Groups were concerned. In effect, each of these Groups had the nucleus of a Script Department of its own. The reorganisation of popular, generic television formats as an equal term with 'Plays' was a symbolic recognition that popular dramatic fiction was an equally valid, cultural form.

Barry's departure as Head of Drama during 1961 offered the Documentary Department a 'window of opportunity' in terms of the freedom to 'do its own thing' until Sydney Newman took up his post. Norman Rutherford was appointed acting head, and Elwyn Jones, who had previously been in charge of Documentary Drama, was appointed as his assistant. Jones and Robert Barr together reinstated documentary within the Drama Department. 1962 has been called one of the great years of television, when such 'classics' as *Steptoe and Son*, *Z Cars*, *Dr Finlay's Casebook* and *Maigret* were transmitted. It is highly significant that the last three were produced within the Documentary Department, which Barr describes as:

> just like the early days of documentary – when talent talked with talent and there were no Heads of Department to interfere … Just having four people whose only interest was in programmes, in stories and writing, we summoned out of the air three winning series … In that short time we had done an about turn and these new programmes were in one sense a continuation of the old dramatised documentaries – series based on truth but with the old PR element removed so that you did it fictionally.[21]

But, before it was possible to remove the 'PR' element, Barr had to negotiate a difficult hurdle in producing a pre-planned production about 'the Met'.

Locating *Z Cars*

According to Peter Lewis, the idea for the *Z Cars* series came about because Troy Kennedy Martin, one of its earliest writers, had mumps. Sitting in bed, listening to VHF radio (a common occupation during the early 1960s when it was newly accessible on ordinary receivers), he began monitoring the police.[22] Elwyn Jones went up to Liverpool to show Colin Morris's celebrated story-documentary *Who, Me?*, about police interrogation methods, to a group of Lancashire detectives who had thought it so realistic they requested it as a training film. The trip gave Jones the idea of using the county as the base for a new series. He asked the Lancashire County Police division whether they used car patrols and what they were called. The answer was 'Crime Cars'. Robert Barr claims that *Z Cars*' title was his own invention: 'I used it first of all as a working title. The planner of course laughed and said "Surely that's not what you're going to call it?" ... "It will never sell in America", they said "because over there Z is pronounced Zee"'.[23] BBC relations with the Lancashire County Police were already close, after not only *Who, Me?*, but also the four-part series that followed it, *Jacks and Knaves*.[24] Kennedy Martin was sent by Jones to Lancashire on a 'recce' and came back with a good report on the the possibilities. In the autumn he went back with co-writer Allan Prior to live among the police and write the first scripts.

From the start, great emphasis was placed on the documentary approach. Of the first 13 scripts, three were based directly on case-book material. Once more, these were supplied by DCI Prendergast whilst the remainder were improvised from situations typical of crime car work in the police division of Lancashire.[25] Much trouble was taken over minutiae, emphasising television's instructional and demonstrative roles. How to handle gelignite, for example, was portrayed to vivid effect in the third episode, 'Handle With Care', about some stolen gelignite; what brings the police out on typical Friday nights, as in the sixth episode 'Friday Night'; and just which officers take charge of operations in a prison break-out, in 'Jail Break', the 11th episode.[26]

The series was set in a fictionalised Liverpool, where Seaforth became 'Seaport' and Kirkby New Town was shortened to 'Newtown'. Newtown itself was portrayed as rootless, 'displaced'. It was as far from Dock Green's pastoral connotation, itself inherited from the suburban 'Green Leaf' ideology of the Ealing comedy, as imaginable. The character which was to create the biggest fuss was 'Newtown nick's bully boy': Detective Inspector 'Charlie' Barlow, played by Stratford Johns. The complete opposite to Dixon, Barlow was 'a bear of a man', and like his forerunner in *Who, Me?*, once more inspired by that real-life 'most unusual' Bill Prendergast. Stratford Johns stated he decided to make Barlow abrasive because:

> I was annoyed that the police had always been portrayed as pipe-smoking bunglers who occasionally stumbled over a corpse ... I was bored with it. I had two lines as a detective in a film, *Across the Bridge*, in which I was supposed to indicate that I wasn't overpowered by Steiger. I brought a little reality into it, did a rather bad-tempered act. It got a good reaction. So I tried it on *Z Cars*.[27]

Indeed, the new series did 'bang in some reality'. So much so that its arrival was like throwing a stone into the press millpond, producing ever-

16. Brian Blessed as Fancy Smith, with Jock Weir in *Z Cars*.

increasing rings of indignant public response claiming that it tarnished the force's image. 'Now the police are in the dock', ran one typical newspaper headline.[28] The remarks by an 'anonymous' senior police officer from Lancashire, quoted by the *Guardian* following the first episode, 'Four of a Kind', are typical of the police response:

> You can say there have been heated arguments … It was awful. We all thought it made us look fools. And our wives thought it made them look fools too, I mean, it made it look as though we're always running into each other's houses, eating each other's dinners. We never meet each other's wives. No, never. Things aren't like that at all.[29]

When *Z Cars* was originally mooted by Elwyn Jones, Head of the Documentary Department, Chief Constable, Colonel Eric St John welcomed the idea of a new BBC series based in the North of England. He expected it to run along similar lines to the *Scotland Yard* series, doing for the ordinary police regional force what that series had done for the elite 'Met'. But *Z Cars* caused offence because, unlike *Scotland Yard*, *Fabian* or *Dixon of Dock Green*, it put policemen on the same moral level as those they were policing, portraying them as ordinary, working-class men. In addition, the new series' dialogue was narrated across authentic regional accents. By contrast, its predecessors were shown up as representing the working classes in condescending stereotypical terms, using caricatured 'stage' accents.[30]

Although unloved by police and public, the injection of *Z Cars'* 'grainy' new realism into the police series genre did not go unappreciated by the press, whose reception was mostly favourable, as this extract from the *Bolton Evening News* demonstrates:

> Looking at the programme, members of the county constabulary seem to have seen the television constables only as so many scallywags. They need not take things so tragically. That is not how these constables looked to the layman. For the most part they looked like a set of hearty North-country lads.[31]

To many newspaper critics, it seemed as if, for the first time, *Z Cars* presented the police force realistically in terms of being no better or worse than the rest of the population. They focused their analyses on comparing the new series to its predecessor which, rather like the BBC itself, had become a national institution. As the *Liverpool Daily Post* put it:

> The police constables in *Z Cars* are drawn from life. They have the failings of ordinary men in sharp contrast with old 'Dixon', that paragon of immaculate virtue who surely never cheeked an inspector, never asked a civilian for the winner of the three-thirty and never went on duty needing a haircut.[32]

There was, however, some adverse criticism, especially concerning the lack of a strongly consensual narrative line. For example, Donald Soper in the *Tribune* complained that: '*Z Cars* destroys genuine respect for the law by blurring the real divisions between right and wrong.'[33] The *Manchester Evening News* went even further, and expressed concern that 'programmes like "Z-Cars" could be providing a "blue-print for crime"', arguing that a series of local incidents was traceable to the influence of recent episodes.[34] This notion of television as a causative agent of a breakdown in law and order was linked to 1960s sociological theories, including the 'hypodermic effect' model.[35]

Even practitioners had their doubts. Arthur Swinson, the 1950s television critic and documentarist, stated that although the '*Z Cars* series has been a great triumph for documentary writers ... it is in some ways a pity that it has come by fusing the documentary with the crime story, of which violence and suspense are natural ingredients'.[36] Quoting a BBC spokesman, the *Daily Telegraph* gets to the heart of the *Z Cars* reception angst: it states that whilst

17. Virginia Stride as Katy Hoskins, radio control operator in *Z Cars*.

people 'thought the series was a documentary [programme] because of the acknowledgement', it was in fact 'a *fictional* one with factual overtones'.[37] This comment raised problems about the television drama-documentary's status, which, from its earliest days, had been beset by an insecurity about the weighting of its terms. In *Z Cars* this angst reaches an apotheosis. While the 'mixed messages' or 'codes', when incorporated into the consensus film of the war in the form of the story-documentary, seemed to cause little problem, when transferred to television they became a cause for prolonged debate. Consensus war films such as *Target for Tonight* had, by definition, promoted the interests of the state but it was difficult to see exactly whose interests *Z Cars* served. The equivocal status of the BBC itself, so far as its independence was concerned, added to the controversy. For the writers themselves, the dilemma was between the programme's generic status versus its cultural verisimilitude: or, in documentary terms, between its 'dramatic' and its 'actuality' interest. It was a fruitful opposition which gave rise to much good writing.

Troy Kennedy Martin, joint first scriptwriter of the series with Allan Prior, stated that the idea behind *Z Cars* was 'to use a Highway Patrol format, but to use the cops as a key or way of getting into a whole society'.[38] The American series *Highway Patrol* was shown on ITV, first in the London area in 1956 and again on Anglia television in 1960.[39] Robert Barr, the Group Producer, was more concerned with documentary verisimilitude. As he stated, 'One of the qualities of *Z Cars* comes from a constant war between me, who wants it to be documentary and Troy, who wants to write fiction'.[40] From this brief discussion we can see that *Z Cars* is implicated in two major, interconnected discussions: first it picked up on the 'drama-documentary' debate, one which gave voice to the growing concern throughout the 1950s about what television should represent; secondly, it was concerned with television violence (which lies outside this book's scope). In order to contextualise the drama-documentary debate, I shall now discuss *Z Cars*, both in comparison to *Dixon of Dock Green* and its other predecessors, and within the programme's institutional, technological and ideological contexts. My focus here, as in the case of the Dixon series, will be primarily on the first season: the 'be-ginnings' of the *Z Cars* series.

Institutional contexts

As its title suggests, *Z Cars* is 'about' the exploits of a *group* of patrol-car policemen. The series represents a move away from presenting the police as individual subjects – like 'Dixon' or 'Fabian', each located in their respective communities of 'Dock Green' and 'the Yard' – towards a new collective identity and a more mobile environment. *Z Cars*' collaborationist status necessitated a quantitative expansion of its production team. This quickly grew from its original nucleus of Barr and Elwyn Jones until there were at least eight people working on the series at any one time.[41] Like its predecessor, *Scotland Yard*, *Z Cars* was originally planned in 13 episodes.

The multiples of 13 used in television series were copied from the American practice of dividing the television year into two seasons. During the 13-week summer season, when audiences declined, ratings fell and advertisement revenue diminished. Whereas the target for a season was previously 39 weeks (13 x 3), the lengths of series runs were increasingly reduced by competition on either side, so that by the 1970s, it was more common to make 26 episodes in a British television series.[42] The original *Z Cars* series ran into five seasons before it ceased production during December 1965.

During its first season, *Z Cars'* production team consisted of the following:

Executive Producer	David Rose
Group Producers	Elwyn Jones, Robert Barr
Directors	M Barry (4), E Hills (1), John McGrath (5), J Moxey (3), S Case Sutton (2), H Wise (2)
Casting Director	John McGrath
Writers	M Ashe (1), R Barr (1), RH Dunnbobbin (1), J Hopkins (4), TK Martin (6), Alan Prior (7)
Script Editor	John Hopkins (from 29 February 1962)

As is evident from the chart above, John McGrath and Michael Barry directed the greatest number of performances each, despite Barry's resignation as Head of Drama in 1960. Troy Kennedy Martin and Alan Prior emerge as the most prolific writers. *Z Cars* was produced weekly, live from Studio 3 or 4, in the newly opened BBC Television Centre at White City, whilst the filmed sequences were shot at Ealing Studios, acquired by the BBC in 1955. *Z Cars'* first season was broadcast from 2 January 1962 to July 1962 and was extended from an initial 13 episodes to 31. The initial 13 programmes ended with Kennedy Martin's 'Sudden Death' (27 March 1962).

When McGrath and Kennedy Martin left after the first series, the second series was notably dominated by John Hopkins, who wrote 46 of the original episodes between 1962 and 1963 and also acted as Script Editor. Allan Prior wrote 12 episodes for the second season but only four for the third. At this time, *Z Cars'* audience reached almost 17 million, three million more than for *Dixon*, although it was some way behind the hugely successful *Steptoe and Son*. *Z Cars'* second, third and fourth seasons, designated by critics as 'classic *Z Cars*', lasted from September 1962 to 2 December 1964. Additionally, from September 1962, regular repeats were shown on Sunday afternoons. In all, over a hundred episodes were retransmitted. The repeat was a new phenomenon providing cheap programming and greater access. *Z Cars'* peak audience during early 1963 was 16.65 million average weekly viewers.[43] This figure included those watching repeats. In 1964, Hopkins left the series. During its last season, Alan Plater was *Z Cars'* most prolific scriptwriter. By then the audience figures had dropped to 11.8 million, barely ahead of *Dixon* and below the 13.2 million of *Dr Finlay's Casebook*.[44] During 1965, *Z Cars* was 'rested' but it continued from 1966 and ran on until 1978, just outrunning *Dixon*, which ended during 1976.

New iconographies

At first sight, *Z Cars* hardly seems the answer to Maschwitz's plea for another 'story show'. It little resembles his exemplary *Dixon, Coronation Street* or even *Emergency Ward 10*, on the 'other side'. The production shifts right away from the exemplary Dixon mode of address: the pointing finger implying a collusive citizenship. *Z Cars'* technique, as seen from the opening titles of each episode, closes up the distance between performance and spectator. Whereas the Dixon persona seemed to 'speak for' the state, in a classic gesture of interpellation, 'hailing' the audience, in *Z Cars* the device is much subtler. The series' 'signature tune', a term derived from early radio, resorts to its original function of simply marking the beginning and end of the episode in order to distinguish it from the 'flow' of other programmes. It is no longer part of the diegesis as was *Dixon*'s theme-tune, whistled by the protagonist himself. No longer is the performance carried by an individual protagonist, as was again the case in *Dixon* or *Fabian of the Yard*. *Z Cars* is topped and tailed by a North Country march song, played on Northumbrian bagpipes, in a plaintive minor key. Its opening titles are synchronised with graphics which plot out a triangular diagram, indicating the route of the two crime patrol cars, labelled 'Z Victor 1' (ZV1) and 'Z Victor 2' (ZV2). The apex of the diagram, 'HQ', signifies the Headquarters of the Lancashire police force. The figure swiftly transforms into two parallel lines, starting from diametrically opposed directions, moving across the diagonal to complete the 'Z' of the title.

The first programme, 'Four of a Kind', was not the fast-cutting, montage aesthetic we have come to expect from the *Z Cars* series. It looks more like a filmed play, or early *Dixon* episode, in terms of its mise-en-scene and iconography, than a copshow. But with one important difference. Instead of the 'generic' 'stereotypes' which tended to be constructed in *Dixon of Dock Green*, especially in the minor roles, there are fully 'rounded' characters. Despite its immediately perceptible difference, *Z Cars* contains elegiac references. An old-style policeman Reggie Farrow, an ordinary 'Bobby on the Beat' – one of the bicycle brigade – killed on duty, whilst defending a man who raised the alarm when his factory was attacked. The murder of a policeman immediately establishes a powerful connection with *The Blue Lamp*, the Ealing film in which the 'Dixon' character originates. The culprit, also a 'tearaway', has now been captured. By now, we are familiar with this phenomenon, as introduced in Colin Morris's eponymously named production. The scene's narrative interests are centred upon a need for crime cars, as introduced into other police units. As Watt says to Barlow:

> If we'd had crime patrols like other divisions Reggie Farrow would be alive today. If we had crime patrols in Newtown when t'alarm went off in't factory, there'd have been two tough commandos at Tearaway.

This topic connects to a 'real-life' police problem. During the 1960s, the police had become increasingly vulnerable to attack. As early as the end of the 1940s, police cars were introduced to combat a 'sharp upward trend in crime'. Clive Emsley maintains that:

> In their attempts to combat this the police developed new, more technologically developed tactics with the Unit Beat System, known popularly as 'fire-brigade policing'. The constable patrolling a beat was increasingly replaced by constables in cars 'responding' to crime rather than just seeking to 'prevent' it.[45]

Barlow and Watt discuss who will be in the two patrol cars, or 'Z Cars', which make up the crime patrol unit. In a resonant moment during the first and second shots, we see the person who later materialises into Barlow in a felt hat reading a memorial stone bearing the enscription: 'To P.C.Reginald Farrow, shot down in execution of his duty, Newtown Co-operative Society'.

Speaking an entirely different kind of dialogue to the increasingly 'Southern' pronunciation of the embourgeoisied *Dixon* series, *Z Cars*' protagonists use local dialogue: Barlow states that criminals 'come back like victims to a smell'. The culprit, 'a tearaway from Liverpool', had 'coughed the lot', 'enough to top him', but 'if he's a nut case they won't top him'. As Watt and Barlow drive back from the cemetery, they take a detour past Newtown. As audience, we do not see the scene. Instead, we are shown a series of reaction head shots in response to the spoken dialogue. Barlow describes Newtown's lack of a sense of community: the buildings 'mushrooming up' everywhere, providing 'just good hiding places for tearaways, and villains'. Repeated talk of 'tearaways' and 'villains' is reminiscent of *Jacks and Knaves*. The rootlessness of Newtown is the reverse side of the coin to that of Dock Green, characterised by its 'safe' village atmosphere.

In the next scene we are introduced to Lynch and Steele, two potential members of the *Z Cars* 'team'. Janey, married to Lynch, is giving Steele lunch whilst waiting for her husband to return from duty. The dialogue is mediated across slow, reaction shots and the scene is obviously done in the studio.

Although, like *Dixon* and *The Blue Lamp*, *Z Cars* differs from the detective series in showing the 'behind-the-scenes' domestic life of the Z Cars men, it is very different indeed to both. Far from portraying a picture of harmony, *Z Cars* shows domestic violence. Lynch alludes to Janey's facial contusion: 'You know you're married to a Barbarian'. She defensively replies, 'It was an accident.' He persists in asking about the mark on the wall:

> *Steele*   Is this the stain the hot pot made? It looks to me like the stain a
> hot pot makes when thrown by an angry wife.

Here Janey is seen as a wife who, whilst devoted to her policeman husband, takes the rough – quite literally – with the smooth. As she ironically quips to Fancy Smith, the black eye will 'do me some good'. In terms of establishing Janey's credibility as a Newtown wife, it will serve her 'better than a stretch in Strangeways'. Following this notable appearance, the feminine disappears from what subsequently becomes a primarily masculinist discourse: a tendency, begun in *Dixon*, by presenting the protagonist as a widower and continuing not only through *Z Cars*, but also into *Softly, Softly*. From this perspective the male-partnership theme which commenced between Barlow and Watt may be seen as a sublimation. With its American 'buddy' influence, this was to become a generic trait of the mainstream British television police series throughout the 1970s, most notably with the John Thaw/Dennis Waterman partnership in *The Sweeney*, and also the 1980s, with Lewis and Inspector Morse. The 1980s also saw the first British woman's police series appear, with *Juliet Bravo* (1980) as a sort of feminised *Dixon of Dock Green*. Not until the 1990s was any genuine empowerment given to the feminine in terms of the law, with the introduction of the feisty Jane Tenison, played by Helen Mirren in *Prime Suspect* (1991).

In *Z Cars*' masculinist wilderness, women are seen mostly as wives or switchboard operators, not as police personnel. Dorothy White who played the unfortunate Janey Steele stated, 'I just can't bear it when Jeremy says "Janey where's me dinner?" I feel so irritated I really want to throw things'. She was however pleased 'to be playing a wife', since most of her previous parts were of 'young girls on the wrong side of the law'.[46] Other depictions of women in *Z Cars* are as worn-down wives (as in 'Handle with Care') or prostitutes. Virginia Stride, the actress who took the part of Katie Hoskins the radio-telephone operator, was symbolically encased in the glass box of her telephone kiosk. She hoped her part would develop into something more than just saying 'HG to Z Victor One'. During the second episode, 'Handle with Care', DI John Watt attempts to chat up Katie, asking her to the fireman's ball; she turns him down flat, as she has, we are made to feel, upon other occasions. After her function of controlling the Z Cars had been demonstrated, Stride's part was diminished to such an extent that after the last episode of the first series, she resigned. She explained to a newspaper reporter: 'At first I thought I could make something of the part. Some of the officers tried to date me and so on, but my scripts have got smaller and smaller and now even that doesn't happen'.[47] The way in which the feminine is literally 'written out' not just of the individual episode, but the series, is projected during the first episode. As they ride along in the Ford Zephyr, Barlow interrogates Watt about the break up from his wife, Mary, and says 'You should've married somebody who understood CID work'. Watt replies that it 'din't suit her', and, 'She won't come back, not from London'. Here, the feminine is seen as escaping 'South' to the razzle-dazzle allure of the metropolis, which may offer her a better deal in life than being a policeman's wife.

Audience response

Kinematograph Weekly stated that when *Z Cars* 'started as a cautious six-episode experiment by the BBC' it had viewing figures of 16 million: this represented a jump of seven million since its opening in January.[48] The official BBC Audience Research Report estimated that for the first episode, 'Four of a Kind', the audience constituted 18 per cent of the total viewing public. According to the BBC Audience Research Department, this represented 40 per cent of the Band 1/3 public (classes a, b, c) as compared to programmes on ITV, which at the time were seen by 35 per cent across the same 'Band'.

Although there was so much press fuss about the first episode, the audience report reveals that the action in 'Four of a Kind' was 'laggardly', especially at the beginning, and that some incidents added little to the main theme ('too many side-tracks'), besides being introduced, it was said, in a somewhat clumsy and confusing fashion. In addition, a number of viewers did not care for the way the members of the Newtown police force were portrayed ('as wife-beaters and gluttons') and hoped that such details as 'the undignified eating' were not meant to be true to life. It was hardly likely, they maintained, that many real policemen would behave so unattractively, and therefore the whole thing seemed 'unbelievable and false'. One or two critics also felt there was a surfeit of features and plays about crime and its detection ('about as prolific as Westerns') and noted that this first episode of *Z Cars* did not suggest that the series would bring anything fresh to a theme that a Sports Journalist, for one, saw as 'a "Dixon of Dock Green" on wheels'.[49]

Figures in the Reaction Index of subsequent programmes during the first season show a marked improvement. 'Handle with Care' (No. 3) and 'Stab in the Dark' (No. 4) reached 65. The last programme, about the stabbing of a young girl on her doorstep and traced to a youth whose mind was disturbed by a bullying father, was found to be more widely accepted. As the Audience Report itself stated:

> it was thought a truer picture of the police at work than some other dramatisations in which they featured ('Goody goody Dixon' was cited in this connection by two or three viewers). The Script this week (which several of the sample described as the best so far) was enjoyed for its feasibility and down to earth qualities, for the interest and excitement of participating in the investigation into the crime, and for the touches of humour which helped in getting the story and characters over convincingly.[50]

Some viewers, however, were 'disturbed by the Detective Inspector's questioning of the shocked and injured girl, saying that it seemed rather too tough and not altogether credible'. 'Friday Night' about a typical end of the week scenario out on the town, was considered 'the best, if not the best in a notable series. Here was all the drama, tragedy, humour and sheer 'slog' of routine police procedure, made all the more effective for being presented with commendable realism and with never a suggestion of romanticism or mock heroics'.[51]

Despite claims for *Z Cars*' 'liveness', it is a little-known fact that the first episode, 'Four of a Kind', was unusually shot almost entirely on film. By the beginning of the 1960s, video technology was used to record entire performances, but because of the difficulties of editing it, filmed inserts were still the norm. There was a strong feeling that television's essential characteristic was its immediacy, the reason *Z Cars*' predominantly 'live' performance was deliberately prolonged. Filmed scenes were done at Ealing Studios on a special stage and usually included around eight per episode. Stylistically too, *Z Cars* was a cross-generic product, melding the experiments of both dramatists like Duncan Ross and Michael Barry himself with those of documentarists like Robert Barr.

The move away from a theatrical mode of production which subordinated live performance to the narrative action was partly to do with institutional changes. Between 1957 and 1960, ITV maintained a 2:1 lead over the BBC and the number of viewers with both channels was 75 per cent. Stuart Hood, the new BBC Controller of Television, was appointed in 1961 and an acknowledgement that series drama was to become a cornerstone of the television schedule caused a shift away from the BBC's endorsement of 'high cultural' values, which tended to connote discrete forms of production, such as the single play. The Pilkington Report and Carleton Greene's new policy begun to exert a certain pressure to move towards more industrialised practices. It was also realised that in order to become more populist, new performative modes, such as the dramatised-documentary form needed to be actively promoted. Yet at the same time, this development was anathema to a move, made during the mid-1960s by Kennedy Martin himself. Fighting a rearguard action against 'naturalism' he denigrated the privatised, highly subjective and individualist view of such theatrical pieces as Osborne's foundational *Look Back in Anger* and saw the whole documentary-realism project as lulling the viewer into a false sense of 'the real'. His primary project, however, was anti-New Wave in terms of its individuation of character. As the *Z Cars* series proceeded and the characters took on a life of their own, Kennedy Martin felt that it too was lapsing into a kind of television naturalism, parallel to that of the stage.

Technologies of performance

Although *Z Cars* did not burst onto the screen with a screeching car chase, its televisual style gradually became characterised by its fast cutting style, with up to six cameras and 14 sets per week. To achieve this, it utilised a hybrid of techniques: montage devices from the documentary film, the use of sophisticated studio techniques such as back projection and cars mounted on rollers – techniques which had been developed by documentary and feature-film makers alike. Such mass production methods are very close to those of the Independent Frame (IF), introduced by David Rawnsley at Rank during the 1940s, which, as we noted in the case of *I Made News*, were more realised in early television production than in film. But there was a crucial difference: it was IF produced *live*, a circumstance which in the police series, often an 'action' genre, necessitated deft footwork and a rigorous production schedule.[52] As such, the central metaphor for *Z Cars* production is that of *performance*. Laing talks of a 'rhythm' of production which emphasises the need for an acuity of choreographic skills. As director John McGrath revealed:

> Stylistically, I went for one rigid rule: no camera move, no cut, until the next piece of story was to be revealed. But the stories unfolded very quickly, so there were a lot of cuts, and a lot of locations ... We placed a conscious emphasis on narrative – society, real and recognisable, but in motion. No

slick tie-ups. No reassuring ending, where decency and family life triumphed.[53]

The rehearsal schedule for *Z Cars* was complex and showed live television at its most professional. According to Peter Black:

It amounted to the presentation week after week of a fast-moving feature film in fifty minutes flat with no retakes, their only cushion against disaster, two recorded programmes. With something like 250 changes of shot in each episode, an average of five a minute, the actor's hardest problem was to remember which scene he was in.

To produce a series in this way meant split-second timing. It only went into the studio for final rehearsal during the two days immediately before transmission. For the rest of the time, rehearsals were normally held in the main hall of a boys' club rented by the BBC.

Technically, *Z Cars* was more complex than its predecessors. As for the 'Film Requirements' specification for a typical episode, 'Birds of the Air' demonstrates that there were, as stated previously, usually at least eight separate film sequences in each programme: locations had to be found and permission obtained from the police and local authorities in advance. Scenes which were filmed in the BBC Film Studios at Ealing also had to be booked in advance and were usually allocated only one-and-a-half days' filming time. All other scenes were specially shot on location. It was these which caused a problem. In a letter to Stuart Hood, then controller of the BBC, Mr W Byron, Clerk to Kirkby Urban Council, stated that public reaction had been 'quite clearly to identify the town of Kirby with "Newtown" referred to in the programme' and that the references to 'North, South and West estates' were clearly identifiable with the Northwood, Southdene and Westvale neighbourhood units of Kirby.[54]

Robert Barr's boast about the importance to his creative process of 'authenticity' is backed up by written and oral evidence. The latter implies the tension between 'creativity' and 'actuality'. This was spelled out in an interview, conducted between researcher Colin Francis King and Barr himself, when the latter describes how he had to co-ordinate the efforts of the *Z Cars* writing team. Allan Prior, who was born in Blackpool, had worked as a newspaper reporter, whereas Kennedy Martin was the dramatist. Prior could provide 'the facts', Kennedy Martin, the 'story'. But Kennedy Martin found it very difficult to 'get going'. Barr tells the interviewer:

I remember that I phoned the Hotel after a week and spoke to Allan and said, 'How's Troy getting along, and he said, 'He hasn't written a word but walks around most of the day and night saying, "I can't do it, I can't do it."' Well I'd already taken a twenty-six week commitment on this series and there was the deadline to meet so I told them both they had just better get on with it.[55]

An undated Report on file headed 'Lancashire County Constabulary', held at the BBC Written Archive, is of considerable interest in showing how writers actually researched their subject.[56] It closely details Lancashire County Constabulary's departmental set-up. Seaforth divisional 'HQ', on which the fictitious 'Seaport' was obviously modelled, is described as being made up of two Sub-Divisions: Seaforth and Kirkby. Seaforth police station is described as 'old, with irregular lay-out, small rooms, battered furniture, and not even sufficient space for a canteen'. By contrast, Kirkby sub-division is described as 'very new' with a recreation room, a covered garage, a section house and new, expensive-looking office furniture. A note observes that there is no strict dividing line between uniformed and plain clothes branches, as there is in the metropolis, so that:

> It is possible for men in all ranks to move between the two – for example, a detective constable may become a uniformed constable. Also it is very likely that men may be transferred regularly within the County: this seems to be considered by the men to be a good thing in that it maintains their interest, but they do say the there are difficulties in the case of married men – house moving, children's schools, etc.[57]

The Report cites the opinion that county policemen have to 'know' far more than city policemen, as their duties are more varied: he instances the case of a county policeman having to be in attendance at sheep dipping, and also having to supervise the building of pyres for the destroying of animals with foot and mouth disease or anthrax. Precise details on 'Crime Patrol Men' and the make of car are given:

> Young men are chosen for this work; keen men with their way to make in the force; they have to be good drivers. The minimum age is 22. At the start of the scheme, it was the practice to put a more experienced older man with a young one and this still seems to happen in certain cases ... The Seaforth Crime Patrol use a Ford Zephyr, and the Kirkby Crime Payroll a Morris Oxford. These cars are distinguished by twin aerials on the boot.

The collective image of the police force in *Z Cars* began to allow for a greater *intraepisodic* interest between characters and events than was possible in individualist series dramas like *Dixon* or *Fabian*. This was exemplified by 'Friday Night' (6 February 1962), which dovetailed eight or nine mini-narratives, about a typical Friday night's work.[58] It was agreed that *Z Cars* should have a minimum of six heroes, so that if one of them wanted to leave, or took sick, there would still be the characters to provide enough narrative interest to allow the series to remain. The strategy was to prove useful when Desk Sergeant Twentyman's part collapsed after actor Leonard Williams died of a heart attack. The way in which the authentic dialogue was arrived at was also indicated in a list of 'slang or local terms': 'stupid ... *barmpot*', 'odd character ... *funny ossity*' are expressions attributed, in parenthesis, to 'Parkinson', alias Barlow.[59]

Although stories were still taken from police files, *Z Cars* inaugurated a thoroughly 'documentary' approach to researching the characters and their environment, basing them on real members of the police force and then modifying them as necessary when the actors were cast. Brian Blessed, in the character of 'Fancy Smith', is a case in point. Allan Prior describes the process:

> At the very beginning, before the actors were cast, we wrote words on paper that one day somebody would speak. They had no reality. When the actors arrived all that changed. Fancy Smith we first visualised as a bit of a dandy. After Brian Blessed was cast, we forget that one, too – he's just the wrong shape![60]

The report previously mentioned not only contains detailed location notes, it also comprises a list of 'characters' at the Lancashire County Constabulary. WJH Palfry and Bill Roberts feature respectively as Assistant Chief Constable and Detective Chief Superintendent, responsible for the running of the force. Palfry is described as, 'bluff, rather like an ex-boxer; ... prides himself on his toughness of speech and attitude. He has been very helpful to us. His concern is that he should do for us every bit as much as Scotland Yard did – and that his Force should get as much credit'. Bill Roberts is described as working 'directly to Palfrey'. He too is, 'big, bluff, tough – but more gentle than his boss, more of the seemingly sympathetic investigator, but with the top policeman's hard look between the eyes [sic]'.[61] Alongside Roberts' description is written, in parenthesis, 'script name, *Robins*': *Z Cars*' 'real-life' Detective Chief Superintendent. Further down the list is a description of 'Det. Chief Inspector Ronny Parkinson, Head of "Q" Division CID at Seaforth, answerable to Mr. Roberts': again, in parenthesis, 'script name, *Barlow*'. He is profiled as:

Tall, dark hair what's left of it, bald patch on top, wears specs with dark half rims. Very nice fatherly type with soft Lancashire accent. Has a few plants on his office window ledge, 'contemporary' wallpaper, and a couple of photographs on wall. Easy to talk to, but no softie.

What is of interest is the evidence that Barlow's characterisation is following earlier practice, based on a real-life policeman. Kennedy Martin saw Barlow as usefully erasing Dixon as a figure of authority, but was concerned at the 'avidity' with which he felt the press greeted the concept of 'the stern face of authority, the vengeful father'.[62]

This effect was amplified by the relatively unknown Stratford Johns, who decided to interpret the character as 'a rather bad-tempered act'. The Report further details Detective Sergeant Carter, 'real-life' Crime Prevention Officer as responsible for 'immediate contact for Z-car men – their problems, duties, etc.' Described as 'a sort of Mavis Johnson' (obviously, some kind of 'in' departmental reference) it is he who is designated as the model for the Sergeant Watt character. His appearance is given as 'Greying thick dark hair, dark moustache, dark eyebrow. White stiff shiny-collar, white handkerchief in breast pocket'. Here is evidence of an even greater discrepancy between the actor Frank Windsor who was eventually chosen to play the part, than that between Brian Blessed and 'Fancy Smith'.

John McGrath, the Casting Director, looked for a particular kind of actor. No-one starring in the *Z Cars* series was of name-value. This was an important difference to the 'star vehicle' of *Dixon of Dock Green* and served to align the new series with a strong 'documentary' style. The same had been true of *Pilgrim Street* (1952), which also had no 'stars'. Even *Coronation Street*, on 'the other side', had allegedly begun in this fashion. However, as the series grew, it took on a different 'character' or, more accurately, characters. For all their research, once the programmes were transmitted, the characters took on a life of their own. As in the case of *Coronation Street*, created by Tony Warren as 'a working class series without any stars', in *Z Cars* also, 'viewers and the press made the characters – and therefore the players – into stars'.

'Nats' coming home

Not only does *Z Cars* mark the end of the story-documentary trajectory in terms of its 'live' performance, it also shifts radically away from post-war reconstructionism, no longer colluding with the status quo. There is a constant tension between its social and documentary aims. On the one hand, seeing 'the cops' as 'a key or way of getting into a whole society'; on the other, its narrative interest encourages a close look at the police themselves. This can be seen in the previously mentioned tension between Barr, the documentarist and Kennedy Martin the dramatist. To understand this ideological shift, it is helpful here to address the so-called 'naturalist debate' which lies at the centre of the 'drama-documentary' controversy and is revived in *Z Cars*.

Broadly defined, the 'naturalist debate' concerns two different epistemologies concerning representation: those of 'naturalism' and 'social realism'. Each arises from nineteenth century theatre, literature and painting. The first is characterised by a determination to capture the rhythms and situations of real life as lived by ordinary people rather than the artificial lives of the 'great and the good'. These different approaches are best illustrated in the critical debate offered by Lukacs and Brecht. Lukacs idealised the nineteenth-century novel as a model literary form, maintaining that this should register not individual objects or events seen through the consciousness of a central protagonist but instead give 'the full process of life'. Bertolt Brecht profoundly disagreed with Lukacs and introduced an anti-naturalist concept to combat what, in his view, led to atrophy and stasis. He further held up naturalist theatre, because of its illusion of reality, as falsely producing audience empathy. The only genuine way to create effective communication between the dramatist and the audience, in Brecht's view, was by means of distancing techniques.[63]

Brecht's theatrical rebellion was revived by early television dramatists who saw that early post-war drama continued within the same structure as naturalist theatre. Playwrights of an older generation were influenced by left-wing companies such as Unity Theatre or the London based Vital Theatre Movement, of which Ted Willis was a member, which created a forum for attempting to promote an alternative form of social realism and 'naturalism pure'. Whilst realising the shortcomings of overt propaganda, Willis himself believed that theatre should be, in the Gramscian sense, a hegemonic process: 'a battleground for warring ideas ... not a parade in which only one regiment is mustered'.[64]

Ted Willis defines the 'finest television as that which is concentrated in time and space and character, which takes one or at the most two characters and makes their nature known'.[65] In Willis's eyes, television is theatre brought into close vision: that he was deeply influenced by Chayevsky is undoubted, although critics have averred that his use of the new realism occasionally testifies somewhat more to the 'ordinary' than the 'marvellous'.[66] His stance clashes with Troy Kennedy Martin's idea of television, which holds that it should not be 'theatre in close-up.' In his manifesto, 'Nats Go Home', he excoriated television naturalism. His prime reason for doing so was because he believed it perpetuated a theatrical legacy, in which the production tells a story through means of dialogue, roughly uses studio time as equivalent to real time and photographs 'faces talking and faces reacting': from all of which, he implies, it should be escaping.[67] 'Nats Go Home' called for a 'new TV grammar' based upon image rather than word: a release of dramatic structure from the constraints of real time and from the tendency to accord dialogue more importance than mise en scene.

In a *Movie* interview 25 years later, when asked about how far he felt *Z Cars* had broken with the naturalist tradition of drama, Kennedy Martin replied that, on the contrary:

> I thought it was absolutely in line with naturalism. One of the reasons why I didn't go overboard about *Z Cars* was that all I felt I was doing was contributing to what I thought then were the death throes of naturalism. People said it was a breakthrough but I never thought it was.[68]

Some producers felt *Z Cars* was 'semi-radical' in that, as Kennedy Martin explained, 'it had at least early on, a political attitude which I suppose can be described as left wing'. Later on, though, both he and others of his ideological persuasion felt the series became entirely conformist. They saw this lapse as entirely due to the insistence of 'department heads' in sticking to exactly the same format. This led to the situation in which, as John McGrath stated:

> After the Cops kept appearing week after week people began to fall in love with them, and they became stars. So the pressure was on to make them the subjects, rather than the device and when the BBC finally decided that's what they were going to do, then Troy and I decided we'd had enough.[69]

This was not just a problem with *Z Cars*; it was a generic shortcoming of the series format itself. As McGrath further argued, 'A series is a living thing, always twisting and turning. But if they insist on this sameness week after week then the characters tend to become caricatures of themselves. After a time you get hollowness and nothing'.[70] Albert Casey further cited the beginnings of a problem in maintaining a critical distance between the producers and the police protagonists. He stated, 'You don't have to pretend to be *Dixon of Dock Green* anymore. You can play it down and say "Oh I've seen that on

TV … on *Z Cars*". So eventually in my view *Z Cars* became an instrument which could confirm police practices and was no longer critical'.[71] During 1965, the year that Sergeant Flint played by Arthur Rigby – but not Dixon himself – retired from *Dixon of Dock Green*, there were problems about the quality of *Z Cars*, which seemed to fulfil Troy Kennedy Martin's predictions of its inevitable demise. 'Isn't it sad to see this once brilliant series teetering out in fumbling ineptitude?' asked TC Worsley in the *Financial Times* in January 1965.[72]

It is interesting to note how we have come full circle. In order to redeem 'character', so lacking in early documentaries, *Z Cars* travelled into new generic terrain – that of the 'series-al'. This was a long-running series with a strongly built-in continuing element which, at the same time, gave the strong impression of offering a complete story each week, which became a major characteristic of its 'spin-off' series and successor, *Softly, Softly* (1966). Meanwhile, the final episode of the original 'live' *Z Cars* series to be transmitted was Alan Plater's 'That's the Way it Is', transmitted on 21 December 1965.

Softly, Softly was the way in which the BBC averted the problem of losing its 'nice little earner'. The first ever British series 'spin-off', the new police series dealt with a very different range of crimes, in a new location, but featured some of the same characters. Elwyn Jones had told the BBC representative in the North-West that 'if we can keep *Z Cars* singing until the summer of '65 we might well do a Crime Squad series as a spin-off with some of the characters, as early as the autumn of next year'.[73] But even that wasn't strictly the end of the story. The *Z Cars* title was revived in March 1967 and continued to be broadcast until September 1978. It was however, no longer produced 'live'. Meanwhile, its *Softly, Softly* successor, relocated to the South, was a very different product, as will be discussed in the next chapter.

And this was its main problem: in terms of answering Hoggart's wish that programmes should perform the ideological 'work' of uniting society, the British television police series had become a fundamentally Southern initiative. *Z Cars*, it seems, was riven with contradictions and conflicts, especially in terms of its representation of Northerness. Whereas its (mostly Southern-based) producers saw the series, initially at least, as representing a critical new realism, the police, the local press and residents viewed it more in terms of a *mis*representation: one in which the North was portrayed in an unflattering light. It was not until the next generation – in the 1990s – with the arrival of an entirely different post-Annan broadcasting economy and an ideology in which diversity was celebrated, that the conflicts engendered around the binary opposition of centre and periphery and North and South become resolved. In the meantime, there appeared to be this impetus which sought to retrieve a more conservative, Southern version of the television police series, at the same time, retaining the Northern characterisations which *Z Cars* had so popularised. As we shall see in the final chapter, the success of the British television police series' first ever 'spin-off' – *Softly, Softly* – although once again popular with the audience, was, both in terms of generic development and geography, a return South.

18. Members of *Softly, Softly, Task Force* outside their headquarters:
Terence Rigby as PC Snow, with 'Inky'; Norman Bowler as
Detective Inspector Hawkins.

6

Softly, Softly, back-pedalling South

The BBC's new television crime series, '*Softly, Softly*', which opened on BBC1 last night, is a legitimate, well-bred offspring of its predecessor '*Z Cars*'. It has the same rough, abrasive realism, the same sharp, prickly dialogue, the same terse economy of style. But it is also a development of the original taking some of the better qualities and moulding them to a new format. It will not have the same impact that '*Z Cars*' made when it first appeared for the new ground has already been broken. All the new series can now do is explore the tracks.

Peter Knight, *Daily Telegraph* (1966)[1]

I don't quite know [why] I have stopped watching *Softly Softly;* for the same reason, perhaps, that one stops seeing the face of a wife or husband.

Nancy Banks-Smith, *Sun* (1969)[2]

The *Daily Telegraph* quotation above picks up the contradictions inherent in *Z Cars*' spin-off successor. Although *Softly, Softly* (1966) offered continuities with its predecessor's documentary realism, it was at the same time a more 'polished' version, especially in terms of its central character, Charlie Barlow. As will become evident, *Softly, Softly*'s paradoxical qualities were the manifestation of a fundamental transition which resulted not only in its geographical relocation South, but in the rescinding of *Z Cars*' 'gritty' realism. Part of this alteration is due to the social and cultural changes introduced by the 'swinging sixties'. Jeffrey Richards writes that during this time, in terms of representation:

> Sober realism and earnest social comment gave way to fantasy, extravaganza and escapism; black and white photography and Northern locations to colour and the lure of the metropolis; Puritanical self-discipline to hedonistic self-indulgence; plain truthful settings to flamboyant, unrealistic decorativeness.[3]

Certainly, *Softly, Softly*'s relocation South and its change to colour in 1969 are testament to these views.[4] In addition, the realignment of the BBC Drama Department, the accessibility of new recording technology and the end of consensus politics were all important contributory factors. In terms of the latter, according to Krishnan Kumar:

> Politicians, moralists and sociologists on all sides were talking about the break-up of 'the consensus' that had been the underlying force in the stability of the political and social system – and so of the BBC – up to the end of the 1950s.[5]

As we have seen, the increasingly commercial ethos of the BBC had been crucially informed by the arrival of 'the Competitor'. At a programme level, the demise of consensus politics was expressed by a shift in ideological values. Whereas the hegemonic values in both *Dixon of Dock Green* and *Z Cars* (despite its iconoclasm) were identifiable as those of community, fairness and citizens' rights, in *Softly, Softly* they modulate into those of freedom, enterprise and property-owning democracy. Richard Buxton has argued that police series like *Z Cars* and *Softly, Softly*:

> aligned themselves with the technocratic, managerial reformism of the 1960s Labour government ... Modern police work, a judicious compound of technology and human experience, was a pragmatic solution to particular problems without the authoritarian illusion of totally stamping out crime through moral injunctions and repression.[6]

He further states that the close association between this selective realism and liberal humanism and the underlying strategy of legitimising modern police techniques in the fight against crime is evident in actor Stratford Johns' assessment of the new programme as:

> the most realistic of television police programmes. It is also, I think, the most human ... Living off the backs of serving police officers, we strive never to cheapen their attitudes, betray their confidences or underrate the magnitude of the tasks they face on our behalf.[7]

Z Cars' humanist 'warts and all' portrayal, incarnated in Barlow's 'angry' characterisation, is notably toned down in *Softly, Softly*. In addition, whereas its predecessor portrayed the police as an integral part of society, in *Softly, Softly* they begin to stand *apart* from it. This alteration is monitored by the programme's different narrative concerns. As correspondence states, *Softly, Softly* portrays a different calibre of criminal to *Z Cars*, and is less concerned with the investigation of non-petty crime.

At an institutional level, *Softly, Softly* represents a crossover point, and a final assimilation of mainstream values. This chapter commences with a brief examination of the realignment of BBC Drama, before examining the new series' remit, strategies and more writerly attitude towards characterisation. Finally, it traces the way in which the documentary impulse is redirected to BBC Drama within the single play slot, exemplified by Ken Loach's 'Cathy Come Home', an early *Wednesday Play*, which seeks to define – not altogether successfully – its auteurist interests against *Softly, Softly*'s more collaborative methods of production. My overall aim here is not so much to provide an analysis of the individual programmes of *Softly, Softly* as to trace the trajectory of this development in the context of changing institutional, technological and cultural contingencies, both at the BBC and within the wider cultural framework of 1960s British television.

Institutionalising the task force

Running for ten years and 264 episodes, *Softly, Softly* was proof that by treating the television episodic series as 'product' and with the application of marketing and narrative planning, it was possible to prolong a genre's active shelf-life. The way in which the BBC averted the problem of losing its 'nice little earner' in *Z Cars*, when viewing figures began to decline, was by producing the first-ever British television series 'spin-off'. What this amounted to was a new police series dealing with a different range of crimes and location, but featuring some of the same characters.

A new phenomenon in the history of British television imported from America, the *Softly, Softly* spin-off represented not only a move towards greater commercialism but a final assimilation into mainstream collaborative – rather than singly authored – production methods. This series was the ultimate in 'teamwork', with its increasingly rationalised, mass industrialised *modus operandi*, even if separate episodes were still written by individual writers.

Re-allocated to BBC Drama Series, *Softly, Softly*'s production team consisted of a stable of producers, directors and writers, in the same way as its predecessor. Whilst continuing to act as a seed-bed for talent, including playwrights such as Alan Plater and Allan Prior, *Softly, Softly*'s processes were more rationalised, with an even more established core staff. For clarity's sake, I have once again set down the personnel in chart form:

Executive Producer	David Rose
Group Producers	Elwyn Jones, Robert Barr
Producer	Leonard Lewis
Directors	Vere Lorrimer, Peter Cregeen, Ben Rea, David Proudfoot, Leonard Lewis
Writers	Robert Barr, Elwyn Jones, Alan Plater, Allan Prior, Don Shaw
Story Editor	Ralph Yarrow

As will be seen, designations frequently overlapped (eg Lewis doubles as Director and Group Producer). It is this process, whereby roles are often interchangeable in television drama production, which makes the concept of auteurship somewhat complex; a point which will later be pursued.

During its first season, *Softly, Softly*'s locale was based upon two offices, 'District', which was located at Deneford County (alias Gloucester), and 'Squad' at Wyvern, near Bristol (just as *Z Cars*' 'Newtown' was close to Liverpool). In narrative terms, Charlie Barlow and John Watt leave Liverpool and Newtown to join a regional crime squad, Wyvern, supposedly near Bristol. This geographical relocation was paralleled by a social shift back towards the upper echelons of the police force. Many of the storylines were generated by Barlow and Watts' working relationship, augmented by a miscellany of other characters, such as local Detective Inspector Harry Hawkins, played by Norman Bowler; Welshman Sergeant Evans, played by Lloyd Meredith; and dog-handler PC Henry Snow, played by Terence Rigby. Desk Sergeant Blackitt also returned, now simply 'Mr Blackitt', played by Robert Keegan, accompanied everywhere by his dog, Pandy.[8] Similar in format to its predecessors, *Softly, Softly* was put out as a weekly series of 50-minute episodes. It continued for a ten-year run, until December 1976 (barely outlasting *Dixon*. Stratford Johns went on to star in two further spin-off series, *Barlow at Large* (1971–1973) and *Barlow* (1974–1975). From 2 November 1966, the main show's title was changed to *Softly, Softly, Task Force* (although its content remained the same). The series never topped *Z Cars*' early 14 million viewing-figures, pulling in an audience of over 9 million at the height of its popularity. But, of course, that wasn't the end of the story so far as its predecessor was concerned. The *Z Cars* title was revived in March 1967 and continued to be broadcast until September 1978, with one very different feature which I shall shortly be taking up – it was no longer produced 'live'.

I have previously discussed how, following Sydney Newman's arrival, BBC Drama became reorganised into a tripartite formation. What the division meant so far as Robert Barr's former Documentary Department was concerned was that its practitioners' briefs tended to be much more proscribed. Whereas previously television documentarists' work had been courageously experimental, in the new climate there was no longer the space for what had, on occasion, proved to be hit-and-miss tactics.

In the new post-Consensus climate it was the Single Play which took over from the story-documentary series in providing a space for the articulation of generic innovation. It is no coincidence that in the wake of this transmigration went much of the practical talent nurtured by the Documentary Department. Leading pioneers, apprenticed within the television documentary tradition, who crossed over from series production, included such primary figures as John McGrath, James McTaggart, Troy Kennedy Martin and Tony Garnett, in fact all of those who had previously worked on and trained in *Z Cars*. Ken Loach, who also contributed to a couple of *Z Cars* episodes, was the leading exponent, producing the groundbreaking 'Cathy Come Home' (1966).

So far as the series' overall design was concerned, *Softly, Softly*'s 'programme plan' begins with Barlow as the newly-appointed Detective Chief Superintendent, in charge of the CID of Deneford County, described as a:

> medium-size force not overly efficient. It is, for example, a County which just hasn't caught up with its recent, and rather savage, overspill towns; which has had rather a gentlemanly approach to crime; which almost automatically calls in the Yard when anything big happens. Barlow wants to change all that, making his Force so efficient he need hardly ever call upon outside help. Watt arrives in Deneford County with the rank of Detective Superintendent and the job of heading one of the County's two Task Forces. Just as it was assumed in *Z Cars* that there was an industrial state, a port, a wealthy suburb and real rural communities within reach – these were also assumed to exist within the Kingley district over which Watt has overall control.[9]

The Centre of programme operations in the early *Softly, Softly* series is County Headquarters, a genuine mansion in near-rural surroundings, some three miles from the centre of Kingley. Narrative interest derived from the interaction between the Co-ordinator of the District Office, Assistant Chief Constable Austin Gilbert, and the Deputy Co-ordinator, Detective Chief Superintendent Charles Barlow. Detective Chief Inspector John Watt is in charge of the Branch Office at Wyvern and, as we will recall from *Z Cars*, is separated from his wife Mary. A brief attachment to Gwen Lloyd, Gilbert's secretary, has already faded, even before she leaves the office.

Softly, Softly shifted away from the portrayal of ordinary, regional crime in order to focus upon the new Task Forces. In the interests of analysis, it is worth examining this new 'real life' police development a little further. Task Forces constituted the roving units which were – somewhat ironically – first initiated in Lancashire, as a large dossier put together by Elwyn Jones, dated 29 March 1968 and marked 'Confidential', explains:

> In Lancashire Task Forces are the very latest organisational development in the continuing war against crime. They have previously existed in Chicago; they bear some slight resemblance to the Metropolitan Police's Special Patrol Groups.[10]

Leonard Lewis, in an internal memorandum, described the Task Force's 'real-life' National set-up in the South Midlands as comprising nine Police districts, including the Metropolitan area. It states that the series' two districts, or 'zones', will encroach on at least three of the national districts, 'thereby not identifying precisely with any Home Office distinctions nor impersonating any particular serving Officers recently appointed'. This remark is of interest when we recollect the numerous complaints made over 'identifiable locations' in the *Z Cars* series. As the document further relates, 'The general impression will be a Squad of some 100 or more detectives operating through a network of cells in teams of eight down to two.' These were controlled by a Chief Co-ordinator whose office was at New Scotland Yard, London.

Not only is the control by the Metropolitan police a return to the Metro-politan centre, the fact of the Force's answerability to Scotland Yard is another indication of generic assimilation into a newly defined mainstream, one that involves serious rather than, as previously, minor crime (as such, this repre-sents another generic recuperation). At a more general level, the mobility of the Task Force units contrasts with the rootedness of the single 'manor' as exemplified by *Dixon of Dock Green*, and earlier on, by *Pilgrim Street*. Furthermore, it outlines their special capabilities as mobile forces able to move in strength into any area. Not only can Task Forces tackle any single major crime (murder, rape, bank robbery) they can also deal with minor crime, but only where there is an unusual preponderance. As the document states, 'they will not go, as such, to tackle a minor robbery: they will go on to tackle one of a *series* of minor robberies.' Once more, we are reminded of *Softly, Softly*'s new remit not to portray small, everyday crime.

Despite the earlier Chicago reference, in terms of achieving transnational appeal, *Softly, Softly* like its predecessor, was popular only with European and foreign language-speaking countries because it could be dubbed or subtitled: American networks found the series unintelligible. In addition, *Softly, Softly* failed to convey an image of Britishness with which they were familiar, unlike those of *Scotland Yard*, or new, popular 1960s Brit-product like *The Avengers*, with its self-conscious Carnaby Street 'pop' appeal. Until the arrival of the 1970s and *The Sweeney* (itself influenced by American imports), transatlantic traffic in terms of the television police series (unlike the *Scotland Yard* film) was manifestly one-way.

Under the subheading 'The Job', the Programme Dossier states that the programme's main *raison d'être*, in terms of its 'take' on the police, is the 'investigation of the criminal – rather than the crime'. Significantly, the Crime Squad men of the Task Force are on the same *level* as the local CID. The dossier states that the Barlow character is 'determined to break down barriers between the CID and the uniformed branch'. This is a new departure, offering dramatic opportunities in terms of conflict between departments, as well as suggesting an assimilation within them. Detective Inspector Hawkins, who is to serve under Watt, is to be 'the one likely to be caught in any cross-fire between Barlow and Watt', thereby affording many narrative opportunities.

Softly, Softly's storylines rarely featured very serious crime, but during week four of the second season, 'Pressure', written by Elwyn Jones, was atypically centred upon a murder enquiry. The programme was a device to show the air of lethargy that has descended on the Murder HQ and on the Crime Squad officers assisting the investigation into the death of Alfred Cameron: even Watt shows an unusual tendency to allow his personal affairs to take a parallel interest with the job in hand. But when the local CID Chief Superintendent in charge goes sick, Barlow takes over and 'the pressure' is at once stepped up. The episode was instrumental in introducing the character of Dr Jean Morrow, played by Gay Hamilton, to be seen in subsequent episodes. John Watt first meets Morrow when she is called in to certify the death of the murdered man, and their acquaintance is continued in the course of the investigation. Once again, we can see from the storyline synopses new forward-looking narrative strategies, in terms of a development running across individual programmes. 'Assistance' (1966) another Elwyn Jones script, features a shift in the usual regime at Wyvern, when Gilbert has to be away for an indeterminate length of time whilst carrying out an official investigation into allegations against a senior police officer. Barlow is appointed to deputise for Gilbert, and Detective Superintendent Jones of the local CID is brought in to do likewise for Barlow. Jones has worked with the Squad on previous occasions and was also, with Barlow, one of the candidates for the post of Co-ordinator at the time that Gilbert was appointed. His views on the running of a Crime Squad bring him into conflict at once with Barlow over the degree of assistance the Squad should provide in response to a request by another local Force investigating a murder. A note on file comments that the 'Gilbert/Barlow/Watt inter-relationship is probably the most complex in the Squad, leaning heavily on the men's personalities as much as on their respective functions'.[11]

So as to avoid *Z Cars'* 'shape' so far as the uniformed side of the Task Force was concerned, it was thought best to deploy two-men-in-a-car, but underplay this element. In addition, according to the programme file, Elwyn Jones states the need to move away from the idea of a team and 'to focus our interest instead on one Crime Patrol Sergeant, out in a car on his own, sometimes in uniform sometimes not'. This particular individual is to be Robert Evans, who has come to Deneford County because:

> he was just that much too small for Glamorgan County. He's a bright and thrusting Sergeant, a former detective constable who thought his only chance of promotion lay in the uniform branch: he may change his mind about this now that Barlow is around. He is one of those natural thief catchers; one of those whose every step seems to take him into places where crime is being committed.[12]

An episode written by Keith Dewhurst, called 'The Bombay Doctor' (1967), features Box the 'ugly' PC, and only member of the lower ranks of the Squad who is married and has a family. When Box gets a tip-off from his 'snout' George Milton that a big platinum robbery is going to be pulled, what he doesn't know is that Milton is depending on the tip-off money to entice away with him the young daughter of the woman with whom he has been asso-ciating.[13] All these synopses feature stories which are pretty universal and are not necessarily directed at their local area. The last programme in the first series of the Wyvern Crime Squad, was appropriately called 'Write Off' (1969) and was written by Alan Plater.

Characterisation

Rightly or wrongly, *Softly, Softly* confirms the way in which generic characters always seem to become dominant because of the iterative nature of its format. This leads to an abandonment of the documentary idea of using them as 'a key to a whole society'. The fact is that, they, rather than the wider social view, become the main dramatic interest. As will be seen, this tendency is exploited to the hilt by the series' writers. Here, there is no documentary portrayal of character, constructed from 'real' dossiers on men and women, taken from a real police division. Unlike that process, traced in *Z Cars*, the writing is that of the make-believe, constructed world of the television dramatist. In terms of characterisation, this is observable in the newly imaginary construction of Barlow's assistant Chief Constable Arthur Cullen. He is, as the document emphasises 'not a smooth Henley type; he's crusty, but sophisticated, a suave rough diamond – if the contradiction can be grasped'. There is a further contradiction here, Cullen, in many ways seems to be drawn from an earlier, *Z Cars* version of the Barlow character. However, unlike his predecessor, he is not drawn from real life.

Another transmigration can be seen in the way in which Watt, like Barlow, is 'brought back to somewhere near his home vicinity with the rank of Detective Superintendent with the job of heading one of the County's two Task Forces'. Henry Snow, as before, provided what Joe Mounsey, real-life Head of Lancashire CID, warningly described as the 'Rin Tin Tin touch'. He works on his own except for Union his Alsatian dog which he grooms as meticulously as he grooms himself. The document further suggests that care should be taken to ensure that Snow is a Midlander and 'not the most intelligent man in the world; he is brave; he is not very resourceful; he's having trouble in passing his examination for sergeant. He is a bachelor'. This description once again reinforces the constructed nature of this new type of characterisation. The new Barlow character is now portrayed not only as smoother but as 'going soft', with connotations not only of succumbing to middle age, but also to (softer) middle-class values. This is represented by the series' very different ambience and mise-en-scene to those of *Z Cars*. It is most tellingly represented by Barlow's new Headquarters at Kingley Hall, described in the Story Development Document as 'a genuine mansion', with:

> a really lush office in it – handsome desk, deepish carpet, fine mullioned windows. This is almost one of our symbols: the force is soft; the food in the Officers' Mess is very good; its wine cellar is more than tolerable. Barlow, curiously, will relish this more than his Chief Constable.[14]

In an interview with Michael Williams, Stratford Johns stated that he felt that:

> Barlow always hankered secretly after this sort of life. Even in Newtown, he was great at seeking out the odd interesting little restaurant whenever his

pay would run to it … Now that he's moved into another financial bracket he's become that little bit more confident, that little bit less rough in the tongue. And I make sure that he's dressing to fit the new part too – I've got him a new wardrobe of better suits. Not Saville Row of course, but good. About the thirty-guinea mark.[15]

Arguably, it is the 'softening' of Barlow which led to Nancy Banks Smith's comments cited above, in the *Sun*, whose headline, 'Give me awful old Barlow, warts and all', echoed the sentiments of many. Such pundits felt the series' assimilation into the generic values of the mainstream was at a cost to its critical realism. Watching *Softly, Softly* was – to extend the metaphor – like playing *Z Cars pianissimo*. Later, again with reference to the Barlow characterisation, documentation on file states 'there is a strong feeling that a "shaking up" of character would be advantageous.' One narrative strategy suggested was that since Barlow had 'reached his natural elevation' it might be time for him to discover new challenges. It could be that this would devolve on Barlow's taking temporary administrative control of the Squad with rather less ease and success than he had anticipated; or that a temporary co-ordinator be appointed to the post from outside, to Barlow's mortification.

Such developments are clearly indicative of a more co-ordinated and professionalised editorial approach. *Softly, Softly*'s narrative stories certainly proceeded from a more pre-planned and fictionalised base than those of *Z Cars*, especially as far as characterisation was concerned. This was not created – as it had been in *Z Cars* – from the raw material of the police themselves, but from the writer's – in this case Elwyn Jones's – own imagination. A dossier compiled by Jones entitled 'The Facts', exemplifies the process. Under a sub-section entitled 'The Men', Detective Constable William Digby, is described as:

Aged 25–26 years. Single; tall; blonde. Attractive to women whose company he enjoys – though, in the final analysis he can take 'em or leave 'em. This seeming independence only serves to enhance his attraction. He is a native Bristolian – a city-dweller all his life. Comes from a poor family. Left school at the first available moment, and joined his father as an employee of a local cigarette manufacturing company. He has worked there from the age of 15 – rising to become assistant packaging supervisor … a job offering little possibilities for future advancement. He has two brothers, and a sister … all of whom are living away from home. Mother and father have moved to a new estate on the outskirts of Bristol. His salary … would be about £1,200.[16]

A new addition is a female detective with a special responsibility for dealing with cases involving children and females whilst also 'performing duties similar to those of her male colleagues'. Leonard Lewis states: 'She becomes my plea for youth and beauty'. He goes on to justify this casting by stating:

> there were women detectives employed in the Kray case who were not a day over 24 and there is no reason why ours should be any older. She should also be pretty. Her name is Betty Donald. She is local, born and bred in the County; she is also working-class – her father is a fitter in one of the local motor car factories. She missed out on her eleven-plus, went into an office from secondary modern school, then into the Police Service.

The reference to the notorious gangland Kray Brothers' arrest in 1968 is of interest, in terms of providing a real-life index. Lewis is at pains to construct a credible female character. Betty is certainly no 'bimbo'. According to the dossier 'she goes to evening classes whenever she can; plays Linguaphone records at the slightest opportunity, is more liable to be reading a French grammar than a woman's magazine'.[17] She is to turn up in several incarnations throughout the 1970s and 1980s, both in the US and Britain, finally arriving at a definitive version in the DCI Tenison persona, played by Helen Mirren in *Prime Suspect* (1991). After the hundredth edition of *Softly, Softly*, written by Elwyn Jones and teasingly entitled 'Departure' (Barlow's aircraft was reported missing), Julian Critchley rated it 'by far the best of police programmes.'[18] But, as he nonetheless points out, unlike *Z Cars* 'it is a writers' show'.

Spinning off a new aesthetic

In narrative terms, the implications of having two offices, at Bristol and Gloucester, proved too complex. The Audience Research Report for 'Off Beat' by Martin Hall, the first programme, gave it a Reaction Index of 62. The comments from a retired Civil Servant are quoted as being typical. He stated that it 'took me a long time to sort out who was who and what was going on. However, I think the series is going to be alright'. For some, 'Off Beat' opened in such a quiet manner as to be dull. A bank manager stated that the programme 'had none of the impact of the initial programme of *Z Cars*'. A Civil Servant remarked that in *Softly, Softly* 'the "new boys" will have to live up to the idols they have ousted'. Other viewers felt that the performance of certain members of the cast (notably the three detectives) was only 'fair to middling', as yet. Stratford Johns (Barlow) took the honours as appearing 'right on form'. The main problem was that viewers were often confused as to what was going on. A Student opined that there was, 'too much talking between the many detectives attached to the district office of this West Regional Crime Squad', with a Technical Assistant adding:

> we were confused by characters quoting the names of others with whom we are not yet familiar, and the combination of West Country accents and fast dialogue was a little difficult to grasp at times.[19]

During the second series (2 November 1966–31 May 1967), a BBC Press Service release announced that '*Softly, Softly* ... returns on November 2, with a new face a new opening and a few changes'. At this time the series' title changed. A new opening sequence featured a monkey dominating an aerial view, which replaced the titles wiping up the screen. Apart from the slightly surrealist appearance of the zoo-animal, there were two cast changes. First, Detective Chief Inspector Lewis played by Garfield Morgan, left: he was not replaced. Internal correspondence from David Rose states 'we are not stressing the series reason, but for the record, he has returned to his old Force on promotion to Superintendent'. Second, PC Greenly, played by Cavan Kendall, was replaced by PC Tanner, played by David Quilter. The Press Release further states that 'Watt, who takes over from Gilbert Lewis, Barlow, Blackitt, Calderwood, Box, Dwyer and Hawkins (regulars) will a now operate under one roof in the Bristol area which we call Wyvern.' Another memo from David Rose stated that the Squad was to remain located on the ground floor, with the District Offices immediately overhead, with Detective Inspector, now senior officer on the Squad, in charge. The Press Release promised that in future 'the stories will be clearer and some of them will be in two parts'.

The second series was scheduled for 31 episodes and included one double; Parts 1 and II by Robert Barr and one treble, featuring Barlow; geared to Christmas, weeks, 51, 52 and week 1/67. This development, which had begun in *Z Cars*, allowed for much greater narrative development, as in the feature film. Meticulously pre-planned by a team, working in unison, the new *Softly, Softly* reflected an even more conscious effort at pre-planning.

A memo, following a meeting held in 1967, discusses the results of the introduction of a new system of four designers and two design assistants, instead of three designers and three design assistants to work to the four directors on the weekly production. With the directors working on a four week round, the production cycles for two successive productions by the same director overlapped, since the script for the second production had to be available while the first was still in rehearsal. A memo from David Rose, written as early as 1967, concerning the new series, demonstrates its greater sense of pre-planning. It also states that:

> There is a feeling that the present high level of quality and achievement might be built on by an increasing awareness of the possibilities of continuing development over the series as a whole: development of character relationships, of official relationships within the Squad and with outside organisations, and of the Crime Squad's operational methods.[20]

This suggests a very new approach to the episodic series form. It shifts from the definition supplied by John Tulloch et al, in which each episode consists of complete and discrete narratives, with only the main protagonists and main locations (offices, homes) providing continuity between episodes.[21] Now, there is continuity between the episodes, so that it more represents the series-al: the cross-over between the soap and the series format. The document goes on to discuss that whilst such an 'awareness' cannot be imposed upon individual scripts, it may be 'reflected' through being shared by everyone concerned, in individual scripts.

Accessing video-recording technology

Softly, Softly's rationalisation of its production methods was assisted by the utilisation of recording technology. This ultimately replaced live studio broadcast transmission with fully-recorded programmes allowing for an even greater degree of pre-planning and industrialised mode of production than in *Z Cars*. At the same time it enabled a stylistics and mise-en-scene markedly more cinematic than those of its immediate predecessor. As a result, the BBC's television aesthetic moved away from the drama in close-up, so much the stylistic of early *Z Cars*, to a more filmic language, one that appeared no longer limited by the demands of continuous 'live' performance.

By the mid-1960s, television had passed out of John Ellis's designated 'era of scarcity', and film was used more frequently by the BBC Drama Department in order to compete with ITV. In order to show the change in climate, it is worth noting that during *Softly, Softly*'s second season, a couple of episodes were not only filmed – an extremely unusual occurrence – but were advertised as being so. As an Early Warning Synopsis from the Director, Leonard Lewis, used for publicity purposes, stated:

> Two programmes have already been filmed entirely on location in the West Country: 'Dead Aboard' by Elwyn Jones, which has a dockside background,

and 'Error of Judgement' by Ben Bassett, which features private flying, filmed on the ground and in the air … these stories break away from the Early Television tradition of programmes recorded in the television studios with only a small amount of filmed content, in order to give full value to stories which deal extensively with the 'outdoor' aspect of Regional Crime Squad work.[22]

It is clear from this announcement that not only producers but also the general public were sufficiently *au fait* with television technology for this to be a big break in the continuity of the television documentary-drama tradition. From an aesthetic and stylistic point of view, it seems evident that film could still supply what a mixed economy of studio television production and small amounts of film inserts could not: 'action'. Despite several devices which simulated movement, such as the use of back projections, cars on rollers, as well as multiple changes of shot, it was still not possible to achieve speed. *Z Cars*, despite all the restrictions residing in early live television production, nonetheless aimed to simulate the aesthetic of 'a fast-moving feature film'. In the interests of *Softly, Softly*'s subsequent development, it is important to register its anticipation of this important move to film. Indeed, because of its more rationalised methods of production, compared to most other contemporary popular BBC series formats (for example *Dixon of Dock Green*) the average shot length in *Softly, Softly* was – as in later *Z Cars* episodes – appreciably faster (12 seconds, against ten seconds for cinema film).

Hitherto, film had been the sole preserve of the current affairs documentary, notably Rotha's *Special Enquiry*. So far as either BBC Drama or the Documentary Department was concerned, it was not on the agenda. By contrast, it was not to film but to an extended use of VTR which *Softly, Softly* and other series were relegated, right up until the 1970s, when video itself began to simulate the qualities of film. The use of VTR in the uniform police series pointed towards a new direction and marked a departure from that particular moment of 'live' television drama, of which *Z Cars* had been its fullest realisation. In sum, this development was linked to a privileging of productivity over aesthetics, where the previous hegemony of 'immediacy' was finally abandoned.

In terms of publicity and production pre-planning, Early Warning Drama Synopsis were circulated in advance to all personnel. A memo put out from David Rose to the Presentation Editor, Pictorial Publicity and the *Radio Times* Television Editor shows this new, co-ordinated approach. It states that 'An interesting change that comes about in the episodes to be seen in Weeks 11 and 12 during its second year of production is significant'. It also states that in Week 11:

> The Co-ordinator, Assistant Chief Constable Calderwood (John Welsh) relinquishes his post to become Chief Constable of a nearby Force. This is his last appearance as a 'regular' member of the cast. The episode, 'Selection' (by Elwyn Jones), as the title suggests concerns the appointment of his successor. Barlow is in the running – the choice made is Deputy Chief Constable Gilbert – a fact which should be withheld from the viewers in pre-publicity. It will be remembered that Gilbert (John Barron) was one of the officers who investigated Barlow's suspected corruption at the turn of the year.

The episode referred to is 'Barlow was There', the two-parter put out on 28 December and 4 January, respectively. Once again, this phenomenon was another 'first': what it allowed for was a more extended development occurring within the same time-frame as a feature film. This elaborate narrative strategy, looking ahead to the development of plot and characters over the whole series, is made possible due to the implementation of recording technology. By now, after the use of film for several episodes, together with the availability of video-recording technology, the use of pre-recording the programme in terms of scheduling exigencies and pre-planning had become self-evident. The same memo referred to above, which demonstrates a much greater, forward-looking approach to narrative continuity in *Softly, Softly* than in any other previous British television police series, states that the production of the programme in 'week 12 is live, but Episode 11 is to be recorded in Week 8: This recording should prove very useful pictorially for *Radio Times*, Publicity and Trails in promoting both episodes 11 and 12'. Such forward co-ordinated planning was unheard of in *Z Cars*, where each episode was more or less an entity.

Softly, Softly was very important in marking that transitional stage, in which 'live' transmission was gradually replaced by fully taped programmes (although these were recorded 'as live'). A note on file from Leonard Lewis to the Head of Series indicates that the decision to go over to video-tape was not unchallenged. It states:

> I would like to express the concern I feel over the decision to make *Softly, Softly* a totally recorded programme. There are many arguments that could be gone into concerning the virtues of 'live' or 'recording' but these arguments do not seem to have been aired, and I think they should be.[23]

He adds further that a 'decision to stop doing any "live" series must surely be a historic decision' (in television terms). In response, Peter Raleigh, Series Planning Manager replies that 'Softly, Softly could in fact be transmitted live'. But recalls the fearful contortions which the production team had undergone trying to achieve it. The main difficulty was the requirement that only the working-week should be utilised. As he states, 'we were balked by the requirement that rehearsal days for Drama Series should not fall during the weekends'. In the same memo, Raleigh puts the matter bluntly, at the same time framing the situation in an interrogative context:

> C.BBC [Controller BBC1] will be grateful for your advice as to where in Drama Group, in your view, the balance of advantage lies – keeping *The Wednesday Play* on its present recording day or transmitting *Softly, Softly* live. Which of the two do you prefer?[24]

This juxtaposition is interesting and ironic in terms of the way in which the two productions are seen to be competing for space. However, a couple of years later, a new technological development eclipsed the live/recorded debate. After a six months break the fifth *Softly, Softly* series returned with Episode No. 111, entitled 'Recovery', written by Elwyn Jones and directed by Leonard Lewis. It announced that although the first ten episodes were to be transmitted in monochrome, 'from Week 47 the transmissions will be in colour'. Furthermore, 'all episodes will be on tape'.[25] Finally, it was the endless shifting around of other shows, including *Dixon of Dock Green*, because of the availability, or lack, of studio space which brought the argument to a head. By this time, there was no contest. In terms of kudos, *The Wednesday Play* now took precedence, although some programmes, including 'Cathy Come Home' were in fact shot on film.

During the early 1970s, a number of changes took place: Stratford Johns went off to co-star in the two further spin off series, *Barlow at Large* and *Barlow*, from 1971. Once Barlow finally left the Wyvern area and the series itself, to 'go on his own' in *Barlow* – produced by Keith Williams – the genre whose moment had been realised in *Z Cars* began to implode. Now, as Lorna Sage has stated, 'The series is no longer how the police operate but what being a policeman is all about. Not so much how it's done, but why.'[26] Once again, that pull between the documentary exigencies of the public service discourse (know your legal rights, illegal firearms and so on) and the drama of human existence is made clearly visible. For Troy Kennedy Martin, it is this contradiction which constitutes the fate of the genre because 'As soon as a series becomes successful you're on the tail of a comet. You can't start destroying the characters you have created – because now they belong to the public'.[27] Like Dixon, Barlow became an enduring figure, so much so that Nancy Banks-Smith, writing during 1969 in the *Sun*, stated: 'I feel as though Barlow and I have been together now for 40 years'. He was to last until 1975; a mere 13 years, when set against Dixon's unbelievable 21.

By the time the whole cycle of *Z Cars* and its spin-offs was near completion, not only had Barlow become an established character, he also became reabsorbed into the southern Metropolis, enmeshed in the secretive Whitehall machine where as Sage, again, has so eloquently put it, 'he never seemed less sure of what being a policeman is all about'. And so it was that the South finally absorbed and subordinated the 'grittiness' that had been *Z Cars'* hallmark, turning it into a blander portrayal. Meanwhile, the remit for innovation that had characterised the drama and story-documentary was transferred to the single play.

Homing in on the single play

It will be recalled that one of the Documentary Department's earliest accolades, apart from translating the Griersonian manifesto into television, was considered to be the way in which it combined documentary form with series. It is somewhat ironic therefore, that its experiments resulted in a shift to the mainstream whilst the personnel they had trained, along with their entire repertoire of documentary values, were appropriated by Plays. Even more ironic is the fact that the generic newcomer, *Softly, Softly,* anticipates a more cinematic production although still being shot on video and film, whilst the occasionally film-originated *Wednesday Play* arguably preserved the immediacy aesthetic of television. Dramatists, who had served an early apprenticeship within the documentary department, such as Ken Loach – who directed three episodes of *Z Cars* – went on to direct in this slot, introduced by Sydney Newman who had been 'poached' from ABC Television and its highly popular *Saturday Theatre*. Attached both to *The Wednesday Play* and single drama generally was a definite concept of authorship which had not been present in the documentary series.

There has famously been doubt about the concept of auteurism and television. Rosalind Coward has questioned press constructions of Dennis Potter as TV *auteur*, suggesting that the industrialised nature of the medium and its 'complexity of production and division of labour' has rendered the transparent communication between one author and his or her audience hard to credit.[28] However, as we have already seen, in British television, such designations are down to history and television's close relationship to theatre and radio. As in the case of each of these predecessors, it was the producer and writer who were privileged. We only have to recall radio's regime of producer-writers, whose function was to oversee the whole process of early programmes from start to finish, to see how this was established by practice. Within this division of labour, a directorial role in the film sense was subsumed within that of the Producer. Indeed, the role of director in the *film* sense was unknown until it was introduced by Robert Barr in *I Made News*, in order to facilitate the weekly turnaround: however, it was not until the arrival of *Z Cars* that it was acknowledged as such. Earlier BBC policy had been against the use of the words 'Director' or 'Directed by' because it was thought better to follow theatre rather than film practice, due to the poor relations between the film-industry and television.[29] Once producers in the *film* sense were introduced, it became possible to reassign the designations. By contrast, in the one-off single play the role of director in the film sense began to be introduced, although the divisions of labour between writer, producer and director were much fuzzier and it was therefore difficult to assign authorship to any one function. For example, 'Cathy Come Home' is unusual in that it is Ken Loach the director, over both the writer (Jeremy Sandford) and producer (Tony Garnett) upon whom the laurels of auteur are usually conferred. An Oxford graduate who became a BBC trainee, Loach was a notable example of the success of the recently instituted BBC training course. Like Tony Garnett, Loach worked on both *Z Cars* and *The Wednesday Play*, the former acting as we have also seen, as a 'seed-bed' for young dramatists. In doing so, they crossed over between popular and élite forms of drama.

It is worth staking out the claim that a cross-fertilisation of techniques across the departments under Drama as a result of the new designations – in particular between Series and Plays – resulted in a generic hybridity and proliferation. *The Wednesday Play*, and later *Play for Today*, continued the ideology and aesthetics of early programmes like *Z Cars* in terms of their critical realism. Conjoined with Sydney Newman's own desire to show social change in contemporary Britain, alongside a new story-editor system in a rationalised slot, they took up the old documentary 'torch'. Writers, directors and producers, inside the discrete slot of *The Wednesday Play*, had the advantage of being able to express controversial views that would not have been sustainable over a series of any length. The fact that a television aesthetic was passed over to film is important in terms of establishing a relationship between the two media that is not hierarchical so much as symbiotic.

As John Cook has argued, shifts in emphasis gradually took place in *The Wednesday Play*. During the first season, under the direction of James

MacTaggart (an early director of *Z Cars*) and Roger Smith, it was more 'expressionist' in style than in later years when, with Loach's chief collaborator, Tony Garnett, as story editor and then subsequently one of the producers, it became much more documentary.[30] 'Cathy Come Home' has been seen as definitive in terms of this move. It exercised an equivalent iconoclastic effect on the British public to that of *Z Cars*, and met with similar criticism. Featuring the story of a young provincial woman who hitchhikes to London, the play follows the adventures of the eponymous heroine (played by the actress Carol White) as she meets and marries delivery-driver Ray. She shortly discovers – unlike Julie Christie in *Darling* (1965) – that the city streets are not as she had hitherto thought, paved with gold. Following the birth of her baby, she moves with her family first into a squalid tenement, followed by a dilapidated caravan and then into a hostel for the homeless, before being evicted and finally seeing her children taken away from her. 'Cathy Come Home' surely must remain as the exemplar par excellence of John Ellis's television as Witness, its presence on the small screen seemingly testifying to a sense of co-presence unavailable at the cinema, hence its being taken up by Shelter, the charitable foundation for the homeless.

As George McKnight suggests, the central theme of 'Cathy Come Home' follows Loach's preoccupation with the concern of human betrayal, played out within organisations out of sight of public scrutiny. From this perspective, Loach carries on the television tradition of using documentary to critique the processes of state, the very reverse of the public service documentary film. In McKnight's own words the narrative voice over:

> is not the conventional third-person omniscient voice of reassurance – the kind of voice that is often otherwise employed to reinforce social norms – but a voice that points to the failure of current housing policies and calls for a new policy.[31]

Inverting its conventions, documentary no longer props up the status quo but exposes the more unacceptable face of the state. Arguably, it was because of the production's left-wing political stance that it met with criticism, in particular, about the nature of its 'evidence' relating to homelessness. For, as McKnight further suggests, 'these accusations seem to arise when Loach has set out to counter an already existing imbalance of opinion in the broadcast media, favouring a point of view that supports dominant political attitudes'.[32]

If Loach's stance within the space allowed by the *Wednesday Play* slot was highly polemical, it was not without precedent. Shifting away from consensus attitudes, in common with novelists, playwrights and earlier television dramatists, Loach was interested in portraying settings which reflected his own working-class background. 'Cathy Come Home' was about the false allure of London and the way in which it could destroy the hopeful aspirations of ordinary young people. One year before its transmission, Peter Watkins' highly controversial visualisation of a nuclear attack on Britain, 'The War Game' (1965) – also shot on film – was withdrawn and apart from the press preview, remained publicly unshown until 1985. What caused the fuss was not only the dramatisation of scenes that were too terrible for domestic consumption, but also the use of so-called 'experts' appearing as witnesses. According to Tom Pocock in the *Evening Standard*:

> The film is in the guise of a documentary and the action sequences are broken by the comments of doctors, psychiatrists, churchmen and strategists. Whilst the presentation seems authoritative, the film is straight propaganda for the Campaign for Nuclear Disarmament.

Here we have a demonstration of the problem with Television as Witness, in writer-led drama. Above all, it was the way in which the 'codes' used to represent the categories separately designated as 'drama' and 'documentary' seemed to have been deliberately blurred and, to add insult to injury, any passages featuring dramatised reconstructions were not indicated as such.[33] James Thomas wrote, after viewing *In Two Minds* by David Mercer, about a young woman from a middle-class home driven mad by her environment:

> Inside BBC television a new battle is blowing up between the men who deal with fact and the men who deal with fiction. Producers are expressing open anxiety at the way the line between drama and documentary is being blurred, leaving the public in doubt about whether they are watching truth or fantasy and exposing them to a new and potentially alarming method of propaganda ... It is not before time that the dangers of some of the new forms of so-called drama are coming under discussion at the BBC. Too often the drama spots are being used by writers and producers to air opinions so way out that they should not be shown to a massive lay audience without balance.[34]

Thomas, writing in the *Daily Express*, further demanded that, 'the BBC should make it a rule that every play which might be confused with a serious features programme must carry announcements before and after to make it clear to the public that they are watching fiction'.[35]

As we have also seen, hitherto, the BBC had been punctilious in explaining to the British television public, the status of its productions, especially in

19. Discovering that London's streets are not, after all, paved with gold.
'Cathy Come Home', with Carol White (1966).

the case of story-documentaries. However, reconstructions had been the name of the documentary-game from the beginning. What was new was that in *The War Game* they were used to dramatise controversial material in a production whose overall status was uncertain. Was it fact or fiction? Was it a play or a documentary?

According to Julian Petley, 'The War Game' was not banned because it was too shocking to show, but because it was the victim of intense Establishment pressure and that the press preview was not organised to publicise the film, but as a cynical ploy to 'justify its suppression on the grounds of bowing to "public opinion" since the press was, as ever, in an anti-BBC mood, and the Corporation must have realised that the majority of papers would clamour for a ban'.[36]

It will be recalled that earlier film documentarists were accused of 'selling out' to the establishment in terms of promoting the public service interests of the state. Here, Watkins is being accused of precisely the opposite. As we have seen, television producers and the authorities were in fact highly aware from the beginning of its potential for political subversion, the latter of whom had sought to separate out 'the social' from 'the political'. Yet, at the same time, Reith at the inception of broadcasting history had sought to procure 'balance'.

By contrast to Watkins who – like Rotha – only worked with film, Loach was well-schooled in a mixed economy of 'live' transmission with film inserts. As a result, his early documentaries have a more distinctly televisual 'feel' about them. By deploying the methods originally devised by television documentarists, in particular the 2–shot in mid close up, and applying them to the one-off drama, he succeeds in producing something at least as iconoclastic in terms of generic innovation as *Z Cars*. 'Cathy Come Home' continued the social exploration of the working class, in line with the novels and television story-documentaries of the 1950s, only this time the myth about the North literally came home to roost. The storyline takes pains to reveal that the South, and in particular the Metropolis, is an equal urban wilderness if you are homeless. At the same time as being a departure within the discourse of its time, 'Cathy Come Home' is also a continuation, containing within itself the memories of Henry Mayhew's *London Labour and the London Poor* (1851). For just like the earlier book and other studies carried out within the previously mentioned nineteenth-century anthropologist framework, it revealed that behind the prosperous hinterland of contemporary 'swinging' London, existed a deep penumbra of poverty.

Finally, it is important to note that during the 1960s the usual subordination of television by film is reversed: television is seen as the originator of a new form of documentary realism. Loach's career, from 'Cathy Come Home', through *Kes* to *Carla's Song* is exemplary, as are those of such distinguished producers as James MacTaggart and Tony Garnett. All worked on *Z Cars* and *The Wednesday Play*, thereby crossing the line between what had hitherto been separately perceived as popular and élite forms of drama. On this occasion at least, they demonstrated that the traditional hierarchy and succession, which placed the single play above that of the series form, was reversed. But whatever the arguments for and against, the important outcome of these conjunctures was the creation of today's distinctive British television and film product. This was achieved through a mutually enhancing relationship, both between film and television and between popular and élite forms of culture, which was forged through the 1950s and achieved fruition in the 1960s.

CONCLUSION
Blue endnotes

The replacement of the older narration by information, of
information by sensation, reflects the increasing atrophy of
experience. In turn there is a contrast between all these
forms and the story, which is one of the oldest forms of
communication. It is not the object of the story to convey a
happening per se, which is the purpose of information;
rather, it embeds it in the life of the storyteller in order to
pass it on as experience to those listening.

Walter Benjamin[1]

Now that I hope, like a real life detective, to have discovered at least
some of 'the facts' in the process of writing this book, I would like, to
conclude with a few thoughts concerning their possible meaning. Throughout
the trajectory of 'telling the story' of the British television police series in
Beyond Dixon of Dock Green, three main strands have emerged. Since these
seem to show that the British television police series performs an important
ontological, ideological and identificatory function, I want, by way of
concluding, to consider each in turn.

In terms of ontology, Walter Benjamin's views cited above are worth
consideration. Although this member of the so-called Frankfurt School of
'pessimists' had the press in mind when he posited that the story in modernity
was in decline, his argument can also be applied to television. Benjamin's
stance arose because of what he considered to be the surfeit of sensationalist
information being showered upon the public. In terms of today's television,
with its never-ending diet of 'reality TV' in endless *Big Brother* and *Survivor*-
type programmes, there seems much here that we can identify with. However,
other critics argue just the opposite, that there is in fact a proliferation of
stories. They see this as occurring because of the way in which an increased
blurring of the boundaries between information and entertainment, facts and

stories gives rise to an even greater proliferation of narratives. Of course, this 'fuzziness' leads us back into the old 'drama-documentary' debate, especially with accusations of trickery and fakery in such programmes as *The Connection* (1998) and *Daddy's Girl* (1998).[2] However, still more so in terms of their stain of dishonesty, such critics claim that they are still 'stories'. It all depends on our definition of terms. As John Hill sums it up, 'the conventions associated with realism do not remain fixed and are subject to historical variation and change'.[3]

As this book has implicitly argued, it is the transitional form of the story-documentary which undermines the traditional polarity between fact and fiction and whose occurrence argues for a reassessment of the 'documentary idea'. We traced the two-phase cycle of documentary's assimilation into mainstream narratives, first during a pre-television period and second in television itself. However, it is important to note that the trajectory which advances the 'fact' of the documentary into the 'fiction' of mainstream narratives, including the British television police series, has antecedents. The nineteenth-century novel was similarly concerned with the relationship between fact and fiction, particularly in regard to modern life. What each generic innovation has in common is a concern to show the ordinary, everyday event, as well as an essential human-interest factor. By contrast, we recall the difficulties consecutively addressed by film and television documentarists Pat Jackson and Norman Swallow, both of whom complained that 'what was missing' from documentary films such as *Night Mail* and BBC current affairs programme *Special Enquiry*, was 'people'. Today's television soaps and series fulfil this requirement in abundance. Indeed one of the problems with the iterative form of the series is just the opposite to that of documentary. As was noted by John McGrath, a writer on *Z Cars*, no sooner had the BBC realised they had a winner on their hands than the pressure was on writers to build narratives around the characters rather than the social issues, with the result that it lost its radical edge.

John Caughie's article in *Screen*, written during the early 1990s, which moves on from his earlier concerns with the 'documentary-drama' debate, suggests that one way we might poeticise televisions soaps and series is to regard them as 'an historical development of the complex theoretical genre of novelistic discourse' and that:

> Just as Bakhtin ... traces the rise of the novel back to the romances and
> adventure narratives of Hellenistic Greece, so it may be useful ... to think
> of film and television narratives as forward projections of the same novelistic

discourse into the new media using radically different technologies of transmission and reception.[4]

Here, at the conclusion, it is worth considering ways forward including the exciting enterprise to create a television poetics in which television's popular generic fictions are central. Caughie perceives the difficulties involved, and includes that of the absence in television studies of the film studies equivalent of the Hollywood movie's 'classical formation' (another allusion to the need to construct a Bordwellian history). As we have seen, this difficulty has recently been surpassed by new television scholarship that constructs a periodisation in which television's 'golden age' may be regarded as an equivalent construction. At the same time, we need to be fully aware that this concept, as with the 'Dixon' figure, tends once more to be seen through a veil of nostalgia. A new poetics needs to look forward, as much as backwards or at least to interpret the past in terms of the present, rather than remain in a state of denial. More importantly in terms of Caughie's suggested project is the necessity to take into consideration *local conditions*. To proceed in ignorance of these, especially the specificities of particular national televisions, for example the prolonged period of 'liveness' in British television, is to commit the error of elision. By tracing the thread of one strand within the tapestry of television generic fiction, that of the British television police series, I hope to have addressed some of these issues, especially those of local difference. At the same time as Raymond Williams' crucial distinction between 'residual and emergent practices' makes clear, new species of cultural practice always carry continuities with older formations, however innovative they may first seem.[5]

With this in mind, and moving on to ideological considerations, it is worth recalling television's intervention in promoting post-war consensus. During the post-war period it was revealed that petty crime – which had continued throughout the war – was still a problem. As this book has traced, the production of story-documentaries like *It's Your Money They're After*, *First Time Ever* (1946, thief caught by radio), *For the Housewife* (1946, keeping burglars out) and *War on Crime* (1951) were instrumental in 'interpellating' the viewer, at the same time serving as a warning to potential miscreants. The British television police series, which devolved from these forms, became implicated in the hegemonic process whereby the state achieved consensus. In this respect, we have only to evoke the spectacle of 'Dixon's' address to camera to see that it is, in effect, a dramatised translation of Lord Kitchener's famous poster, to the end of keeping the post-war Peace.

Just as Peel's original conception of policing emphasised preventive patrol by uniformed constables, so their appearance on the television screen in the post-war period contributed to the notion of the bobby on the beat 'as the essential bedrock of the force, to which all other specialisms are ancilliary'.[6] With the end of post-war consensus, the television police series began to reflect the way in which the meaning of crime prevention shifted away from the 'scarecrow function' of uniform patrol to the development of specialist crime-prevention departments. We have seen this move in *Z Cars*, where both sets of interests are represented and more fully still in *Softly, Softly*, which featured the new, regional crime-prevention squads of which Barlow and Watt were central figures. In television terms at least, the oft-recited account of the police series' succession runs against the grain of the idea of an eternally resurrected 'Dixon'. This runs something along the lines of 'first there was *Dixon of Dock Green* and then there was *Z Cars*', as if the second erased the first. Not only is this normative account paradoxical, it is profoundly misleading. Although *Z Cars* defined itself very differently, focusing upon the more spectacular effects of increasing police mobility, neither that series, nor its spin-off successor, *Softly, Softly*, replaced the earlier series. Not even when *The Sweeney* (1975) was showing on 'the other side'.

In terms of the British police series, the situation is nicely summed up by a 1970s *Radio Times* feature entitled 'Well, Which one do they love, *Dixon of Dock Green*, *Z Cars*, or *Softly, Softly*?' Whilst all three productions ran concurrently on BBC television, the gist of the article is that each presents a different type of police work.[7] *Dixon of Dock Green* is the earliest metropolitan 'classic' exponent of life on the beat; *Z Cars* is the original British patrol cars series; and *Softly, Softly* is the first programme concerned with regional crime squads. It is not therefore a case of which representation is 'better' or more realistic than another, but, in television terms, one of choice: a new notion of addressing a differentiated, rather than a mass audience, made possible by the move away from a homogenised BBC culture. In policing terms, the dramatisation of different modes of crime prevention, both traditional and progressive is surely most efficacious. As we have seen, the police themselves were always highly aware of the effectiveness of television in terms of public relations.

By way of summing up, it may well be that the British television police series, more than any other popular genre, registers the changing relationship between the broadcast audience and National Identity. As we have discovered, within the broader paradigm of the British police/detective series there was a bifurcation between those élite narratives based upon the myth of Scotland

Yard with a literary connotation, as in 'golden-age' detective narratives such as *Sherlock Holmes*, and those culled from real-life case-files in new, made-for-television series, including Robert Barr's *Scotland Yard* (1960). Whilst there exists in the British Scotland Yard detective story of any era, a ready-made *international* cultural export, in terms of the self-originated British television police series, which emerged and defined itself against the élitist Scotland Yard genre, from *Dixon of Dock Green* (1955) to *Z Cars* (1962), the opportunities were almost non-existent. However, these 'home-produced' products act as a litmus paper by which to test national notions of 'Britishness', especially regarding the classic division between North and South, in which the North is seen as 'Other' in terms of being everything that the South is not. As we have seen, *Z Cars* and its antecedents anticipated the 'Angry Young Man' realism of the 1960s, mirroring its translation to misogyny, in the 'writing out' of female narratives, as in the case of the actress Virgina Stride, whose part dried up. This attitude, partly a result of the distributive structures of the BBC, which had earlier privileged the metropolis over the regions, had associations with the felt sense during the 1950s and 1960s of the loss of Empire. A remasculinisation of narratives and the privileging of 'the centre' over the margins, sought to dramatise internal control. Not that, as we also saw, the Empire didn't fight back some! As BBC Audience Reception proves, so far as the regions themselves were concerned, such representations seemed a travesty of their real lives.

Finally, and to reiterate, it is necessary to reverse the assumption whereby it is the single play rather than the television series which is regarded as 'leading edge'. Television story-documentaries were experimenting with new writers several years before Sydney Newman allegedly 'saw the light to Damascus', after watching a theatre performance of *Look Back in Anger*, ironically, *with* Michael Barry.[8] Barry himself, as we also saw, always promoted the interests of the drama or story-documentary against the latter. All in all, right through from *A Woman Alone* to *Z Cars*, television had negotiated a 'worm's eye view of society' since its reopening. In particular, it was the dramatised – or story – documentary, which not only engendered the British television police series from *Pilgrim Street*, through *Dixon of Dock Green*, to *Z Cars* and beyond, but acted as seedbeds for new television writers who subsequently moved on to the single play. For example, Ken Loach cut his directorial teeth on three episodes of *Z Cars* and went on to direct *The Wednesday Play*, making his mark with 'Cathy Come Home'. Bearing in mind that the directorial function in television was also introduced by documentary practice, for which Robert Barr's *I Made News* series acted as a prototype, it is important to register its centrality. The television story-documentary was fundamental in introducing new forms of practice, from the British television police series to a rearticulation of the single play.

There is after all, nothing novel in the development of new forms of television novelistic – today's soaps and series, despite their radically altered modes of 'transposition'. As I have suggested, the trajectory which advances the 'facts' of documentary into the 'fiction' of the television police series is similar to that of the nineteenth-century novel and its connection to the news. We can therefore see that there is no hierarchy of accession between what is perceived as fact and fiction: they are equally weighted terms, shifting their emphasis according to local, national and, today, global exigencies. As we have also seen, the prioritisation of one term over another has to do with legitimation factors, which itself constitutes the trajectory of a frequently repeated struggle. During the ascent of the mass media, it first occurred in the case of the printing industry which had to wrestle to print the news; next in radio which in its turn, had to fight the press for the same right; and finally television, whose right to present its own, self-originated fictions, was a hard-won battle.

Today, incorporated within so many different genres, from docu-soap – *Blues and Twos* (1998) – to soap-opera, or both, as suggested by the very title of *Undercover Heart* (1998), the British television police series can be almost anything desired.[9] Indeed the phrase 'continuous emergence' is appropriate to both television and the police series itself. The sheer proliferation of the genre, both through the 1990s and in the new millennium, offers food for thought. Change is as axiomatic of genre as it is of television, the most onto-logically unstable and therefore, perhaps, the most productive of all media.

Notes

Introduction

1. Inserted in the *Guardian*, Wednesday 6 October 1993, p 8.
2. R Barthes, *Mythologies* (1973) p 141.
3. Horace Newcomb, *TV: The Most Popular Art* (1974) p 258.
4. The programmes include *The House that Reith Built, 1922–1945, Growing Pains, 1945–1960* and *Making Waves, 1960–1970*. At the time of writing, they are only available off-air, but enquiries may be made to BBC Television at Bush House in London.
5. Newcomb, p 202.
6. Tim O'Sullivan, *Nostalgia, Revelation and Intimacy*, cited in Christine Geraghty and David Lusted, *The Television Studies Book* (1998) p 202.
7. There is a comprehensive 'Golden Age' literature. See Ernest Mandel, *Delightful Murder: A Social History of the Crime Story* (1985); John G Cawelti, *Adventure, Mystery and Romance: Formula Stories as Art and Popular Culture* (1976).
8. The scene was replayed on the BBC News, 8 June 1999, the day of Sir Dirk Bogarde's death.
9. Charles Barr, *All Our Yesterdays* (1977) p 83.
10. Charles Barr, 'Television on Television', *Sight and Sound* (1986) p 159.
11. Charlotte Brunsdon compares this volume with his 1993 collection, *British Television Drama in the 1980s*, which is no longer grouped solely by writers, 'What is the "Television" of Television Studies?', in Geraghty and Lusted, p 97.
12. This is to greatly oversimplify the position. Fiske's reworking of uses and gratifications theory is critiqued by David Buxton, who argues that it too is 'tarred with the brush of "effects theory"'. See *From the Avengers to Miami Vice: Form and ideology in television series* (1990) p 19.
13. Although the juxtaposition of feminism and soap opera seems a contradiction in terms, the new scholarship was concerned with the different ways in which female viewers consumed this previously derided form.
14. John Caughie, 'Television Criticism: "A Discourse in Search of An Object"', *Screen* (1984) pp 119–120.
15. Jerry Palmer, *Potboilers: Methods, Concepts and Case Studies in Popular Fiction* (1992) p 127.
16. John Corner and Sylvia Harvey (eds) *Television Times: A Reader* (1996) p xvi.
17. James Chapman, 'Cinema, propaganda and national identity: British film and the Second World War', in Justine Ashby and Andrew Higson (eds) *British Cinema, Past and Present* (2000) pp 193–196.
18. See bibliography for full details of all these authors.
19. See bibliography for details of titles within the *Oxford Television Studies* series. In addition for some extremely good short pieces on the latest scholarship, see:

G Branston, 'Histories of British Television', in Geraghty and Lusted; Charles Barr, '"They Think It's All Over": The Dramatic Legacy of Live Television', in J Hill and M McLoone (eds) *Big Picture, Small Screen: The Relations Between Film and Television* (1997) pp 47–75.

20. Jason Jacobs, *The Intimate Screen: Early Television Drama*, (2000) p 1.

21. ibid, p 29.

22. ibid, p 28.

23. Stuart Hall, 'Technics of the medium' in John Corner and Sylvia Harvey (eds) *Television Times: A Reader* (1996) p 7.

24. Gerbner's cultivation hypothesis that television cultivates a frightening perception of the world has formed a vast literature of its own. See Richard Sparks, *Television and the Drama of Crime: Moral tales and the place of crime in public life* (1992) pp 86–9.

25. See *Screen Education* 20 (1976).

26. For a further discussion on the Dixon 'phenomenon' see Alan Clarke, 'Holding the Blue Lamp: Television and the Police in Britain' (1983) vol. 19 *Crime and Social Justice*, no. 44, and Colin Sparks, *Television and the Drama of Crime* (1983) pp 25–30. More generally, see G Hurd, 'The television presentation of the police' in S Holdaway (ed.) *The British Police* (1979). For *Z Cars*, see Stuart Laing, 'Banging in Some Reality: The Original "Z Cars"', in J Corner (ed.) *Popular Television in Britain: Studies in Culture* (1991). For *The Sweeney*, see *Screen Education* (1976) and A Clarke, 'This is not the boy scouts: television police series and definitions of law and order', in T Bennett et al (eds) *Popular Culture and Social Relations* (1981).

27. Buxton, writing at the beginning of the 1990s, argues that there was little critical analysis of series carried out both because television represented a non-legitimate object of research and because of weaknesses in the structuralist approach, op cit, p 5.

28. For the best comparative account to date, see Barr, '"They Think It's All Over"', p 21.

29. The classic story of this development is to be found in Eric Barnouw, *Tube of Plenty* (1975).

30. For comprehensive details see Steven Bryant, *The Television Heritage* (1989).

31. Peter Nichols in 'Back Bites', *Independent Magazine*, 14 August 1993, p 43.

32. Note that such accounts are not always reliable. Peter Nichols goes on to discuss how 'fuzzy grey pictures of us went out to millions of tiny sets that had been switched on to watch the Coronation and never turned off since'. Since the programme was transmitted a year *before* the event of the Coronation (1953) this is a typical example of the way in which memoirist accounts can be inaccurate.

33. Charles Barr discusses the *Panorama* programme and compares the clock with that used in *Marty* (1953) op cit.

34. John Ellis, *Visible Fiction* (1982) p 146.

35. For the definitive account, see Paddy Scannell's chapter, '"The Stuff of Radio": Developments in Radio Features and Documentaries before the War', in John Corner (ed.) *Documentary and the Mass Media* (1986).

36. John Caughie, 'Progressive Television and Documentry Drama', in *Screen* (1980) p 23.

37. Hayden White, 'The Modernist Event', in Vivian Sobchack (ed.) *The Persistence of History* (1996) p 16.

38. Arthur Swinson, *Writing for Television* (1955) p 78.

39. John Ellis, *Seeing Things: Television in the Age of Uncertainty* (2000) p 9.

40. ibid, p 13.

41. ibid, p 25.
42. John Caughie, 'Progressive Television and Documentary Drama', pp 9–35.
43. Peter Black, *The Mirror in the Corner – People's Television*, (1972) p 19.
44. Caughie, op cit, pp 9–35.
45. John Corner and Sylvia Harvey (eds) *Television Times: A Reader*, op cit.
46. Douglas Couzens Hoy, *Foucault: A Critical Reader* (1986) p 7.
47. Michel Foucault, *The Archaeology of Knowledge* (1972) p 22.
48. 'Before the Golden Age: Early Television Drama', in John Corner (ed.) *Popular Television in Britain* (1991) p 25.
49. Programme Board Minutes, 9 May 1930, cited in Asa Briggs, *The History of Broadcasting in the UK*, Vol. 2: 'The Golden Age of Wireless' (1965) p 259.
50. *Public Opinion Quarterly*, Spring 1950, p 148.
51. Quoted in Briggs, op cit, p 259.
52. ibid, p 267.
53. *BBC Handbook* (1955) p 41.
54. ibid.
55. An Audience Research Report carried out on *Dixon of Dock Green*, Episode 6, 'London Pride'. The Reaction Index is based on questionnaires completed by a sample of the audience. As stated, the sample audience represents 35% of the TV Viewing Panel. The final figure is arrived at from the numbers of individual scores distributed between five categories A+, A, B, C and C-. BBC Written Archive T/12/75/1.
56. Jason Jacobs, *The Intimate Screen*, p 99.
57. Fred Cook, 'Now PC Dixon hasn't got his man'. The information comes from the BBC Information Department, in the form of an uncredited press cutting. T12/75/1.
58. Robert Reiner, 'Policing a Postmodern Society', *Modern Law Review* (1992) p 763.
59. ibid, p 762.
60. Jacobs, *The Intimate Screen*, p 159.
61. John Caughie, 'Before the Golden Age', in John Corner (ed.) *Popular Television in Britain* (1991) p 40.

Chapter One: Telling stories of the realm

1. Sir Stephen Tallents, then First Press Officer of the BBC (1938) in a talk to the Institute of Journalists, October, 1937. Cited in Asa Briggs, *The History of Broadcasting in the UK*, Vol. 3: 'The Sounds of War' (1970) p 160.
2. See John Cain, 'Television Arrives', in *The BBC: 70 Years of Broadcasting*, London, BBC Publications (1992) p 31.
3. It was closed because its elevated position at Alexandra Palace, together with its tall mast, made it a security risk.
4. For a full account, see DL LeMahieu, *A Culture for Democracy, Mass Communication and the Cultivated Mind in Britain Between the Wars*, Oxford, Clarendon Press (1988).
5. For an excellent account of this process, see Lawrence Napper in Justine Ashby and Andrew Higson (eds) *British Cinema Past and Present*, (2000) pp 110–124.
6. See Jeffrey Richards, *Films and British National Identity: From Dickens to Dad's Army* (1997) pp 31–59.
7. Basil Maine, 'Is America Killing Our Sense of Humour?', *Radio Times*, 3 July 1931, p 3. Cited in DL LeMahieu, *A Culture for Democracy* (1988) p 189.

8. The BBC was soon considered a National Institution, like the Bank of England. During the Second World War, it doubled in size, and emerged with an even greater standing.

9. Arnold felt that the best palliative for nineteenth-century discontent was culture, hence the title of his book *Culture and Anarchy* (first published in 1932).

10. The Agreement between the Newspaper Proprietors' Association and the Newspaper Society (March 1938) confirmed the BBC's policy of broadcasting news bulletins between 6pm and 2am. Cited in Asa Briggs, *The History of Broadcasting*, Vol. 3: 'The Sands of War', p 160.

11. In 1936, Stephen Tallents became the first ever Public Relations Officer at the BBC and instituted BBC Audience Research.

12. John Reith, *Into the Wind* (1949) p 103.

13. John Reith, *Broadcast Over Britain* (1924) p 34.

14. Andrew Crisell, *An Introductory History of British Broadcasting* (1997) p 29.

15. Consult index of Paddy Cardiff and David Scannell, *A Social History of Broadcasting* (1991).

16. Jurgens Habermas, *The Structural Transformation of the Public Sphere* (1989).

17. Walter Lippmann, *Public Opinion*, New York and London, Allen and Unwin (1922) pp 78–9.

18. The Listener Research Section was set up under Robert Silvey, who introduced a system of random sampling, described in this book's Introduction.

19. Just as in television later, early radio was characterised in terms of its 'relay' potential, perceived as a 'witness' to events, rather than a self-originating source of fiction.

20. Briggs, 'The Birth of Broadcasting' (1961) pp 280–3.

21. Quoted in Lance Sieveking, *The Stuff of Radio* (1934) pp 383–4.

22. Paddy Scannell, 'The Stuff of Radio', in John Corner (ed.) *Documentary and the Mass Media* (1986) p 31.

23. Colin Chambers, *The Story of Unity Theatre* (1989) p 25.

24. Such debates go back to Bertolt Brecht who originally argued against theatrical illusionism because it lulled the audience into a false sense of security which he felt should be interrupted by different devices, including the use of montage, placards and chants.

25. Reith, *Into the Wind* (1949) p 136.

26. In order to breach the gap in the House, Reith issued the notorious syllogism: 'Since the BBC was a national institution, and since the Government in this crisis were acting for the people, the BBC was for the Government in this crisis too'. The statement has gone down in the annals of broadcasting history as a display of the finest brinkmanship. Cited in Briggs, 'The Birth of Broadcasting', p 158.

27. Cited in Briggs, 'The Birth of Broadcasting', pp 68–71.

28. In *Formations of Pleasure* (1983) p 115.

29. Andrew Crissell, *Introduction to the History of Broadcasting* (1997) p 25.

30. Peter M Lewis, 'Referable Words in Radio Drama', in Paddy Scannell (ed.) *Broadcast Talk* (1991) p 14.

31. Paddy Scannell, 'The Stuff of Radio', in Corner (ed.) *Documentary and the Mass Media* (1986) p 8.

32. *Harry Hopeful* was to go on to become *Billy Welcome* during the Second World War.

33. Cited in Scannell, 'The Stuff of Radio', p 17.

34. ibid, p 21.

35. It was famously put on just after Eisenstein's *Battleship Potemkin* at the Film Society (1929).

36. Paul Rotha, *Documentary Diary: An Informal History of the British Documentary Film, 1928–1939* (1973) p 30.

37. John Caughie, 'Progressive Television and Documentary Drama', *Screen* 21/3 (1980) pp 26–27.

38. ibid.

39. When challenged on this point, Grierson replied that he had really wished to say that it was 'the labour of men that was being boxed and barrelled'. Cited in Brian Winston, *Claiming the Real: The Documentary Film Revisited* (1994) p 37.

40. John Mackenzie, *Propaganda and Empire: The manipulation of British public opinion, 1889–1960* (1984) p 10.

41. Sir James Parr in an address to the Empire Film Institute, cited in Paul Swann, *The British Documentary Film Movement, 1926–1946* (1989) p 125.

42. Peter Stead, 'The people and the pictures' in Nicholas Pronay and DW Spring (eds) *Propaganda, Politics and Film 1918–45* (1982) p 92.

43. See Patrick Wright, *On Living in an Old Country: The National Past in Contemporary Britain* (1985) p 2.

44. Jeffrey Richards, *The Age of the Dream Palace: Cinema and Society in Britain, 1930–1939* (1984) p 248.

45. ibid, p 136.

46. Cited in Jeffrey Richards, *Films and British National Identity: From Dickens to Dad's Army* (1997) p 35.

47. The name given to the GPO film unit after it was taken over by the MOI in 1940.

48. According to Charles Barr, who cites the example of *The Good Companions* (1933) which noticeably brought together Priestley, Balcon and Dalrymple, this process of collaboration therefore began earlier than has previously been acknowledged. See Charles Barr, 'Desperate Yearnings: Victor Saville and Gainsborough' in P Cook (ed.) *Gainsborough Pictures* (1997) pp 47–59.

49. Charles Barr, *Ealing Studios* (1977) p 6.

50. ibid.

51. See Ian Aitken, *Film and Reform: John Grierson and the Documentary Film Movement* (1990) p 127.

52. Cited in Swann, *The British Documentary Film Movement, 1926–1946* (1989) p 56.

53. Public relations policies emerged in 1906, when the Pennsylvanian Railroad Company hired a public relations consultant named Ivy Lee to represent them over a serious railway accident: by subtle manipulation of the press and public opinion the criticism was successfully defused. Cited in Ian Aitken, *Film and Reform*, pp 151–2.

54. Philip M Taylor, 'British official attitudes towards propaganda abroad, 1928–1939', in Nicholas Pronay and DW Spring (1982) p 38.

55. Unlike the BBC, whose access extended to millions by the end of the 1930s, documentary films during the 1920s to mid-1930s suffered from a lack of public audience. The EMB Library (1931) loaned out 517,000 film copies during its first year, but this method of distribution was cumbersome.

56. Swann, *The British Documentary Film Movement, 1926–1946*, p 157.

57. Paul Rotha, *Documentary Diary* (1976) pp 220–1.

58. Cited in Forsyth Hardy, *John Grierson, a Documentary Biography* (1979) p 80.

59. For an interesting discussion of *Night Mail* and the story-documentary generally, see Andrew Higson, *Waving the Flag: Constructing a National Cinema in Britain* (1995) pp 203–212.

60. Elizabeth Sussex, *The Rise and Fall of British Documentary* (1974) p 76.
61. Ian Aitken, *Film and Reform: John Grierson and the Documentary Film Movement*, p 65.
62. ibid.
63. John Beveridge, *John Grierson: Film Master* (1978) p 29.
64. For an understanding of containment strategy see Frederic Jameson, 'Reification and Utopia in Mass Culture', *Social Text*, 1/1 (1979).
65. Antonia Lant, *Blackout: Reinventing Women for Wartime British Cinema* (1991) p 44.
66. Antonia Lant, p 44.
67. See Antony Aldgate and Jeffrey Richards, *Britain Can Take It: The British cinema in the Second World War* (1994) p 23.
68. Cited in Sussex, op cit, pp 140–1.
69. Entitled 'International Propaganda and Broadcasting Enquiry'. See Philip Taylor, *Historical Journal of Film and Television History*, 1/1 (1981).
70. Cited in DW Ellwood, 'Showing the world what is owed to Britain: Foreign policy and cultural propaganda, 1935–45', in Pronay and Spring (eds) p 63.
71. The news became compulsory listening after the 'real' war opened up, with the German invasion of Holland and Belgium. During the phoney war, there was widespread criticism of the tedious aspect of broadcasting generally. Clement Attlee told the House of Commons on 26 September, 'I am not a habitual listener but I must say that at times I am depressed when I listen in'. Cited in Asa Briggs, *The BBC: The First Fifty Years* (1985) p 179.
72. It is general knowledge that 'Lord Haw-Haw' was a name invented for the anonymous broadcaster, William Joyce, by the *Daily Express*. See Briggs, *The BBC: The First Fifty Years*, p 190.
73. Paddy Scannell, 'The Stuff of Radio', p 25.
74. This is a gloss on LeMahieu's excellent account in *A Culture for Democracy* (1988) pp 317–333.
75. Briggs, 'The Sands of War', p 212.
76. Crissell provides a clear synopsis of these developments. Andrew Crissell, *An Introductory History of British Broadcasting*, pp 47–54.
77. Cardiff and Scannell, cited in Bennett et al (eds) *Popular Culture and Social Relations*, p 99.
78. Cited in Briggs, 'The Sands of War', p 133.
79. Steve Neale and Frank Krutnik, *Popular Film and Television Comedy* (1990) p 221.
80. Asa Briggs, 'The Sands of War', p 109.
81. David Cardiff and Paddy Scannell, *The Historical Development of Popular Culture in Britain, Radio in World War II* (1981) pp 31–79.
82. For a more detailed discussion of these radio cross-overs, see Aldgate and Richards, *Britain Can Take It*, p 91.
83. James Chapman, *The British at War: Cinema, State and Propaganda, 1939–1945* (2000) p 179.
84. John Grierson, *Eyes of Democracy* (1990) p 83.
85. See Michael Paris, *From the Wright Brothers to Top Gun* (1995) pp 127–173.
86. Aldgate and Richards, *Britain Can Take It*, p 328.
87. The MOI saw a doubtful use of propaganda in a film that celebrated a lost battle and featured a shipwreck.
88. *Daily Express*, 24 September 1941.

89. This story famously caused a Middle Eastern nation, Saudi Arabia, to break off diplomatic relations with Britain.

90. Quoted in *Halliwell's Film Guide*, 1992, p 561.

91. See Geoffrey MacNab, *Arthur Rank and the British Film Industry* (1993) p 123.

92. Clive Coultass, 'British Cinema and the Reality of War', in Philip M Taylor (ed.) *Britain and the Cinema in the Second World War* (1988) p 84.

93. Charles Barr, *Ealing Studios*, pp 4, 5, 13, 27.

94. Jeffrey Richards, *Films and British National Identity: From Dickens to Dad's Army*, p 106.

95. George Orwell, *Collected Essays, Journalism and Letters 2*, Harmondsworth, 1971, p 88.

96. See Wendy Webster's perceptive account in *Imagining Home: Gender 'Race' and National Identity, 1945–1964* (1998) p 1.

97. Andy Medhurst, 'Music Hall and British Cinema' in Charles Barr (ed.) *All Our Yesterdays*, p 179.

98. Robert Murphy, *Realism and Tinsel*, p 176.

99. John Hill, *Sex, Class and Realism: British Cinema, 1956–1963* (1986) pp 67–127.

100. ibid.

101. Andy Medhurst, in the Barr (ed.) *All our Yesterdays*, p 184.

102. Jeffrey Richards and Tony Aldgate, *Best of British* (1999) p 127.

103. The authors refer to Scott's autobiography, in which the Commissioner emphasises the film's propoganda value. Sir Harold Scott, *Scotland Yard* (1954) pp 90–1.

104. ibid, p 130.

105. Aldgate and Richards usefully detail how the shooting of Dixon will have recalled the shooting in Southgate in 1946 of PC Nathaniel Edgar, who was the first policeman to be shot in many years. ibid.

106. Charles Barr, *Ealing Studios*, p 85.

107. As opposed to the detective genre established by film.

108. Tony Aldgate and Jeffrey Richards, *Best of British*, p 138.

Chapter Two: New forms for old

1. Cited in *From the Palace to the Grove* (1992) p 71.

2. Duncan Ross, 'The Documentary in Television', *BBC Quarterly*, 5/1 (1950) pp 22–23.

3. Caryl Doncaster, 'The Story Documentary', from Paul Rotha (ed.) *Television in the Making* (1956) p 36.

4. Doncaster's statement relates to the empire-building tactics of Talks, previously referred to.

5. Michael Barry, 'Problems of a Producer', *BBC Quarterly*, 3/3, Autumn, 1951, p 167.

6. See George McKnight (ed.) *Agent of Challenge and Defiance: The Films of Ken Loach* (1998).

7. Briggs gives a detailed account of the structure of the BBC at this time in 'Sound and Vision' pp 454–5.

8. See Roger Sales, 'An Introduction to Broadcasting History', in D Punter (ed.) *Introduction to Contemporary Cultural Studies* (1986) pp 54–6.

9. Grace Wyndham Goldie of Talks aptly compares this move to 'appointing two generals

to crush a rebellion, only to find they promptly joined the rebels'. Cited in Bell, 'The Origins of British Television Documentary: The BBC 1946–1955', in Corner (ed.) *Documentary and the Mass Media*, p 69.

10. Collins left BBC television in 1950 and joined ITV. See Briggs, 'Sound and Vision', p 455.

11. Elaine Bell, 'The Origins of British Television Documentary', in Corner (ed.) *Documentary and the Mass Media*, p 77.

12. The Forces programme remained, transformed into the new Light Programme after the war had ended.

13. John Caughie, 'Broadcasting and Cinema, 1: Converging histories', in Barr (ed.) *All Our Yesterdays*, p 71.

14. Paddy Scannell, 'The Social Eye of Television 1946–55', in *Media Culture and Society* (1979) p 97.

15. ibid.

16. Duncan Ross, 'The Documentary in Television', *BBC Quarterly*, 5/1, (1950) pp 19–29.

17. Grierson's statement is cited in 'Documentary on Unesco', *Radio Times*, 2 April 1948, p 25. Grierson and Robert Barr collaborated on the television documentary film *Unesco* (1948) introduced by JB Priestley.

18. Although Grierson's appointment was sought by the BBC, he refused it, not wanting a full-time commitment.

19. Cited in Jan Bussell, *The Art of Television* (1952) p 136.

20. Steve McCormack, from interview with Elaine Bell (July, 1979). Cited in Bell, 'The Origins of British Television Documentary', in Corner (ed.), *Documentary and the Mass Media*, p 73.

21. See *Radio Times*, 2 January 1948.

22. Entry in *Radio Times*, Friday 23 April 1948. See Appendix 2a.

23. Asa Briggs, *The History of Broadcasting in the UK*, Vol. 4: 'Sound and Vision', p 282.

24. In Michael Barry, *From the Palace to the Grove* (1992) p 97.

25. Duncan Ross, 'The Documentary in Television', *BBC Quarterly*, 5/1 (1950) Spring.

26. Memo from Duncan Ross to Robert Barr and Ian Atkins, 4 February 1953, BBC WA T4/75/Z.

27. ibid.

28. ibid.

29. The programmes, in order, are 'Juvenile Court' (Monday 27 November), 'Probation Officer' (Tuesday 22 December) and 'Who's to Blame?' (Monday 22 January); I have been unable to locate the fourth the fifth was 'The Assizes' (Tuesday 21 July 1953). The time-slot varied from 9.10pm ('Juvenile Court') to 8.30pm ('The Assizes').

30. *Radio Times*, 15 December 1950.

31. Quoted in Arthur Swinson, *Writing for Television* (1955) pp 81–2.

32. Duncan Ross to C. Tel P., 'Letter from National Association of Probation Officers', dated 19 December 1950. BBC WA T4/75/1.

33. 'Critic on the Hearth', in the *Listener*, 29 March 1951.

34. Ian Atkins, 'The Course of Justice' in *Radio Times*, 26 November–2 December 1950.

35. Caryl Doncaster, 'The Story Documentary', in Paul Rotha (ed.) *Television in the Making*, p 36.

36. Letter to the author from Robert Barr, dated 20 September 1993.

37. Letter from Robert Barr, op cit.

38. Jason Jacobs, *The Intimate Screen: Early British Television Drama*, p 100.

39. Scotland Yard file memo, dated 20 October 1954. BBC WA T16/577.

40. *War on Crime*: 'Gold Thieves', 'Woman Unknown', 'Death Rings the Doorbell', 'Gunman', 'Burn the Evidence', 'Interpol'. For dates of transmission, see Appendix.

41. *Radio Times*, 14 April 1950.

42. Duncan Ross, 'The Documentary in Television', *BBC Quarterly*, 5/1, pp 450–151.

43. ibid.

44. ibid.

45. *War on Crime*. BBC WA T4/75/1.

46. ibid.

47. Memo from Cecil McGivern to Robert Barr, dated 7 March 1950. BBC WA T4/75/1.

48. ibid.

49. *Daily Mail*, 7 March 1950.

50. 'Woman Unknown' script BBC WA T4/75/1.

51. ibid.

52. *War on Crime* Press Notices on file. No. 2: 'Woman Unknown'. BBC WA T4/75/1.

53. Memo from H. Tel. P. (McGivern) dated 20 April 1950, to Robert Barr.

54. Memo from McGivern to Barr, 20 April 1950. BBC WA T4/75/Z.

55. ibid.

56. Memo from Barr to McGivern, 24 April 1950. BBC WA T4/75/2.

57. ibid.

58. ibid.

59. Letter from New Scotland Yard (R Jackson), 12 May 1950. BBC WA.

60. ibid.

61. Undated, cited in internal correspondence. BBC WA T4/75/2.

62. Memo from Leonard Brett, 'Short Report on Weekly Documentary Scheme as Worked with Producer and 2 Directors in "I Made News" series'. BBC WA T/4/24.

63. Robert Barr's own Report on *I Made News*. BBC WA T/4/24.

64. Cited in memo from Robert Barr to Cecil Madden (Programme Organiser) dated 17 December 1951. BBC WA T4/24.

65. Cited in *I Made News* Audience Report, 18 December 1951. BBC WA T4/24.

66. Letter to the author from Robert Barr, dated 19 October 1993.

67. 'Critic on the Hearth', in the *Listener*, 29 March 1951, p 990.

68. ibid.

69. Letter from Robert Barr to the author, 29 September 1993.

70. Colin Francis King, in a recorded interview with Robert Barr. Cited in *The Influence of Documentary Methods upon BBC Television Drama*, University of Hull, 1975, p 250.

71. ibid.

72. See Appendix 2a for details of transmission.

73. See the end of Chapter 1 for a discussion of *The Blue Lamp*.

74. *Radio Times*, 30 May 1952, p 41.

75. ibid.

76. Memo from Cecil McGivern, Controller, Television Programmes, 18 February 1952. BBC WA T32/274/l.

77. First Draft Script 'Police Station', or *Pilgrim Street* as the series came to be called. BBC WA T32/2741.

78. *Evening Standard*, 5 February 1952.

79. Memo from Robert Barr to Cecil Madden, 15 May 1952. BBC WA T32/2741.

80. First Draft script 'Police Station' (*Pilgrim Street*). BBC WA T32/274.

81. ibid.
82. ibid.
83. A Viewer Research Report on 'On Our Manor', para 3. T32/272.
84. Norman Swallow, 'Paul Rotha and Television', in *Paul Rotha*, BFI Dossier 16 (1962) pp 34–35.
85. ibid.
86. ibid, p 88.
87. Bell, in Corner (ed.) p 80.
88. For *Special Enquiry* see John Corner, 'Documentary Voices', in John Caughie (ed.) *Popular Television in Britain*, p 42.
89. Letter from Robert Barr to the author, 29 September 1993.

Chapter Three: Entertaining Lightly

1. Programme note to the BBC *Crimewriters* series (1978).
2. John Hill defines the Social Problem Film in, *Sex, Class and Realism: British Cinema, 1956–1963* (1986).
3. It is no accident that the *Pilgrim Street* series, as discussed in the previous chapter, was written by Jan Read, inventor of the 'Dixon' character, or that its working-title was *The Blue Lamp*.
4. Krishnan Kumar, 'Holding the middle ground: the BBC, the public and the professional broadcaster', in James Curran, Michael Gurevitch and Janet Woollacott (eds) *Mass Communication and Society* (1977) p 241.
5. Grace Wyndham Goldie, *Facing the Nation* (1977) p 11.
6. John Caughie, 'Before the Golden Age', in John Corner (ed.) *Popular Television in Britain*, (1990) p 40.
7. Asa Briggs, *The History of Broadcasting in the United Kingdom*, Vol. 4: 'Sound and Vision', OUP, p 458.
8. Tim O'Sullivan states that radio and television broadcasts of the Coronation on 13 June 1953 produced the largest domestic audience of viewers and listeners recorded to that date. BBC research suggested that 88 per cent of the adult population of the United Kingdom saw or listened to some part of the service. The TV audience was estimated at 41 per cent of the broadcast audience, as against 37 per cent listening to radio (said to have numbered nearly 20 million viewers). See 'Television Memories and Cultures of Viewing, 1950–65', in John Corner (ed.) *Popular Television in Britain*, p 79.
9. Quoted in TF Lindsay and Michael Harrington, *The Conservative Party: 1918–1970*, London, Macmillan (1974) p 202, cited in John Hill, *Sex, Class and Realism*, p 5.
10. The Report was some 18 pages long, only three of which were dedicated to television. For a concise account of the implications of the Beveridge Report see Andrew Crisell, *An Introductory History of British Broadcasting* (1997) p 76.
11. Reith, reporting to the Committee, likened ITV's arrival to 'Smallpox, Bubonic Plague and the Black Death'. House of Lord Debates, 176: 1297, 22 May 1952, cited in John Corner (ed.) *Popular Television in Britain*, p 5.
12. Curran and Seaton argue that Beveridge was to have 2 marked effects on the commercial broadcasting it disfavoured: a) ITV would carry 'spot' commercials, not

sponsorship; b) its disapproval of the BBC's metropolitanism inspired ITV's regional structure. Cited in Crisell, ibid, p 77.

13. A more pluralist era was not to come into force until the Annan Committee (1977) made possible the arrival of Channel 4 with its use of independent producers.

14. Unfortunately, I have been unable to find out the exact circumstances of this 'occurrence', nonetheless it is illustrative of contemporary attitudes.

15. Peter Black, *The Mirror in the Corner* (1972) p 25.

16. ibid, p 24.

17. 'Light Entertainment Policy'. Memo dated 6 April 1951 from R Waldman. T16/91/1.

18. ibid.

19. According to Briggs, by 1956, this was the only BBC programme challenging top ITV ratings. 'The Competitor', p 521.

20. Peter Black, *The Mirror in the Corner* p 24.

21. R Waldman, 'The Variety of Television Variety', in the *Radio Times Annual* (1954) pp 56–7.

22. As in the case of Bernard Braden who was prevented from returning to television in a new series written for him by Frank Muir and Dennis Norden. Cited in Peter Black, *The Biggest Aspidistra in the World* (1972) p 161.

23. Peter Goddard, '"Hancock's Half-Hour", A Watershed in British Television Comedy', in Corner (ed.) *Popular Television in Britain*, p 76.

24. Black, *The Biggest Aspidistra in the World*, p 163.

25. Arthur Swinson, *Writing for Television Today* (1963) p 230.

26. Steve Neale and Frank Krutnik, *Popular Film and Television Comedy* (1990) p 248.

27. Cited in Briggs, 'Sound and Vision', p 718.

28. The 'soap' in 'soap opera' derives from the sponsorship of daytime serials by manufacturers of household cleaning products: Procter and Gamble, Colgate-Palmolive and Lever Brothers. Robert C Allen, *Speaking of Soap Opera* (1985) p 8.

29. Note its similarity to *Coronation Street* (1960), which was first produced by a local ITV programme before being networked by Granada Television.

30. Cited in Asa Briggs, *The BBC: The First Fifty Years* (1985) p 100.

31. The Listener Research Report for the first episode, 'The Case of the Drunken Sailor' (27 October, 9.30–10.00pm), states that, although many viewers found the play entertaining, a minority did not care for it, some complaining that it was ridiculous and far-fetched, others that the plot was stereotyped, or 'thin'. A few disliked the characterisation of the hero, who, they felt, was too 'public-school' to be a typical PC. BBC WA R19/16/5.

32. Despite its popularity, Vernon Harris, *PC 49*'s producer had to fight to place the programme.

33. The Shakespeare play cited is, of course, *As You Like It*.

34. '"Up the Pole" in a Police Station', *Radio Times*, 14 October 1949, p 9.

35. Raymond Williams, *Marxism and Literature* (1977) p 121.

36. This was a post-war innovation. Previously, there was no suggestion that each of the three networks should be devoted to a single type of output but rather that each should compete in offering a 'mix' at a distinctive, targeted level. Audiences would constantly find themselves 'stretched'. Cited in John Cain, *The BBC: 70 Years of Broadcasting*, p 60.

37. Briggs, 'Sound and Vision', p 58.

38. See Robert Allen, *Speaking of Soap Opera* (1985).

39. Stephenson to R McCall, Asst. Controller (S), 17 March 1948. Cited in Briggs, 'Sound and Vision', p 693.

40. Cited in Tom Burns, *The BBC: Public Institution and Private World* (1977) p 54.

41. Letters to Robert Barr, dated 17 February 1950 and 26 July 1950, from Howard Thomas, Producer-in-Chief, Associated British Pathe Ltd. Both letters are headed US Television. Correspondence held at the Robert Barr Archive, Exeter University.

42. *I'm the Law* transmitted 8.55–9.25pm from Saturday 19 July 1954 for 24 episodes.

43. First episode, 'The Extra Bullet', transmitted 8.45pm on 13 November 1954.

44. As is by now well-known, the so-called Toddlers' Truce was that period when television was taken off the air between 6.00pm and 7.00pm to enable the children to be put to bed. The practice was ended in 1956, significantly, one year after the arrival of ITV.

45. Letter to the author from Robert Barr, dated 10 September 1994.

46. Letter to the author from Jan Read, dated 31 July 1994.

47. This occurred when a motorcyclist, father of six, was gunned down whilst trying to stop a getaway after a bungled jewel robbery in Charlotte Street, London, in 1947. Cited in Tony Aldgate and Jeffrey Richards, *Best of British*, p 130. Robert Barr, in the letter cited above told me that at this trial, 'Bob was in the dock in charge of one of the accused. When they were asked to stand up to be sentenced Bob's "charge" said "Stand well back mate, or that old bugger will top you as well"'.

48. Details on file state that the radio series title for the six programmes was to be changed to 'Fabian of the Yard'. Memo from JA Camacho to Head of Planning, Light Programme, '"Out of the Blue" – "Fabian of the Yard"', dated 21 April 1959. BBC WA R/1647/1.

49. Conan Doyle, 'A Case of Identity', pp 190–1, cited in Derek Longhurst (ed.) *Gender, Genre and Narrative Pleasure* (1989) p 54.

50. Robert Murphy, *Realism and Tinsel*, p 163.

51. It was ITV which introduced newscasters in vision.

52. In fact, as is observable from details taken from the 'psb' details on *Dixon of Dock Green*, the first production to begin at 6.30pm was not until 2 January 1960.

53. Eric Paice went on to write *The Brothers*. (See British Film Institute archive for Paice scripts, for both *Dixon of Dock Green* and *The Brothers*.)

54. Geoff Tibballs, *Watching the Detectives*, p 127.

55. Audience Research 1 – 'PC Crawford's First Pinch'. BBC WA T12/75/1.

56. ibid.

57. Audience Research 6 – 'London Pride'. BBC WA T12/75/1.

58. Memo from Head of Planning. BBC WA T12/751.

59. Letter to Major-General L de M Thuillier, NSPCC, dated 11 April 1961. BBC WA T12/75.

60. BBC WA T12/75/1.

61. Memo entitled '*Dixon of Dock Green*, Saturday, September 7', dated 12 September 1957. T12/75/1.

62. Cited in Martin McLoone, in 'Boxed In?: The Aesthetics of Film and Television', in John Hill and Martin McLoone (eds) *Big Picture, Small Screen: The Relations between Film and Television*, p 90.

63. Richard Hoggart, 'The "real" world of people: illustrations from popular art – "Peg's Paper" 1957', in David Lodge, *20th Century Literary Criticism* (1972) p 489.

64. Charles Barr, *Ealing Studios*, p 180.

65. See Tony Aldgate and Jeffrey Richards for a good discussion on *The Long Arm* and *Gideon's Day* in *Best of British*, p 136.

66. In *Gideon's Day*, Hawkins' Gideon is the definitive Scotland Yard officer who, according to Richards, unmasks a corrupt sergeant for 'taking bribes from drug-pushers, saves his informer from a razor gang, hunts down an escaped mental patient who rapes and murders an 18 year old girl, breaks up a payroll robbery gang and finally deals with a gang of aristocratic amateurs who rob a safety deposit'. Jeffrey Richards, 'The Thin Blue Line', Best of British pp 138–9.

67. Martin McLoone, 'Boxed In?: The Aesthetics of Film and Television', in John Hill and Martin McLoone (eds) *Big Picture, Small Screen: The Relations between Film and Television*, University of Luton Press (1997) pp 83–84.

Chapter Four: Jacks, Knaves and the 'other' North

1. Jeffrey Richards, *Films and British National Identity: From Dickens to Dad's Army*, p 25.
2. 'Swinging a Very Pretty Pick', *Sunday Times*, 26 November 1961.
3. Richards, op cit, p 353.
4. ibid, p 276.
5. JB Priestley, *English Journey*, 1934. Cited in Terry Lovell, 'Landscapes and Stories in 1960s British Realism', *Screen* (1990) p 159.
6. Quoted in TF Lindsay and Michael Harrington, *The Conservative Party: 1918–1970* (1974) p 202.
7. Theodor W Adorno and Max Horkheimer, 'The industrial production of cultural commodities', in *The Dialectic of Enlightenment* (1972).
8. Richard Hoggart, *The Uses of Literacy* p 246.
9. ibid, p 189.
10. Georg Lukacs, 'Art and Objective Truth', in *Writer and Critic and Other Essays*, ed. and trans. Arthur Kahn, London, Merlin Press (1970) pp 34–43.
11. David Buxton, *From the Avengers to Miami Vice*, pp 2–3.
12. Christine Geraghty differentiates between the series and the soap. In the latter, 'Time rather than action becomes the basis for organising the narrative; the real time that reflects viewers' experience of it in their own lives.' Christine Geraghty, *Women and Soap Opera* (1991) p 12.
13. WJ Weatherby, 'Camino Real', *Contrast* (1961–1962).
14. The 'Angry Young Man' label itself was more a term of of convenience employed by the press than a term used by the writers themselves. It wasn't a 'school' in any organised sense.
15. David Storey, 'Journey Through a Tunnel', the *Listener*, 1 August 1963, pp 159–161, quoted in Kathryn and Philip Dodds, 'Engendering the Nation', in Andrew Higson (ed.) *Dissolving Views*, (1996) p 49.
16. John Hill, *Sex, Class and Realism: British Cinema, 1956–1963*, p 25.
17. Richards goes on to cite Frank Ormerod, who, 'writing in 1915, identified its characteristics as natural independence, candour, a sense of humour and a democratic spirit.' *Films and British National Identity: From Dickens to Dad's Army*, p 255.
18. ibid, p 254.
19. Information from a note by Barr, dated 1958, held at the Robert Barr Archive, Exeter University.

20. Colin Morris interview with Colin King, transcribed in Colin Francis King, *The Influence of Documentary Methods upon BBC Television Drama*, PhD Thesis, p 258.

21. During the 1960s, Colin Morris produced the play *With Love and Tears*, which looked at the impact of the birth of a mongol (Down's Syndrome) child on a family. The production had first been inspired by Brian Rix's experience as the father of a Down's Syndrome child.

22. Interestingly, the plot hinges on three confidence tricksters' scam of luring victims to a hotel by a poster advertising a self-confidence course. See John R Cook, *Dennis Potter, A Life on Screen* (1998) p 24.

23. *New Statesman*, 25 August 1956, p 214, cited in Stuart Laing, *Representations of Working-Class Life, 1957–1964*, p 160.

24. ibid.

25. 'Jacks and Knaves', *Radio Times*, Thursday 9 November, p 47.

26. JB Priestley, *English Journey*, p 253, cited in Jeffrey Richards, *Films and British National Identity*, p 256.

27. 'Reel to real life: Colin Morris', obituary in the *Guardian*, 21 May 1996. Colin Morris, playwright and documentary-filmmaker, born 4 February 1916; died 31 May 1996.

28. 'Tearaway' script, TX 1950.

29. Stuart Laing, *Representations of Working-Class Life: 1957–1964*, p 160.

30. Richards, *Films and British National Identity*, p 254.

31. Television script: *Tearaway* by Colin Morris, TX 1950.

32. 'Who Me?', T5/2428.

33. BBC WA T5/2428.

34. Letter from Chief Constable's Office, Cornwall County Constabulary, Bodmin, dated 17 October 1959, BBC WA T5/2428.

35. 'Who Me?', Audience Research Department, 23 October 1959. BBC WA T2/122.

36. *Radio Times*, 9 November 1961.

37. Memo to Assistant Head of Copyright, 26 August 1960, from Edward Caffery, T5/2121/5.

38. *Radio Times*, 9 November 1969.

39. Advance publicity Weeks 46–49, BBC WA T5/2121/5.

40. Continuity Notes T5/2124/1.

41. Audience Research Report, 4 December 1961, *Jacks and Knaves*: 'The Master Mind', BBC WA T5/2122.

42. Letter to the Hon. Nicholas Ridley, MP, dated 2 May 1962, BBC WA T5/2/2121/5.

43. Correspondence BBC WA T5/2121/1.

44. Colin Francis King, interview with Gilchrist Calder, December 1973. Transcribed in *The Influence of Documentary Methods upon BBC Television Drama*, PhD Thesis, Appendix 48.

45. 'Interview with the Commissioner', September 1959. Present were the Commissioner of the Metropolitan Police, Sir Joseph Simpson, Robert Barr and Percy Fearnley, head of the Public Information Division, BBC WA T16/577.

46. By 1955, the Television Service had five studios at Lime Grove (taken over from Rank in 1950). *Scotland Yard*, like later *Dixon of Dock Green* episodes, was produced at Riverside Studios, Hammersmith, acquired in 1954 and brought into use in June 1956.

47. Script for No. 1 'Nightbeat', *Scotland Yard* series, transmitted 7.55pm 12 April 1960, held at the BBC Written Archive under its title.

48. ibid.

49. A six-week training course for directors was instituted in 1960, and the division of director/producer roles is often an apprenticeship relationship.

50. Don Taylor, *Days of Vision* (1990) p 23.

51. The *Scotland Yard* camera script tallies with Wilson's recollections, although Camera Rehearsal seems to have begun, at least in the case of 'Nightbeat', at 9.30am. Lunch was from 1pm to 2pm; tea, 3.45–4pm; and supper 6.25–7.25pm. The camera line-up was from 7.25 to 7.55pm.

52. Don Taylor, *Days of Vision*, (1990) p 17.

53. ibid, p 22.

54. *Daily Express*, 12 May 1960. Ironically, Percy Hoskins sometime scriptwriter at the Documentary Department, is the writer.

55. Robert Barr is 'Questioned' by police in *Television Today*, May 1960.

Chapter Five: Calling 'Z Vctr 1' and 'Z Vctr 2'

1. John McGrath, quoted in 'Why do Z-men shock the police? TV chief answers that "oafs" criticism', in the *Daily Sketch*, 1 May 1962.

2. ibid.

3. McGrath's affiliation to New Left drama is well known, as is his criticism of Naturalism. For a very useful discussion see John Tulloch, *Television Drama: Agency, Audience and Myth* (1990) pp 166–179.

4. *Times Educational Supplement*, quoted in publicity leaflet 'This is the BBC: a documentary film', 1959. Cited in Briggs, 'Competition', p 235.

5. ibid, p 272.

6. See the Pilkington Committee, *Report of the Committee on Broadcasting* (1969) Cmnd 1753.

7. Charles Barr cites the OED definition of 'candy floss' as 'a blown-up confection on a stick, characterised by sugariness without substance'. Cited in 'Broadcasting and Cinema: Screens within Screens', in Barr (ed.) *All Our Yesterdays: 90 Years of British Cinema*, pp 217–218.

8. Cited in Anthony Davis, *Television: The first forty years* (1976) p 16.

9. See Barr, *All Our Yesterdays*, p 218.

10. 'In emphasising that society shapes television they do not allow nearly enough for the medium's capacity to reveal new perspectives, for the broadcaster's consequent responsibility to realise that capacity – and in so doing, to enable a more fully informed audience to choose more freely.' Cmnd. 1753 (1962) para 164 p 54. Cited in Briggs, 'Competition', p 278.

11. M Wiggin, 'Going the Whole Hoggart', *Sunday Times*, 1 July 1962.

12. 'Notes on the Future of BBC Light Entertainment' by Eric Maschwitz, dated April 1961. BBC WA T16/91/2.

13. ibid.

14. Cited in Asa Briggs, 'Competition', p 265.

15. ibid, p 323.

16. See Andrew Crisell, 'Filth, Sedition and Blasphemy: The Rise and Fall of Television Satire', in Corner (ed.) *Popular Television in Britain*, p 145.

17. *Radio Times*, 26 February 1970.

18. *Daily Express*, 5 January 1963.

19. *The Times*, 11 October 1967. Quoted in Briggs, 'Competition', p 396.

20. Series was to be comprised of members of the old documentary department.
21. Interview between Robert Barr and Colin Francis King, cited in, *The Influence of Documentary Methods upon BBC Television*, p 246.
22. P Lewis, 'Z Cars', *Contrast*, No. 1, 1961–2, p 309.
23. Interview with Colin Francis King, op cit, p 246.
24. Briggs inaccurately refers to *Jacks and Knaves* as comprising a single episode.
25. Peter Lewis, 'Z Cars', ibid, p 309.
26. Directed by J Moxey, written by TK Martin, 13 March 1962.
27. Cited by Geoff Tibballs in the (very useful) *Boxtree Encyclopedia of TV Detectives*, p 451.
28. *Topic*, 13 January 1962.
29. 'Z Cars limelight declined: BBC to drop police', the *Guardian*, Manchester, 5 January 1962.
30. Since it was adopted by the BBC as its 'received pronunciation', the television audience was generally used to hearing the upper-class Southern English accent from which it mostly derived.
31. *Bolton Evening News*, 5 January 1962.
32. 'Z Cars will drive on to further triumphs' by John Chelsfield, TV Critic, *Liverpool Daily Post*, 17 February 1962.
33. Cited in the *Listener*, 3 May 1962, p 787.
34. 'Ideas for criminals in "Z-Cars"', *Manchester Evening News*, 23 March 1962.
35. A famous experiment conducted by Bandura et al (1961), in which children were allowed to observe an 'adult model' under several conditions, one of which involved the adult attacking a clown-doll (Bobo doll) with a hammer. Results showed that they behaved more aggressively than those who had seen a non-aggressive model, or no model at all. Cited in McQueen, *Television: A Media Student's Guide*, p 181.
36. Arthur Swinson, *Writing for Television Today*, London, Black (1963) p 129.
37. My italics, *Daily Telegraph*.
38. J McGrath, 'Better a bad night in Bootle', *Theatre Quarterly*, No. 19 (1975) pp 42–3.
39. Geoff Tibballs, p 185.
40. P Lewis, 'Z Cars', *Contrast*, Vol. 1, p 310.
41. Usually two alternating directors so as to allow for overlapping performances.
42. Generally, a producer makes a 'pilot' film and, if this is successful, obtains a contract to make 13 (a series) with an option of another 13 (second series).
43. *BBC Handbook*, 1964, p 25.
44. *BBC Handbook*, 1966, p 32.
45. Clive Emsley, *The English Bobby*, p 130.
46. 'Message ends for me, says Z-Car Girl', *Grimsby Evening Telegraph*, 16 March 1967.
47. ibid.
48. *Kinematograph Weekly*, April 12 1962.
49. Cited in 'Reaction to Z-Cars' (undated memorandum), BBC WAC T16/734 TVf Policy, Programme Correspondence.
50. Audience Research Report, *Z Cars*, No. 6 'Friday Night', BBC WA 15/22/449/1.
51. ibid.
52. Interestingly, J Arthur Rank, who instituted the Independent Frame method, reported to the secret Hankey committee report published in March 1945, that television should be delivered direct to cinema screens and that the BBC should broadcast its material to cinemas which would also contain their own television studios.

53. J McGrath, 'TV Drama: The Case Against Naturalism', *Sight and Sound*, 46/2 (Spring 1977) p 103.

54. 'Z Cars loses its Touch of Lancashire', *Liverpool Daily Post*, 5 January 1962.

55. 'Origins of Z Cars', transcript of a tape-recorded interview between Colin Francis King and Robert Barr, held at the Robert Barr Archive, Exeter University and reproduced in King's PhD Thesis.

56. *Z Cars* TX 62.01.09. BBC WA T3/244S/1.

57. ibid.

58. Robert C Allen states that a central premise of structural linguistics is that language and narrative are structured along two axes: a syntagmatic (combinatory) axis and a paradigmatic (associative) axis. *Speaking of Soap Operas*, p 69.

59. Taken from a report designated 'Information gleaned between 15 and 19 October, 1961' headed 'Lancashire County Constabulary', in BBC WA T3/2443/1 *Z Cars*.

60. Cited in S. Laing, 'Banging in Some Reality', in John Corner (ed.) *Popular Television in Britain*, p 141.

61. Memo from Acting Assistant Head of Drama, Television to CP Tel, dated 29 December 1961. BBC WA T5/710/4.

62. Troy Kennedy Martin, 'Four of a Kind?', *Crimewriters*, BBC (1978) p 125.

63. As is well known, for Brecht the point of *Verfremdung* was not simply to break the spectator's involvement and empathy in order to draw attention to the artifice of art but also to demonstrate the workings of society, both realities of which are obscured by habitual modes of perception.

64. Cited in 'Look Back in Wonder', *Encore*, No. 13, 1958.

65. Cited in George Brandt, *British Television Drama* (1981) p 143.

66. ibid.

67. Troy Kennedy Martin, 'Nats Go Home', *Encore*, No. 48 (March–April 1964) p 21.

68. ibid.

69. McGrath, 'Better a bad night in Bootle', p 43.

70. Cited in P Lewis, 'Z Cars', *Contrast*, p 315.

71. Albert Casey, 'Blood Without Thunder', *Screen Education*, No. 116 (September–October 1962) p 27.

72. Quoted in Asa Briggs, 'Competition', p 526.

73. Jones to R Jordan, BBC North-West Representative, 'Suggestion for New Crime Series', 8 October 1964, replying to a letter of 24 September 1964. T5/2506/4.

Chapter Six: *Softly, Softly,* back-pedalling South

1. 'New series takes "Z Cars" idea further', Peter Knight, *Daily Telegraph*, 6 January 1966.

2. 'Give me awful old Barlow, warts and all', Nancy Banks-Smith, *Sun*, 19 September 1969.

3. Jeffrey Richards, *Films and British National Identity*, p 157.

4. The Government controlled wavelengths and needed to decide which colour system to adopt, a complex technical problem involving international sensitivities. As a result the target date for colour coming in 1956/7 was severely delayed. It arrived in 1967 under the guidance of David Attenborough. A supplementary £5.00 licence fee for colour television was introduced.

5. Krishnan Kumar, 'Holding the middle ground: the BBC, the public and the professional broadcaster', in James Curran, Michael Gurevitch and Janet Woollacott (eds) *Mass Communication and Society*, London, Arnold (1977) p 73.
6. *Radio Times*, 22 February 1968. Cited in David Buxton, *From the Avengers to Miami Vice*, p 122.
7. ibid.
8. '*Softly, Softly*' Story Developments (undated) see file T5/1943/Z BBC WA.
9. ibid.
10. ibid.
11. ibid.
12. ibid.
13. Programme synopsis.
14. Development Document to Head of Series, Drama, marked Confidential, from Elwyn Jones, undated, T5/1943/Z.
15. *Softly, Softly*, Stratford Johns interview, undated, WAT5/1943/Z.
16. *Softly, Softly*: a series of fifty-minute programmes for television. 'The Facts'. Undated dossier, in file T5/1943/3.
17. *Softly, Softly*: a series of 50-minute programmes for television. 'The Facts'.
18. Julian Critchley, 'Long live Barlow', *Television*, 1969.
19. Audience Research Report for 'Off Beat' the first episode of the *Softly, Softly* series. T5/1943.
20. *Softly, Softly* Story Developments, undated, unsigned memo. T5/1943/Z.
21. John Tulloch and Manual Alvarado, *Doctor Who: The Unfolding Text* (1983) p x.
22. Drama Early Warning Synopsis from Leonard Lewis, 12 September 1969. T5/19433/3.
23. Memo from Leonard Lewis, Producer *Softly, Softly* to H Series D Tel, dated 13 July 1967. T5/1943/Z BBC WA.
24. Memo from Planning Manager, Peter Raleigh to HDG Tel, re 'Softly Softly' Live or Recorded? Dated 19 August 1967. T5/1943/Z.
25. Drama Early Warning Synopsis from Leonard Lewis for Week 12 September 1969. T5/19433/3.
26. Cited in Lorna Sage, 'Kojak and Co.', in *Sight and Sound*, Vol. 44, No. 3, Summer 1975, p 183.
27. Peter Lewis, *Contrast*, 1961–2, Vol. 1, p 315.
28. Cited in John Cook, *Dennis Potter, A Life on Screen*, p 3.
29. See memos from Denis Johnston to Directors, dated 2 July 1946/18 June 1946 re Producers Credits. T/16/911.
30. See John Cook's excellent account in *Dennis Potter, A Life on Screen*, MUP, (1998) p 31.
31. George McKnight, 'Ken Loach's domestic morality tales', ibid, p 84.
32. ibid, p 9.
33. John Corner states that the current sub-genres of documentary are the observational, the testimonial, the combinatory and the visually associative. These types exist within a highly signalled genre and are publicised and announced as 'documentary'. There is therefore a problem when hybrid categories are presented unannounced. See *The Art of Record* (1996).
34. James Thomas, 'Getting a bit blurred on TV … "Drama" and Real life', *Daily Express*, 8 March 1967. Cited by Julian Petley in 'Factual fiction and fictional fallacies: Ken Loach's documentary dramas' in George McKnight, p 33.

35. ibid.
36. ibid. p 29.

Conclusion: Blue Endnotes

1. Walter Benjamin (1970), p 161.
2. Roger Silverstone cites Benjamin in his argument that there is a proliferation of stories. *Why Study the Media?* (1999) p 41.
3. John Hill, 'From New Wave to "Brit-Grit", in Justine Ashby and Andrew Higson (eds), *British Cinema, Past and Present* (2000) p 250.
4. John Caughie 'Adorno's reproach: repetition, difference and television genre', in *Screen* (1991) p 151.
5. Cited in Raymond Williams, *Marxism and Literature* (1977) p 121.
6. Robert Reiner, 'Policing a Postmodern Society', *Modern Law Review*, vol. 55, No. 6 1991, p 768.
7. *Radio Times*, 1 March 1968.
8. It wasn't until an extract was shown on television that it became popular. For this and a discussion about Barry and Newman, see Jason Jacobs, *The Intimate Screen*, p 157.
9. *Blues and Twos* was a 'fly-on-the-wall' series on independent television about the emergency services of the West Midlands Police Operational Support. It followed on directly from *The Bill*, also showing on ITV, and if you switched on late, you could easily have mistaken it for the former.

APPENDIX 1

Bibliography

Addison, P, *The Road to 1945* (London: Cape, 1977)

Adorno, WT, and Horkheimer, M, *The Dialectic of Enlightenment* (New York: Herder and Herder, 1972)

Aitken, I, *Film and Reform: John Grierson and the Documentary Film Movement* (London: Routledge, 1990)

Aldgate, A, and Richards, J, *Britain Can Take It: The British Cinema in the Second World War* (London: Blackwell, 1986; Edinburgh: Edinburgh University Press Ltd, 1994)

Aldgate, A, and Richards, J, *Best of British: Cinema and Society from 1930 to the Present* (London and New York: I.B.Tauris, 1999)

Allen, RC (ed.) *Channels of Discourse Re-Assembled* (London: Routledge, 1992)

Allen, RC, *Speaking of Soap Operas* (Chapel Hill: Universityof North Carolina Press, 1985)

Alvarado, M, and Thompson, J, *The Media Reader* (London: British Film Institute, 1990)

Alvarado, M, and Thompson, J, *Doctor Who: The Unfolding Text* (London: Macmillan, 1983)

Anderson, B, *Imagined Communities* (London: Verso, 1983)

Ang, Ien, *Watching Dallas: Soap Opera and the Melodramatic Imagination* (London: Methuen, 1985)

Annan Committee, *Report of the Committee on the Future of Broadcasting* (London: HMSO, 1977)

Armes, R, *Action and Image* (Manchester: Manchester University Press, 1994)

Arnold, M, *Culture and Anarchy* (Cambridge: Cambridge University Press, 1994)

Ashby J, and A Higson (eds) *British Cinema, Past and Present* (London: Routledge, 2000)

Bailey, K, *Here's Television* (London: Vox Mundi, 1950)

Barnouw, E, *A Tower in Babel* (New York: Oxford University Press, 1966)

Barnouw, E, *The Golden Web* (New York: Oxford University Press, 1968)

Barnouw, E, *Tube of Plenty* (New York: Oxford University Press, 1975)

Barr, C (ed.) *All Our Yesterdays: 90 Years of British Cinema* (London: BFI Publishing, 1986)

Barr, C, *Ealing Studios* (London: Studio Vista, 1977)

Barry, M, *From the Palace to the Grove* (London: Royal Television Society, 1992)

Barthes, R, *Mythologies* (London: Jonathan Cape, 1972)

BBC Handbook (London: BBC Publications, 1955)

BBC Crimewriters Series (London: BFI Publishing, 1978)

Bedarida, F, *A Social History of England, 1851–1990*, 2nd ed. (London: Routledge, 1990)

Benjamin, W, *Illuminations* (London: Fontana, 1992)

Bennett, T, et al (eds) *Popular Television and Film* (London: Open University Press 1981)

Berger, J, *Ways of Seeing* (London: Harmondsworth, 1972)

Beveridge, J, *John Grierson, Film Master* (New York: Macmillan, 1978)

BFI Companion to the Western, The (London: Andre Deutsch, 1988)

Bhabha, HK, *Nation and Narration* (London and New York: Routledge, 1990)

Black, P, *The Biggest Aspidistra in the World* (London: BBC Publications, 1972)

Black, P, *The Mirror in the Corner* (London: Hutchinson, 1972)

Boddy, W, *Fifties Television* (Urbana and Chicago: University of Illinois Press, 1990)

Bogdanor, V, and Skidelsky, R (eds) *The Age of Affluence, 1951–64* (London: Macmillan, 1970)

Bordwell, D, and Thompson, K, *Film Art: An Introduction*, 4th edition (New York: McGraw Hill Inc, 1993)

Bordwell, D, Staiger, J, and Thompson, K, *The Classical Hollywood Cinema: Film Style and Mode of Production to 1960* (London: Routledge and Kegan Paul, 1985)

Brandt, G (ed.) *British Television Drama* (Cambridge: Cambridge University Press, 1981)

Brandt, G (ed.) *British Television Drama in the 1980s* (Cambridge: Cambridge University Press, 1993)

Briggs, A, *The History of Broadcasting in the UK*, vol. 1: 'The Birth of Broadcasting' (London: Oxford University Press, 1961)

Briggs, A, *The History of Broadcasting in the UK*, vol. 2: 'The Golden Age of Wireless' (London: Oxford University Press, 1965)

Briggs, A, *The History of Broadcasting in the UK*, vol. 3: 'The Sounds of War' (London: Oxford University Press, 1970)

Briggs, A, *The History of Broadcasting in the UK*, vol. 4: 'Sound and Vision' (London: Oxford University Press, 1979)

Briggs, A, *The History of Broadcasting in the UK*, vol. 5 'Competition' (London: Oxford University Press, 1995)

Briggs, A, *The BBC: The First Fifty Years* (London: Oxford University Press, 1985)

Bryant, S, *The Television Heritage* (London: British Film Institute, 1989)

Burns, T, *The BBC: Public Institution and Private World* (London: Macmillan Press, 1977)

Burton, P, *British Broadcasting: Radio and Television in the UK* (Minneapolis: University of Minnesota Press, 1956)

Bussell, J, *The Art of Televison* (London: Faber and Faber, 1952)

Buxton, D, *From the Avengers to Miami Vice* (Manchester: Manchester University Press, 1990)

Cain, J, *The BBC: 70 years of broadcasting* (London: BBC, 1992)

Calder, A, *The People's War* (London: The Literary Guild, 1986)

Calder, A, *Myth of the Blitz* (London: 1991)

Cardiff, D and Scannell, P, *The Historical Development of Popular Culture in Britain, Radio in World War II* (Milton Keynes: OU, 1981)

Cardiff, D, and Scannell, P, *A Social History of British Broadcasting* (Oxford: Blackwell, 1991)

Caughie, J, *Theories of Authorship* (London: Routledge and Kegan Paul Ltd, 1981)

Caughie, J, *Television Drama: Realism, Modernism, and British Culture* (Oxford: Oxford University Press, 2000)

Cawelti, JG, *Adventure, Mystery and Romance: Formula Stories as Art and Popular Culture* (Chicago: University of Chicago Press, 1976)

Chambers, C, *The Story of Unity Theatre* (London: Lawrence and Wishart, 1989)

Chapman, J, *The British at War: Cinema, state and propaganda, 1939–1945* (London and New York: I.B.Tauris, 1998)

Contrast on Pilkington, Contrast (London: BFI, 1960)

Cook, J, *Dennis Potter, A Life on Screen* (Manchester: Manchester University Press, 1998)

Cook, P (ed.) *Gainsborough Pictures, Rethinking British Cinema* (London: Cassell, 1997)

Corner, J (ed.) *Documentary and the Mass Media* (London: Edward Arnold, 1986)

Corner, J (ed.) *Popular Television in Britain: Studies in Culture* (London: BFI, 1991)

Corner, J, *Television Form and Public Address* (London: Edward Arnold, 1995)

Corner, J, *The art of record: A critical introduction to documentary* (Manchester and New York: Manchester University Press, 1996)

Corner, J, and Harvey, S, *Enterprise and Heritage: Crosscurrents of National Culture* (London and New York: Routledge, 1991)

Corner, J, and Harvey, S (eds) *Television Times: A Reader* (London: Arnold 1996)

Couzens Hoy, D (ed.) *Foucault: A Critical Reader* (Oxford: Blackwell, 1986)

Crisell, A, *An Introductory History of British Broadcasting* (London and New York: Routledge, 1997)

Curran, J, and Gurevitch, M (eds) *Mass Media and Society* (London: Edward Arnold, 1991)

Curran, J, and Porter, V (eds) *British Cinema History* (London: Weidenfeld and Nicholson, 1983)

Curran, J, and Seaton, J, *Power Without Responsibility: The Press and Broadcasting in Britain* (London: Routledge, 1988)

Davis, A, *Television: The first forty years* (London: Independent Television Publications Ltd, 1976)

Doyle, B, *English and Englishness* (London: Routledge, 1989)

Drummond, P, and Patterson, R (eds) *Television and its Audience* (London: BFI, 1988)

Dyer, R, *Stars* (London: BFI, 1979)

Dyer, R, et al, 'Coronation Street', *Television Monograph*, no. 13 (London: BFI, 1981)

Dyer, R, *Only Entertainment* (London: Routledge, 1992)

Eagleton, T, *Marxism and Literary Criticism* (London: Methuen and Co, 1976)

Ellis, J, *Visible Fictions: Cinema, Television, Video* (London: Routledge, 1982)

Ellis, J, *Seeing Things: Television in the Age of Uncertainty* (London and New York: I.B.Tauris, 2000)

Fielding, R (ed.) *A Technological History of Motion Pictures* (Los Angeles, Berkeley: University of California, 1967)

Fiske, J, *Television Culture* (London: Methuen, 1987)

Fiske, J, and Hartley, J, *Reading Television* (London: Methuen, 1978)

Formations of Nation and People (London: Routledge and Kegan Paul, 1984)

Foucault, M, *The Archaeology of Knowledge* (London: Tavistock, 1972)

Foucault, M, *Discipline and Punish: The Birth of Prison* (New York: Vintage, 1979)

Frith, S, *Formations of Pleasure* (London: Routledge and Kegan Paul, 1983)

Garnham, N, and Bakewell, J, *The New Priesthood: British Television* (London: Allen Lane, 1970)

Garnham, N, 'Structures of Television', *Television Monograph*, no. 1 (London: BFI, 1973)

Geraghty, C, *Women and Soap Opera* (Cambridge: Polity Press, 1991)

Geraghty C, and Lusted, D (eds) *The Television Studies Book* (London: Arnold, 1998)

Gielgud, V, *Years in a Mirror* (London: The Bodley Head, 1965)

Gielgud, V, *British Radio Drama, 1922–1956* (London: Harrap, 1957)

Goldie, GW, *Facing the Nation: Television and Politics* (London: Bodley Head, 1977)

Goodwin, A, and Whannel, G, *Understanding Television* (London: Routledge, 1990)

Goodwin, A, et al, *Drama-Documentary: BFI Dossier 19* (London: BFI, 1983)

Goreham, M, *Sound and Fury* (London: Percival-Maskell, 1948)

Gorham, M, *Broadcasting and Television since 1900* (London: Andrew Dakers Ltd, 1952)

Graham, G, *The Pleasure Dome: The Collected Film Criticism 1935–40*, ed. J Taylor (Oxford: Oxford Univeristy Press, 1980)

Grierson, J, *Eyes of Democracy, The John Grierson Archive* (Stirling: University of Stirling, 1990)

Habermas, J, *The Structural Transformation of the Public Sphere*, trans. Thomas Burger with Frederick Lawrence (Cambridge, Mass: MIT Press, 1989)

Habermas, J, *Legitimation Crisis* (London: Heinemann, 1976)

Hall, S, Clarke, J, Jefferson, T, Critcher, C, and Roberts, B, *Policing the Crisis: Mugging, Law and Order and the State* (London: Macmillan, 1978)

Halliwell's Film Guide, eighth edition (London: Grafton, 1992)

Hardy, F, *John Grierson, a Documentary Biography* (London: Faber, 1979)

Hewison, R, *Culture and Consensus: England, Art and Politics since 1940* (London: Methuen, 1995)

Higson, A, *Waving the Flag: Constructing a National Cinema in Britain* (Oxford: Oxford University Press, 1995)

Higson, A, *Dissolving Views: Key Writings on British Cinema* (London: Cassell, 1996)

Hill, J, *Sex, Class and Realism: British Cinema, 1956–1963* (London: BFI, 1986)

Hill, J, and McLoone, M (eds) *Big Picture, Small Screen: The Relations between Film and Television* (Luton: University of Luton Press, 1997)

Hoggart, R, *The Uses of Literacy* (First published London: Chatto and Windus, 1957; this edition London: Penguin, 1992)

Holdaway, S (ed.) *The British Police* (London: Edward Arnold, 1979)

Hood, S, *On Television* (London: Pluto, 1989)

Hurd, G, *National Fictions: World War Two in British Films and Television* (London: BFI Publishing, 1984)

Jacobs, J, *The Intimate Screen: Early British Television Drama* (Oxford: Oxford University Press, 2000)

Kavanagh, D, and Morris, P, *Consensus Politics: From Attlee to Major* (Oxford: Blackwell, 1989)

Kilborn, R, and Izod, J, *An Introduction to Television Documentary: Confronting Reality* (Manchester: Manchester University Press, 1997)

King, CF, *The Influence of Documentary Methods upon BBC Drama* (Hull University: unpublished PhD, 1976)

Laing, S, *Representations of Working Class Life, 1957–1964* (London: Macmillan, 1986)

Lant, A, *Blackout: Reinventing Women for Wartime British Cinema* (Princeton, Princeton University Press, 1991)

LeMahieu, DL, *A Culture for Democracy* (Oxford: Clarendon Press, 1988)

Light, A, *Forever England: Feminity, literature and conservatism between the wars* (London: Routledge, 1991)

Lindsay, TF, and Harrington, M, *The Conservative Party: 1918–1970* (London: Macmillan, 1974)

Lippmann, W, *The Phantom Public* (New York: Macmillan, 1927)

Lippmann, W, *Public Opinion* (New York and London: Allen and Unwin, 1922)

Livingstone, S, and Lunt, P, *Talk on Television* (London: Routledge, 1993)

Lodge, D (ed.) *20th Century Literary Criticism* (London: Longman, 1972)

Longhurst, D, *Gender, Genre and Narrative Pleasure* (London: Unwin Hyman Ltd, 1989)

Low, R, *The History of the British Film 1929–1939: Documentary and Educational Films of the 1930s* (London: George Allen and Unwin, 1979)

Mackenzie, JM, *Propaganda and Empire: The manipulation of British public opinion, 1880–1960* (Manchester: Manchester University Press, 1984)

Macnab, GJ, *Arthur Rank and the British Film Industry* (London: Routledge, 1993)

McKnight, G (ed.) *Agent of Challenge and Defiance: The Films of Ken Loach* (London: Flicks Books, 1998)

McQueen, D, *Television: A Media Student's Guide* (London: Arnold, 1998)

Mandel, E, *Delightful Murder: A Social History of the Crime Story* (Minneapolis: University of Minnesota Press, 1985)

Marris, P (ed.) *Paul Rotha: BFI Dossier Number 16* (London: British Film Institute, 1982)

Marland, M (ed.) *Z Cars: Four Television Scripts* (London: Longman, 1968)

Marshall, H (ed.) *The Battleship Potemkin* (New York: Avon Books, 1978)

Marwick, A, *British Society since 1945* (Harmondsworth: Penguin, 1982)

Mellencamp, P (ed.) *Logics of Television* (Bloomington: Indiana University Press, 1990)

Michael, T, *The Production of Political Television* (London: Routledge, 1977)

Morley, D, *The 'Nationwide' Audience* (London: BFI, 1980)

Morley, D, *Family Television* (London: Comedia, Routledge, 1986)

Morley, D, *Television, Audiences and Cultural Studies* (London: Routledge, 1992)

Montagu, I, *With Eisenstein in Hollywood: A Chapter of Autobiography* (Berlin: Seven Seas Publishers, 1968)

Mowatt, CL, *Britain between the Wars 1918–1940* (London: Methuen University Paperbacks, 1968)

Murphy, R, *Realism and Tinsel: Cinema and society in Britain 1939–49* (London: Routledge, 1989)

Murphy, R, *British Cinema of the 90s* (London: BFI, 2000)

Neale, S, *Genre* (London, British Film Institute, 1980)

Neale, S, and Krutnik, F, *Popular Film and Television Comedy* (London: Routledge, 1990)

Newcomb, H, *TV: The Most Popular Art* (New York: Anchor Press/Doubleday, 1974)

Nichols, B, *Representing Reality: Issues and Concepts in Documentary* (Bloomington: Indiana Univeristy Press, 1991)

Norden, D (ed.) *Coming to you Live!: Behind-the-screen Memories of Forties and Fifties Television* (London: Methuen, 1985)

Orwell, G, *Collected Essays, Journalism and Letters 2* (Middlesex: Harmondsworth, 1971)

Palmer, J, *Potboilers: Methods, Concepts and Case Studies in Popular Fiction* (London: Routledge, 1992)

Paris, M, *From the Wright Brothers to Top Gun: Aviation, nationalism and popular cinema* (Manchester and New York: Manchester University Press, 1995)

Price, ME, *Television, The Public Sphere, and National Identity* (Oxford: Oxford University Press, 1995)

Pronay, N, and Spring, DW (eds) *Propaganda, Politics and Film, 1918–45* (London: Macmillan, 1982)

Pugh, M, 'The Period of Confusion: Collectivism versus Capitalism 1918–1940', *State and Society, British Political and Social History 1870–1992* (London: Edward Arnold, 1994)

Punter, D (ed.) *Introduction to Contemporary Cultural Studies* (London: Longman, 1986)

Reith, JCW, *Broadcast over Britain* (London: Hodder and Stoughton, 1924)

Reith, JCW, *Into the Wind* (London: Hodder and Stoughton, 1949)

Richards, J, *The Age of the Dream Palace: Cinema and Society in Britain, 1930–1939* (London: Routledge, 1984)

Richards, J, *Films and British National Identity: From Dickens to Dad's Army* (Manchester: Manchester University Press, 1997)

Richards, J, and Sheridan, D (eds) *Mass Observation at the Movies* (London: Routledge, 1987)

Robbins, B, *The Phantom Public Sphere* (Minneapolis: University of Minnesota Press, 1993)

Rockwell, J, *Fact in Fiction* (London: Routledge and Kegan Paul, 1974)

Rotha, P, *Television in the Making* (London: Faber, 1956)

Rotha, P, *The Documentary Film* (London: Faber, 1935)

Rotha, P, *Documentary Diary: An Informal History of the British Documentary Film, 1928–1939* (New York: Hill and Wang, 1973)

Said, E, *The World, The Text, and The Critic* (London: Faber and Faber, 1984)

Saussure, F de, *Course in General Linguistics* (London: Peter Owen, 1960)

Scannell, P, and Cardiff, D, *A Social History of Broadcasting*, vol. 1 (Oxford: Blackwell, 1991)

Scannell, P, *Broadcast Talk* (London: Sage, 1991)

Self, D, *Television Drama: An Introduction* (London: Macmillan, 1984)

Sendall, B, *Independent Television in Britain*, vol. 1, 'Origin and Foundation, 1946–62' (London: Macmillan, 1982)

Seymour-Ure, C, *The British Press and Broadcasting since 1945* (London: Basil Blackwell, 1991)

Shubik, I, *Play For Today: The evolution of television drama* (London: Poynter, 1975)

Sieveking, L, *The Stuff of Radio* (London: Cassell and Co, 1934)

Silverstone, R, *The Message of Television* (London: Heinemann, 1981)

Silverstone, R, *Why Study the Media?* (London: Sage 1999)

Silvey, R, *Who's Listening? The Story of BBC Audience Research* (London: Allen and Unwin, 1974)

Sparks, R, *Television and the Drama of Crime: Moral tales and the place of crime in public life* (Philadelphia, Buckingham: OU, 1992)

Street, S, and Dickinson, M, *Cinema and the State: The Film Industry and the British Government, 1927–1984* (London: British Film Institute, 1985)

Sussex, E, *The Rise and Fall of British Documentary* (Berkeley: University of California Press, 1975)

Sutton, S, *The Largest Theatre in the World: Thirty Years of Television* (London: BBC, 1982)

Swallow, N, *Factual Television* (London: Focal Press, 1966)

Swann, P, *The British Documentary Film Movement 1926–1946* (Cambridge: Cambridge University Press, 1989)

Swift, J, *Adventure in Vision: The first twenty-five years of television* (London: John Lehman, 1950)

Swinson, A, *Writing for Television* (London: A and C Black, 1955)

Swinson, A, *Writing for Television Today* (London: A and C Black, 1963)

Taylor, D, *Days of Vision* (London: Methuen, 1990)

Tracey, M, *The Production of Political Television* (London: Routledge, 1977)

Tibballs, G, *The Encyclopedia of TV Detectives* (London: Boxtree, 1992)

Toderov, T, *The Poetics of Prose* (Oxford: Basil Blackwell, 1977)

Tonqvist, E, *Transposing Drama: Studies in representation* (London: Macmillan, 1991)

Tulloch, J, *Television drama: agency, audience and myth* (London: Routledge, 1990)

Tulloch, J, and Alvarado, M, *Doctor Who: The Unfolding Text* (London: Macmillan, 1983)

Vaughan, D, *Television documentary usage* (London: British Film Institutue, 1976)

Wayne, M, *Dissident Voices: The Politics of Television and Cultural Change* (London and Virginia: Pluto Press, 1998)

Webster, W, *Imagining Home: Gender, 'Race' and Natonal Identity, 1945–1964* (London: UCL, 1998)

Williams, R, *Communications* (Harmondsworth: Penguin, 1962)

Williams, R, *Television Technology and Cultural Form* (London: Fontana, 1974)

Williams, R, *Marxism and Literature* (Oxford: Oxford University Press, 1977)

Williams, R, *Culture and Society 1780–1950* (New York: Columbia University Press, 1983)

Williams, R, *On Television* (London: Routledge, 1989)

Willis, J, and Wollen, T (eds) *The Broadcasting Debate 5: The Neglected Audience* (London: BFI, 1990)

Winston, B, *Misunderstanding Media* (London: Routledge and Kegan Paul, 1986)

Winston, B, *Claiming the Real: The documentary film revisited* (London: BFI Publishing, 1995)

Winston, R, *The Public Eye* (London: Macmillan, Academic and Professional Ltd, 1991)

Wright, P, *On Living in an Old Country: The National Past in Contemporary Britain* (London: 1985)

Wyndham Goldie, G, *Facing the Nation* (London: The Bodley Head, 1977)

Chapters in books

Adorno, Theodor, and Horkheimer, Max 'The Culture Industry: Enlightenment as Mass Deception' (abridged) in Curran, Gurevitch and Woolacott (eds) (1977) qv

Anderson, L, 'Get out and push', in T Maschler (ed.) *Declaration* (London: MacGibbon, 1957)

Barr, C, 'Broadcasting and Cinema, 2: Screens Within Screens', in C Barr (ed.) *All Our Yesterdays* (1986) qv

Barr, C, 'They Think It's All Over: The Dramatic Legacy of Live Television', in J Hill (ed.) (1997) qv

Bell, E, 'The Origins of British Television Documentary', in J Corner (ed.) *Documentary and the Mass Media*) (1986) qv

Branston, G, 'Histories of British Television', in C Geraghty and D Lusted (eds) *The Television Studies Book* (1997) qv

Brunsdon, C, 'Television: Aesthetics and Audiences', in P Mellencamp (ed.) *Logics of Television* (1990) qv

Brunsdon, C, 'What is the "Television" of Television Studies?', in C Geraghty and D Lusted (eds) *The Television Studies Book* (1998) qv

Buscombe, E, 'All Bark and No Bite: The Film Industry's Response to Television', in J Corner (ed.) *Popular Television* (1991) qv

Caughie, J, 'Broadcasting and Cinema, 1: Converging histories', in C Barr (ed.) *All Our Yesterdays* (1986) qv

Caughie, J, 'Before the Golden Age: Early Television Drama', in J Corner (ed.) (1991) qv

Chapman, J, 'Cinema, propaganda and national identity: British film and the Second World War', in Ashby, J, and Higson, A (eds) *British Cinema, Past and Present* (2000) qv

Clarke, A, 'This is not the boy scouts: television police series and definitions of law and order', in T Bennett, C Mercer and J Woollacott (eds) *Popular Culture and Social Relations* (1986) qv

Cook, J, 'Case Studies: Overview', in G Hurd (ed.) *National Fictions: World War* (1984) qv

Corner, J, 'Documentary Voices', in J Corner (ed.) (1991) qv

Crisell, A, 'Filth, Sedition and Blasphemy: The Rise and Fall of Television Satire', in J Corner (ed.) (1991) qv

Dodd, K and P, 'Engendering the Nation: British Documentary Film, 1930–1939' in A Higson (ed.) *Dissolving Views: Key Writings on British Cinema* (1996)

Doncaster, C, 'The Story Documentary' in P Rotha (ed.) *Television in the Making* (1956) qv

Goddard, P, '"Hancock's Half Hour": A Watershed in British Television Comedy', in J Corner (ed.) *Popular Television in Britain* (1991) qv

Hall, S, 'Technics of the medium' in J Corner and S Harvey (eds) *Television Times: A Reader* (1996) qv

Hall, S, 'The Rediscovery of "Ideology": Return of the Repressed in Media Studies', in M Gurevitch et al (eds) qv

Higson, A, 'Britain's Outstanding Contribution to Film', in C Barr (ed.) *All Our Yesterdays: 90 Years of British Cinema* (1986) qv

Hurd, G, 'The television presentation of the police', in S Holdaway (ed.) *The British Police* (1979) qv

Kumar, K, 'Holding the middle ground: the BBC, the public and the professional broadcaster', in J Curran, M Gurevitch and J Woollacott (eds) (1977) qv

Laing, S, 'Banging in Some Reality: The Original "Z Cars"', in J Corner (ed.) (1991) qv

Medhurst, A, '1950s War Films', in G Hurd (ed.) *National Fictions, World War Two in British Films and Television* (1984) qv

Medhurst, A, 'Music Hall and British Cinema', in C Barr (ed.) (1986) qv

McLoone, M, 'Boxed In?: The Aethetics of Film and Television', in J Hill (ed.) *Big Picture, Small Screen* (1997) qv

Murphy, R, 'Riff Raff, British cinema and the underworld', in C Barr (ed.) (1986) qv

O'Sullivan, T, 'Television Memories and Cultures of Viewing, 1950–65', in J Corner (ed.) (1991) qv

O'Sullivan, T, 'Nostalgia, Revelation and Intimacy', in C Geraghty and D Lusted (1998) qv

Pronay, N, 'Political Censorship of Films in Britain between the War', in Pronay and Spring (eds) (1982) qv

Sales, R, 'An introduction to broadcasting history', in D Punter (ed.) *Introduction to Contemporary Cultural Studies* (London: Longmans, 1986)

Scannell, P, 'Public service broadcasting, the history of a concept', in A Goodwin and G Whannel (eds) *Understanding Television* (London: Routledge, 1990)

Scannell, P, 'The Stuff of Radio: Developments in Radio Features and Documentaries before the War', in J Corner (ed.) qv

Taylor, PM, 'British official attitudes towards propaganda abroad, 1918–39, in Pronay and Spring (eds) (1982) qv

Articles

Barry, M, 'Problems of a Producer', *BBC Quarterly*, vol. 3, part 3, Autumn 1951

Barr, C, 'Criticism and TV Drama', *Edinburgh International Television Festival Official Programme*, 1977

Barr, C, 'Television on Television', *Sight and Sound*, vol. 55, no. 3, 1986

Brecht, B, 'Against Georg Lukacs', *New Left Review*, no. 84, 1974

Brunsdon, C, 'Problems with quality', *Screen*, vol. 31, no. 1, 1990

Brunsdon, C, and Morley, D, 'Everyday Television – "Nationwide"', *Television Monograph*, no. 10 (London: British Film Institute, 1978)

Casey, A, 'Blood Without Thunder', *Screen Education*, no. 16, 1962

Caughie, J, 'Progressive Television and Documentary Drama', *Screen*, vol. 2, no. 3, 1980

Caughie, J, 'Progressive Television and Documentary Drama', *Screen*, vol. 1, nos 21/3, 1980

Caughie, J, 'Television Criticism: A Discourse in Search of an Object', *Screen*, vol. 25, nos 4/5, 1984

Caughie, J, 'Adorno's reproach: repetition, difference and television,' *Screen*, vol. 32, no. 2, 1991

Clarke, A, 'Holding the blue lamp: television and the police in Britain', *Crime and Social Justice*, vol. 19, no. 44, 1983

Elsaesser, T, 'The New Film History', *Sight and Sound*, Autumn 1986

Ericson, R, 'Mass media, crime, law and justice: an institutional approach', *British Journal of Criminology*, vol. 31, no. 3, 1991

Gardner, C, and Wyver, J, 'The Single Play: From Reithian Reverance to Cost-Accounting and Censorship', *Edinburgh International Television Festival Official Programme*, 1980

Hall, S, 'Encoding and decoding in the television discourse', Occasional Paper, Birmingham: Centre for Contemporary Cultural Studies, 1975

Higson, A, 'Space, place, spectacle', *Screen*, vol. 25, nos 4/5, 1984

Jacobs, J, 'The Amateur Stage: BBC Television Drama 1938–1952', *Norwich Papers*, no. 1, February 1994

Kennedy Martin, T, 'Nats Go Home', *Encore*, no. 48, 1964

Kerr, P, 'A Response to John Caughie', *Screen*, vol. 22, no. 1

Lewis, P, 'Z Cars', *Contrast*, no. 1, 1961–2

Lovell, T, 'Landscapes and Stories in 1960s British Realism', *Screen*, vol. 31, no. 4, 1990

McCullough, C, 'The Rise and Fall of the Reithian Sunday, 1936–1959', *Europa 1*, vol. 1, 1994

McGrath, J, 'Better a bad night in Bootle', *Theatre Quarterly*, vol. 5, no. 19, 1975

McGrath, J, 'TV Drama: The Case Against Naturalism', *Sight and Sound*, vol. 46, no. 2, 1977

Prior, A, and Hopkins, J, 'Talking about the Z Cars series', *Screen Education*, no. 21, 1963

Pronay, N, 'John Grierson and the Documentary – 60 years on', *Historical Journal of Film, Radio and Television*, vol. 9, no. 3, 1989

Reiner, 'Policing a Postmodern Society', *The Modern Law Review*, vol. 55, no. 6, 1991

Ross, D, 'The Documentary in Television', *BBC Quarterly*, vol. 5, no. 1, 1950

Scannell, P, 'The Social Eye of Television 1946–55', *Media Culture and Society*, vol. 1, no. 1, 1979

Scannell, P, 'Music for the Multitude, The Dilemmas of the BBC's Music Policy, 1923–1946', *Media Culture and Society*, 3, 1981

Taylor, D, 'The Gorbuduc Stage', *Contrast*, vol. 3, no. 4, 1964

Weatherby, WJ, 'Camino Real', *Contrast*, no. 2, 1961–1962

Whiting, J, 'At ease in a bright red tie', *Encore*, vol. 21, 1959

Williams, R, 'Drama and the Left', *Encore*, vol. 19, 1959

Williams, R, 'A Lecture on Realism', *Screen*, vol. 18, no. 1, 1975

Willis, T, 'Look Back in Wonder', *Encore*, vol. 13, 1958

APPENDIX 2a

General Story-Documentaries

Date	Title	Writer/Producer	Director	TTTX (rpt)
08/11/56	**A Man from the Sun**	John Elliot		
09/10/58	**A Shaft of Light**	Ken Alexander		
03/12/48	**Alias**	Robert Barr		
01/04/47	**April the First**			
26/06/47	**Armed Robbery**			
06/10/55	**As Others See Us**	Peter Hamilton		
27/10/52	**Barrister-at-Law**	JamesDowdall/		
		Robert Barr		TTX
21/11/53	**Beat the Burglar** (film)	Derek Wellman		
27/07/47	**Boys in Brown**			
1946	**British Justice**			
1946	**British Zone**			
04/03/58	**Black Furrow**	Elaine Morgan		
13/09/54	**Can I have a Lawyer?**	Jennifer Wayne/	John Moxley	
		Caryl Doncaster		
15/02/54	**Casebook - Loneliness to shop-lifting**			
24/01/63	**Children in Trust**	Caryl Doncaster	John Moxley	
01/08/58	**Children on Trial**	Basil Wright	Jack Lee	
1946	**Chorus Girl**			
	Course of Justice x3			
21/07/53	**Assizes**	Duncan Ross		
28/04/53	**Juvenile Court**	Duncan Ross		
09/06/53	**Magistrates Court**	Duncan Ross		
14/08/58	**Crime Report**	Michael Gilbert		TTX
1947	**D-Day with Wilmot**			
04/10/48	**English Justice**			
26/06/61	**Epidemic**	Robert Barr	Robert Barr	
14/10/46	**First Time Ever** (Thief caught by radio)			
14/02/50	**For the Housewife** (keeping burglars out)			

Date	Title	Writer/Producer	Director	TTTX (rpt)
18/09/46	**Germany Under Control**	Robert Barr		
	***I Made News* (x9)**			
12/10/51	**Case of the Talking Dolls**			
12/10/51	**Rough Diamonds**			
02/11/51	**The Theft of the Pink Diamond**			
09/11/51	**Gunmen in Park Lane**			
16/11/51	**Phantom Millions**			
23/11/51	**The Case That Made the FBI**			
30/11/51	**Double Bill**			
07/12/51	**The Blonde Informer**			
14/12/51	**The Black Butterfly**			
03/11/47	**I Want to be a Doctor**			
21/03/47	**I Want to be a Chorus Girl**	Robert Barr		
06/10/46	**I Want to be an Actor**	Robert Barr		
01/01/55	**In Town Tonight – Interview Bob Fabian**	Robert Barr		
09/12/58	**Incident at Echo Six**	Robert Barr		
17/02/48	***It's Your Money They're After* (x3)**	Robert Barr and Percy Hoskins		
	***Jacks and Knaves* (x4)**			
30/01/61	**The Great Art Robbery**			
16/11/61	**The Master Mind**			
23/11/61	**The Interrogation**			
07/12/61	**It was doing Nothing**	Gilchrist Calder and Colin Morris		
11/06/74	**Just One Kid**	Bernard Kops	John Goldschmidt	
13/07/54	**Leisure and Pleasure** (prison visiting)			
10/04/58	**Loneliness**			
	***Magistrates Court* (x3)**			
27/08/48	**War on Crime**	Duncan Ross		
10/09/48	**On Remand**	Duncan Ross		
24/09/48	**Trial without Jury**	Duncan Ross		
	***Man at the Door* (x4)**			
21/09/54/	**Medical Officer of Health**	Robert Barr		TTX
07/01/59	**Medico**	Robert Barr		
11/01/55	**Missing from Home**	Arthur Swinson/		TTX rptd. 11/01/59
01/04/47	**Mock Auction**	Robert Barr		TTX
23/10/58	**New Editor**	Robert Barr		
1946	**Night at an Inn**	Bellman/Whitney		rptd. 16/07/54

Date	Title	Writer/Producer	Director	TTTx (rpt)
02/05/61	**Night Call**	Arthur Swinson		
1947	**No future in it**			
04/09/48	**No other Woman**			
09/02/60	**On the Road**	Alan White/ John Elliot		
11/04/51	**Other Peoples' Jobs**			
23/03/56	**Outbreak** (gaol break)	John Irving		
	Pilgrim Street **(x6)**			
01/06/52	**On the Run**	Robert Barr	Under new	
04/06/52	**On our Beat**		Director scheme	
18/06/52	**'Rarest of Crimes'**			
25/06/52	**A Medal for Sammy**			
02/07/52	**A Dead Tumble**			
09/07/52	**The Phantom Car**			
22/03	**Reluctant Heroes**	Colin Morris/ Alan Chivers		
02/05/51	**Report on Women**	Caryl Doncaster		TTX
16/02/54	**Return to Living** (rehab. of ex-convicts)	Caryl Doncaster/ John Moxey	Edward Lloyd	TTX
14/02/52	**Rising Twenties**	Patricia Evans/ Caryl Doncaster		TTX
15/10/57	**Rock Bottom**	Colin Morris		
	Roundabout	John Elliot		
	Scotland Yard **(x13)**	Robert Barr	David E Rose and David Wilmott	
12/04/60	**Nightbeat**	Robert Barr	David Rose	
19/04/60	**Information**			
26/04/60	**Title Unknown**	Geoffrey Mathews	David Rose	
03/05/60	**Robbery with Violence**		David Rose	
10/05/60	**Complaints against the Police**	Geoffrey Mathews	David Rose	
17/05/60	**Organised Crime**	A.E. Comet/ Geoffrey Mathews	David Rose	
24/05/60	**Robbery on the A5**		David Wilmot	
31/05/60	**Interpol**	Robert Barr	David Rose	
07/06/60	**Reasonable Doubt**		David Wilmot	
14/06/60	**Special Day**		David Rose	
21/06/60	**Used in Evidence**		David Rose	
05/07/60	**Cheap at the Price**		David Wilmot	
29/09/60	**Protection**		David Rose	
05/01/48	**Searchlight on Crime**			
05/07/54	**Seeing both Sides**			TTX
09/01/47	**Shipwreck**	Robert Barr		
1946	**Silver Jubilee**			

Date	Title	Writer/Producer	Director	TTTX (rpt)
29/10/57	**Skipper's Ticket**	Alan White/ John Elliot		TTX
05/01/66	*Softly, Softly* (see appendix 2b)			
28/04/59	**Some Call me Sister**	Duncan Ross		TTX
02/02/56	**Speech**	Arthur Swinson		TTX
	Spycatcher (**Interpol adventures of Colonel Pinto**)	Robert Barr		
1st series				
17/09/59	**Friend or Foe?** **One Must Die** **Three From Spain**			
2nd series				
18/02/60	**Double Agent** (1st of 7)			
3rd series				
04/10/60	**Left Luggage (1st of 6)**			
4th Series				
02/05/61	**Stooping to Conquer (1st of 7)**			
11/10/56	**Tearaway**	Colin Morris/ Gilchrist Calder		
20/01/50	**Ten Minute Alibi**			
09/10/56	**The Call-up**	Beryl Radley		
06/07/59	**The Case Before You**	John Whitney/ Bellman	Elwyn Jones	TTX
22/07/47	**The Case of Helvig Delbo**	Robert Barr		
07/01/58	**The Challenge**			
04/12/53	**The Connors Case**			
06/10/50	**The Cross and the Arrow**	Albert Maltz		
18/08/52	**The Declining Years**	Patricia Evans/ Caryl Doncaster		TTX
10/08/58	**The Duchess Vanishes**			
03/09/52	**The Family Doctor**	Robert Barr		TTX
23/04/51	**The Hidden Years**	Robert Barr		TTX
23/09/51	**The Loch Ness Monster**	Duncan Ross		
15/05/60	**The Property in Question**	Arthur Swinson		
02/07/59	**The Seventh Age**	John Prebble		
14/02/51	**The Strange Case of Hans Grantzer**	Robert Barr		TTX
09/01/49	**The Trial of Madelaine Smith**			
30/03/61	**The Vet**	Allan Prior		
28/03/87	**The Wharf Road Mob**	Colin Morris		

Date	Title	Writer/Producer	Director	TTTX (rpt)
11/08/60	**They Made History**	Arthur Browne Wilkinson/ Brian Duncalf	Brian Duncalf	TTX
03/05/55	**Those Who Dare**	Caryl Doncaster		
1947	**TV with Cecil McGivern**			
	War on Crime (x6)			
17/04/50	**Woman Unknown**	Robert Barr		
06/05/50	**Gold Thieves**	Robert Barr		
15/05/50	**Death Rings the Doorbell**	Robert Barr		
15/07/50	**Gunman**	Robert Barr		
07/08/50	**Burn the Evidence**	Robert Barr		
04/09/50	**Interpol**	Robert Barr		
08/03/54	**Watch and Ward** (City of London Police)			
15/10/59	**Who Me?**	Colin Morris	Gilchrist Calder	
12/12/58	**Without Love**	Colin Morris		
12/04/54	**Youth Takes a Hand**			
21/01/62	*Z Cars* (see appendix 2b for full details)			

TTX means programme telerecorded.

Appendix 2b:
Police Series

Dixon of Dock Green (9 July 1955–1 May 1976) 1st 5 series shown

Time	Date	Title	Producer	Writer
1st series				
8.15pm	09/07/55	**P.C. Crawford's First Pinch**	Douglas Moodie	Ted Willis
8.15pm	16/0755	**Needle in a Haystack**		
9.15pm	23/07/55	**Night Beat**		
8.51pm	30/07/55	**The Mock Creen Desperado**		
8.15pm	06/08/55	**'Dixie'**		
8.15pm	13/08/55	**'London Pride'**		
2nd series				
10.00pm	09/06/56	**Ladies of the Manor**		
8.46pm	16/06/56	**The Hero**		
8.31pm	23/06/56	**Didey's Dollar**		
8.30pm	30/06/56	**The Little Gold Mine**		
8.31pm	07/06/56	**Eleven Plus**		
8.32pm	18/07/56	**The Gentle Scratcher**		
8.20pm	21/07/56	**Andy Steps Up**		
8.17pm	28/07/56	**On Mother Kelly's Doorstep**		
8.15pm	04/08/56	**Postman's Knock**		
8.15pm	11/08/56	**The Rotten Apple**		
8.00pm	18/08/56	**The Roaring Boy**		
10.04pm	28/08/56	**Pound of Flesh**		
8.46pm	01/09/56	**Father in Law**		
3rd series				
7.20pm	12/01/57	**Give a Dog a Good Name**		
7.33pm	10/01/57	**George and the Dragon**		
7.30pm	26/01/57	**No Place Like Home**		
8.30pm	01/01/57	**The Silent House**		
7.30pm	09/01/57	**The December Boy**		
7.30pm	16/02/57	**The Black Noah**		
7.30pm	23/03/57	**False Alarm**		

Time	Date	Title	Producer	Writer
8.17pm	02/03/57	**The Canon's Gaiters**		
7.30pm	09/03/57	**Rock, Rattle and Roll**		
7.30pm	16/03/57	**The Name is MacNamara**		
7.30pm	23/03/57	**The Gentle Scratcher**		
7.45pm	30/03/57	**Silver Jubilee**		
9.16pm	22/03/57	**Trailer**		

4th series

Time	Date	Title	Producer	Writer
7.30pm	07/09/57	**Presented in Court**		
7.00pm	14/09/57	**The Story of Jimmy Mayo**		
7.31pm	21/09/57	**Notice to Quit**		
7.30pm	38/09/57	**A Woman of Thirty-Eight**		
7.30pm	04/10/57	**The High Price of Radishes**		
7.30pm	12/10/57	**A Slight Case of Ham**		
7.30pm	10/10/57	**The Nelson Touch**		
7.30pm	16/10/57	**The Hall**		
7.31pm	02/11/57	**Fireworks**		
7.30pm	16/11/57	**Boxco and Boxco**		
7.30pm	23/11/57	**The New Skipper**		
7.30pm	30/11/57	**The Love of Phil**		
7.30pm	07/12/57	**The Crooked Key**		
7.30pm	14/12/57	**A Penn'orth of Allsorts**		
7.30pm	21/12/57	**Peace on Earth**		
7.30pm	28/12/57	**Goodwill to Men**		
7.30pm	04/01/58	**The Lady in Red**		
7.30pm	11/01/58	**Duffy's New Boots**		
7.30pm	18/01/58	**The Salvation of Duffy**		
7.30pm	25/01/58	**A Little Bit of French**		
7.30pm	01/02/58	**The Light over the Window**		
7.30pm	08/02/58	**All Buttoned Up**		
7.00pm	15/02/58	**They Don't Like Policemen**		
7.29pm	22/02/58	**The Stargazer**		
7.29pm	29/02/58	**Little Boy Blue**		
7.30pm	08/03/58	**The Case of Mrs X**		
7.30pm	15/03/58	**The Cats and the Fiddle**		
7.30pm	22/03/58	**All my Eye and Elbow**		
7.30pm	29/03/58	**The Key of the Nick**		

5th series

Time	Date	Title	Producer	Writer
7.30pm	27/09/58	**George Sakas Whisky**		
7.30pm	04/10/58	**Tom Brown's Lady**		
7.30pm	11/10/58	**A Whiff of Garlic**		
7.30pm	18/10/58	**Third Time Lucky**		
7.30pm	25/10/58	**Bracelets for the Groom**		
7.30pm	01/11/58	**The Gent from Siberia**		
7.30pm	08/11/58	**The Case of the Stolen Dustbin**		

Time	Date	Title	Producer	Writer
7.30pm	15/11/58	**Strangers at the Same Table**		
7.30pm	22/11/58	**A Little Bit of Luck**		
7.30pm	29/11/58	**The Whisper on the Road**		
7.30pm	16/12/58	**The Pyro Maniac**		
7.30pm	13/12/58	**Genuine Yule Logs**		
7.30pm	20/12/58	**The Old Christmas Spirit**		
7.30pm	27/12/58	**Flint Rides Again**		
6.59pm	03/01/59	**Ride on a Tiger**		
7.00pm	10/01/59	**The Half-Wide Mug**		
7.00pm	17/01/59	**The Magic Eye**		
7.00pm	24/01/59	**The Singer**		
7.00pm	31/01/59	**Trouble on Night Beat**		
7.00pm	07/02/59	**Blues in the Night***		
7.01pm	14/02/59	**The Woman from Kimberley**		
6.59pm	38/02/59	**One for the Milkman***		
7.00pm	07/03/59	**The Whiss Gang***		
7.00pm	14/03/59	**Over and Out**		
7.00pm	21/03/59	**Duffy calls the Tune***		
7.00pm	28/03/59	**Helmet on the Sideboard~**		

*The Published as Broadcast Details at the BBC Written Archive state that these programmes were transmitted 'with film'.

~Series 5 ended with the death of Sergeant Penney

Ted Willis wrote some 229 episodes. Assistant Scriptwriter Rex Edwards was introduced in 1958 and by Series 11 (1964), more rationalised methods of production were in place. A system of writers and directors were introduced, including David Ellis, Gerald Kelsey, Eric Paice and Arthur Swinson, of whom Eric Paice was undoubtedly the most distinguished.

The series first producer was Douglas Moodie (1955–1963) second, Barry Lupino (1963) and the same year, Ronald Marsh took over until 1968. The Final Producer on the series was Joe Waters (1969–1974).

Full details of *Dixon of Dock Green* programmes published as broadcast, are held on microfiche at the BBC Written Archive, Caversham.

Fabian of the Yard (15 November 1954–29 March 1957)

Time	Date	Title	Rpt	1ˢᵗ Date Rpt
8.45pm	15/11/54	The Extra Bullet		
8.14pm	20/11/54	The Unwanted Man		
8.46pm	27/11/54	The Skeleton in the Cupboard		
8.15pm	08/01/55	Against the Evidence		
8.46pm	22/01/55	The Brides of the Firm		
8.15pm	29/01/55	The Troubled Wife		
8.15pm	19/02/55	Written in Dust		
8.15pm	26/02/55	The Purple Mouse		
8.15pm	12/03/55	Little Girl		
8.15pm	19/03/55	The Coward		
7.50pm	30/03/55	Lost Boy		
3.00pm	04/04/55	The Extra Bullet		
8.28pm	06/04/55	The Executioner		
8.35pm	13/04/55	The Poison Machine		
3.00pm	18/04/55	Skeleton in the Cupboard		
8.20pm	20/04/55	The Golden Peacock		
3.00pm	25/04/55	The Unwanted Man		
3.00pm	02/05/55	Against the Evidence		
8.15pm	04/05/55	The Man from Blackpool		
3.00pm	09/05/55	The Troubled Wife		
8.30pm	11/05/55	Robbery in the Museum		
3.00pm	11/05/55	Pride of Fire		
8.15pm	18/05/55	Deadly Pocket Handkerchief		
7.45pm	25/05/55	The Vanishing Cat		
8.15pm	01/06/55	The Pinpoint Signature		
8.15pm	08/06/55	The Innocent Victims		
7.45pm	15/06/55	The Jade Blade		
7.45pm	22/06/55	April Fool		
3.30pm	29/07/55	Written in Dust	Rpt	19/02/55
3.30pm	05/08/55	The Purple Mouse	Rpt	26/02/55
3.30pm	12/08/55	The Little Girl	Rpt	12/03/55
8.30pm	17/08/55	The Hand of Terror		
3.30pm	19/08/55	The Coward File		
3.00pm	26/08/55	Lost Boy	Rpt	30/03/55
3.00pm	02/09/55	The Executioner	Rpt	06/04/55
3.00pm	09/09/55	The Poison Machine	Rpt	13/04/55
3.00pm	16/09/55	The Golden Peacock	Rpt	20/04/55
4.19pm	03/10/55	Man from Blackpool	Rpt	04/05/55
4.16pm	17/10/55	Robbery in them Museum	Rpt	11/05/55
4.17pm	31/10/55	Deadly Pocket Handkerchief	Rpt	18/05/55
3.45pm	12/11/55	No Alibi		

Time	Date	Title	Rpt	1st Date Rpt
4.15pm	14/11/55	The Vanishing Cat	Rpt	25/05/55
3.51pm	19/11/55	Escort for Death		
4.01pm	26/11/55	The Sixth Dagger		
4.15pm	28/11/55	Pinpoint Signature	Rpt	01/06/55
9.33pm	17/01/56	The Ribbon Trap		
7.30pm	02/02/56	The Lover's Knot		
4.15pm	20/02/56	The Innocent Victims		
4.15pm	05/03/56	The Golden Peacock	Rpt(2)	16/09/55
7.30pm	12/03/56	The Masterpiece		
4.15pm	12/03/56	Escort for Death	Rpt	19/11/55
4.16pm	16/03/56	The Hand of Terror	Rpt	17/08/55
4.15pm	19/03/56	No Alibi	Rpt	14/11/55
7.30pm	19/03/56	Cocktail Girl		
7.30pm	26/03/56	The Poison Machine	rpt(2)	13/04/55
7.31pm	23/04/56	The Executioner	Rpt	26/08/55
3.06pm	12/07/56	The Vanishing Cat	rpt(2)	25/05/55
5.27pm	28/07/56	The Ribbon Trap	Rpt	17/01/56
5.30pm	25/08/56	The Man from Blackpool	Rpt	04/05/55
7.30pm	06/09/56	Escort for Death	Rpt	19/11/55
3.15pm	21/09/56	No Alibi	rpt(2)	14/11/55
7.41pm	26/09/56	The Lovers Knot	Rpt	02/02/56
3.23pm	19/10/56	Pinpoint Signature	rpt(2)	01/06/55
3.17pm	26/10/56	Robbery in the Museum	Rpt	11/05/55
3.18pm	02/11/56	The Jade Blade	rpt(2)	15/06/55
3.14pm	09/11/56	The Masterpiece	Rpt	12/03/56
2.50pm	16/11/56	The Hand of Terror	rpt(2)	17/08/55
3.15pm	23/11/56	Cocktail Girl	Rpt	19/03/56
3.16pm	30/11/56	Deadly Pocket Handkerchief	rpt(2)	19/03/56
3.18pm	07/12/56	The Innocent Victims	Rpt	20/02/56
3.15pm	14/12/56	The Sixth Dagger	Rpt	26/11/55
7.50pm	14/12/56	The Sixth Dagger	rpt(2)	26/11/55
3.15pm	21/12/56	April Fool		
3.17pm	11/01/57	The Lover's Knot	Rpt	02/02/56
3.26pm	25/01/57	Ribbon Trap	rpt(2)	17/01/56
3.15pm	01/02/57	The Masterpiece	rpt(2)	12/03/56
3.15pm	15/02/57	The Golden Peacock	rpt(2)	16/09/55
3.25pm	22/02/57	Man from Blackpool	rpt(2)	04/05/55
3.15pm	01/03/57	Cocktail Girl	rpt(2)	19/03/56
3.16pm	08/03/57	No Alibi	rpt(2)	11/05/55
3.15pm	15/03/57	Escort for death	rpt(2)	19/11/55
3.15pm	22/03/57	The Vanishing Cat	rpt(2)	19/11/55
3.15pm	29/03/57	Robbery in the Museum	rpt(2)	11/05/55

Softly, Softly (5 January 1966–15 December 1976) lst 5 series shown

Time	Date	Title	Writer	Rpt
1st series				
8.01pm	05/01/66	**Off Beat**	Martin Hall	
8.00pm	12/01/66	**A Local Touch**	Elwyn Jones	
8.01pm	19/01/66	**The Misinformer**	Eric Coltart	
8.00pm	26/01/66	**It Doesn't Grow on Trees**	Robert Barr	
8.01pm	02/02/66	**Talk to Me**	Kenneth Ware	
8.00pm	09/02/66	**Screws and Drivers**	Martin Hall	
8.00pm	16/02/66	**Take Over**	Elwyn Jones	
8.00pm	23/02/66	**Over-Take**	Elwyn Jones	
8.01pm	02/03/66	**Don't Push Too Hard**	Martin Hall	
8.00pm	09/03/66	**The Key**	Robert Barr	
8.01pm	16/03/66	**Tickle on Wheels**	Allan Prior	
8.00pm	23/03/66	**A Spot of Leave**	Joan Clarke	
8.03pm	30/03/66	**A-Z**	Kenneth Hill	
8.00pm	06/04/66	**Blind Man's Buff**	Martin Hall	
8.00pm	13/04/66	**All the Flowers**	John Foster	
7.59pm	20/04/66	**Do you Believe in Ghosts?**	Robert Barr	
8.00pm	27/04/66	**There's a Lot of it About**	Robert Barr	
7.59pm	04/05/66	**The Gentle Touch**	Elwyn Jones	
8.00pm	11/05/66	**The Short Cut**	Alan Plater	
8.00pm	18/05/66	**Made in Britain**	Joan Clarke	
8.00pm	25/05/66	**Round Trip**	Allan Prior	
8.01pm	01/06/66	**Extraction**	Elwyn Jones	
8.00pm	08/06/66	**Best out of Three**	Alan Plater	
8.00pm	15/06/66	**I Know What I Said**	Robert Barr	
7.59pm	22/06/66	**Conspiracy Pt. 1 -To Rob**	Elwyn Jones	
8.01pm	29/06/66	**Conspiracy Pt. 2 -To Corrupt**	Elwyn Jones	
2nd series				
8.00pm	02/11/66	**Inside Out**	Elwyn Jones	
8.00pm	09/11/66	**All That Glitters**	Allan Prior	
8.00pm	16/11/66	**The Jackpot**	Elwyn Jones	
8.00pm	23/11/66	**Murder Reported**	Elwyn Jones	
8.00pm	30/11/66	**Sleeping Dogs**	Alan Plater	
8.00pm	07/12/66	**Heart of Brass**	Allan Prior	
7.59pm	14/12/66	**Find the Lady**	Robert Barr	
8.01pm	21/12/66	**Barlow Was There Pt. 1 Allegation**	Elwyn Jones	
8.01pm	28/12/66	**Barlow Was There Pt. 2 Enquiry**	Elwyn Jones	
8.00pm	04/01/66	**Barlow Was There Pt. 3 Mischief**	Elwyn Jones	
8.00pm	11/01/66	**Sing a Song of Friendship**	Richard Beynon	

Time	Date	Title	Writer	Rpt
8.00pm	18/01/66	**James McNeil, Aged 23**	Alan Plater	
8.00pm	25/01/66	**The Next Voice You Hear**	Elwyn Jones	
8.00pm	01/02/66	**An Eye For An Eye**	Allan Prior	
8.01pm	08/02/66	**What Colour a Wolf?**	Martin Hall	
8.01pm	15/02/66	**Somebody Important**	Elwyn Jones	
8.00pm	22/02/66	**The Informant Pt. 1 Rough Justice**	Robert Barr	
8.01pm	01/03/66	**The Informant Pt. 2 The Man Inside**	Robert Barr	
7.59pm	08/03/66	**The Same The Whole World Over**	Alan Plater	
7.59pm	15/03/66	**Selection**	Elwyn Jones	
8.00pm	22/03/66	**Appointment in Wyvern**	Elwyn Jones	
8.01pm	29/03/66	**The Investors**	Allan Prior	
8.00pm	05/04/66	**A Piece of Waste Ground**	Alan Plater	
8.00pm	12/04/66	**Proof Positive**	Robert Barr	
8.01pm	19/04/66	**Cash on Deliverance**	Eric Coltart	
7.59pm	26/04/66	**On the Side of the Law**	Elwyn Jones	
8.00pm	03/05/66	**The Linkman**	Allan Prior	
8.00pm	10/05/66	**Blackitt's Round**	Robert Barr	
8.00pm	17/05/66	**See You tomorrow**	Robert Barr	
8.10pm	24/05/66	**The Hole Pt. 1 In the Road**	Elwyn Jones	
10.12pm	31/05/66	**The Hole Pt. 2 In the Head**	Elwyn Jones	

3ʳᵈ series

Time	Date	Title	Writer	Rpt
8.00pm	04/10/67	**The Target Pt. 1 Sighted**	Elwyn Jones	
8.00pm	11/10/67	**The Target Pt. 2 Point Blank**	Elwyn Jones	
8.00pm	18/10/67	**Material Evidence**	Alan Plater	
7.59pm	25/10/67	**Pieces of Silver**	Robert Barr	
8.01pm	08/11/67	**Something Unusual**	Eric Coltart	
8.00pm	15/11/67	**Never Forget a Face**	Allan Prior	
8.00pm	22/11/67	**Inducement**	Elwyn Jones	
8.00pm	29/11/67	**The Mind of the Beholder**	Alan Plater	
7.59pm	06/12/67	**The Hunt**	Elwyn Jones	
8.01pm	13/12/67	**Measure of Tolerance**	Elwyn Jones	
8.02pm	20/12/67	**Who's Mister Smith?**	Alan Plater	
8.00pm	27/12/67	**The Bombay Doctor**	Keith Dewhurst	
8.01pm	04/01/68	**Cause of Death**	Elwyn Jones	
8.00pm	11/01/68	**In Bulk**	Elwyn Jones	
8.00pm	18/01/68	**Complaint**	Robert Barr	
8.00pm	25/01/68	**Landing Whispers**	Martin Hall	
8.00pm	01/02/68	**Major Incidents**	Elwyn Jones	
8.00pm	08/02/68	**Quicker By Rail**	Elwyn Jones	

Time	Date	Title	Writer	Rpt
8.00pm	15/02/68	**The Good Girl**	Allan Prior	
8.00pm	22/02/68	**Identity Unknown**	Robert Barr	
8.0qpm	29/02/68	**Unfinished Business**	Robert Barr	
8.00pm	07/03/68	**Finger of Suspicion**	Allan Prior	
8.01pm	14/03/68	**If I Can Help Somebody**	Alan Plater	
8.00pm	21/03/68	**Don't Tell Me, Let Me Guess**	Robert Barr	
8.00pm	28/03/68	**Fortune on the Move Pt. 1**	Elwyn Jones	
8.00pm	04/04/68	**Fortune on the Move Pt. 2**	Elwyn Jones	

4th series

Time	Date	Title	Writer	Rpt
7.59pm	12/09/68	**Theory**	Elwyn Jones	
7.59pm	19/09/68	**Proof**	Elwyn Jones	
8.00pm	26/09/68	**Bird of Passage**	Allan Prior	
8.00pm	03/10/68	**See the Rabbit**	Alan Plater	
8.02pm	10/10/68	**Take Them in Singles**	Robert Barr	
8.00pm	17/10/68	**Red Herring**	Elwyn Jones	
7.59pm	24/10/68	**Five Pairs of Hands**	Allan Prior	
8.00pm	31/10/68	**Minor Incident**	Elwyn Jones	
8.00pm	07/11/68	**An Old Song**	Alan Plater	
8.00pm	14/11/68	**Big Boats, Little Boats**	Martin Hall	
8.01pm	21/11/68	**For a Rainy Day**	Allan Prior	
8.00pm	28/11/68	**Assistance**	Elwyn Jones	
8.02pm	05/12/68	**Equal Status**	Elwyn Jones	
8.00pm	12/12/68	**Obstruction**	Robert Barr	
8.01pm	19/12/68	**Gong Quietly**	Alan Plater	
8.18pm	27/12/68	**On Christmas Day in the Morning**	Alan Plater	
8.00pm	01/01/69	**Departure**	Elwyn Jones	
8.00pm	09/01/69	**Cross Reference**	Don Shore	
8.00pm	16/01/69	**Run for the Hills**	Robert Barr	
8.00pm	23/01/69	**Pressure**	Elwyn Jones	
8.00pm	30/01/69	**A Quantity of Gelignite**	Allan Prior	
8.00pm	06/03/69	**Critical Path**	Robert Barr	
8.00pm	13/02/69	**Persistence**	Elwyn Jones	
7.55pm	20/02/69	**Second Chance**	Allan Prior	
8.00pm	27/02/69	**How's the Wife, Then?**	Mervyn Haisan	
8.03pm	06/03/69	**Right to Search**	Robert Barr	
7.59pm	13/03/69	**Proved Connection**	Elwyn Jones	
4.58pm	16/03/69	**Star Choice**	David Rose	
5.01pm	13/04/69	**Sleeping Dogs**		APL

5th series

Time	Date	Title	Writer	Rpt
8.00pm	11/09/69	**Recovery**	Elwyn Jones	
8.00pm	18/09/69	**Flash Point**	Allan Prior	
8.01pm	25/09/69	**In at the Death**	Robert Barr	

Time	Date	Title	Writer	Rpt
8.00pm	02/10/69	**Error of Judgement**	Ben Bassett	
8.01pm	09/10/69	**Dead Aboard**	Elwyn Jones	
8.00pm	16/10/69	**One Thing Leads to Another**	Allan Prior	
8.00pm	23/10/69	**General Post**	Elwyn Jones	
7.59pm	30/10/69	**Wild Goose**	Don Shaw	
8.00pm	06/11/69	**We Shall Miss You**	Elwyn Jones	
8.02pm	13/11/69	**Write Off Task Force**	Alan Plater	
8.01pm	20/11/69	**Arrival**	Elwyn Jones	
8.00pm	27/11/69	**The Exercise**	Elwyn Jones	
8.00pm	04/12/69	**Diversion**	Robert Barr	
8.01pm	11/12/69	**The Spilt Ones**	Allan Prior	
8.02pm	18/12/69	**To Protect the Innocent**	Elwyn Jones	
8.01pm	01/01/70	**Any Other Night**	Robert Barr	
8.01pm	08/01/70	**The Aggro Boy**	Allan Prior	
8.01pm	15/01/70	**Standing Orders**	Alan Plater	
8.00pm	22/01/70	**Private Mischief**	Elwyn Jones	
7.59pm	29/01/70	**Open and Shut**	Allan Prior	
8.00pm	05/02/70	**Sprats and Mackerel**	Elwyn Jones	
8.00pm	12/02/70	**Like Any Other Friday**	Robert Barr	
8.00pm	19/02/70	**Power of the Presses**	Elwyn Jones	
8.00pm	26/02/70	**Trust a Woman**	Robert Barr	
8.00pm	05/03/70	**The Hermit**	Allan Prior	
8.00pm	12/03/70	**Escort**	Elwyn Jones	

Full details of *Softly, Softly* programmes published as broadcast (PSB) are held on microfiche at the BBC Written Archive, Caversham.

Z Cars (2ⁿᵈ January 1962–20 September 1978) lst 5 Series shown

From	Date	Title	Writer	Rpt
1ˢᵗ Series				
8.30pm	02/01/62	**Four of a Kind**	Troy Kennedy Martin	
8.31pm	09/01/62	**Limping Rabbit**		
8.30pm	16/01/62	**Handle with Care**	Allan Prior	
8.30pm	23/01/62	**Stab in the Dark**	Robert Barr	
8.29pm	30/01/62	**The Big Catch**	Allan Prior	
8.29pm	06/01/62	**Friday Night**	Troy Kennedy Martin	
8.25pm	13/02/62	**Suspended**	Allan Prior	
			Troy Kennedy Martin	
8.29pm	22/02/62	**Family Feud**	Allan Prior	
8.29pm	27/02/62	**Fire!**	Troy Kennedy Martin	
8.29pm	06/03/62	**Threats and Menaces**	Allan Prior	
8.26pm	13/03/62	**Jail Break**	Allan Prior	
6.42pm	20/03/62	**What Kind of Hero**	Michael Ash	
9.25pm	27/03/62	**Sudden Death**	Troy Kennedy Martin	
2ⁿᵈ Series				
8.25pm	03/04/62	**Found Abandoned**	John Hopkins	
8.30pm	10/04/62	**The Best Days**	John Hopkins	
8.27pm	17/04/62	**Invisible Enemy**	Troy Kennedy Martin	
8.25pm	24/04/62	**Down and Out**	Ray K. Dunbobbin	
8.26pm	01/05/62	**Further Enquiries**	John Hopkins	
8.25pm	08/05/62	**Winner Take All**	Allan Prior	
8.25pm	15/05/62	**People's Property**	John McGrath	
8.21pm	22/05/62	**Hi-Jack!**	Allan Prior	
8.25pm	28/05/62	**Incident Reported**	John Hopkins	
7.55pm	05/06/62	**Never on Wednesdays**	James Doran	
7.54pm	12/06/62	**Day Trip**	Allan Prior	
7.55pm	19/06/62	**Affray**	John Hopkins	
7.55pm	26/06/62	**Contraband**	Allan Prior	
7.55pm	03/07/62	**Team Work**	Troy Kennedy Martin	
7.56pm	10/07/62	**Appearance in Court**	John Hopkins	
7.55pm	17/07/62	**Assault**	Robert Barr	
7.55pm	24/07/62	**Sunday Mornings**	Allan Prior	
7.54pm	31/07/62	**Unconditional Surrender**	Johns Hopkins	
3ʳᵈ series				
8.00pm	10/09/62	**On Watch Newton**	John Hopkins	
2.30pm	23/09/62	*Found Abandoned*		JH
8.00pm	26/09/62	**Full Remission**	Allan Prior	
2.30pm	30/09/62	*Hi-Jack!*		APR
8.00pm	03/10/62	**Truth or Dare**	Lesley Sands	
2.29pm	07/10/62	*Jail Break*		TKM
8.00pm	10/10/62	**Information Received**	John Hopkins	

From	Date	Title	Writer	Rpt
2.29pm	14/10/62	*Threats and Menaces*		APR
8.46pm	17/10/62	**Friendly Relations**	John Hopkins	
8.00pm	24/10/62	**Corroboration**	James Doran	
2.32pm	28/10/62	*Stab in the Dark*		RB
7.30pm	31/10/62	**The Thin Girl**	Allan Prior	
2.19pm	04/11/62	*Contraband*		APR
8.00pm	07/11/62	**Johnny Sailor**	Keith Dewhurst	
8.10pm	15/11/62	**Person Unknown**	John Hopkins	
2.29pm	18/11/62	*Incident Reported*		JH
8.01pm	21/11/62	**Ambush**	Allan Prior	
2.36pm	25/11/62	*Winner Takes All*		APR
8.00pm	28/11/62	**Known to the Police**	Allan Prior	
2.30pm	02/12/62	*Assault*		RB
8.02pm	05/12/62	**The Navigators**	John Hopkins	
2.30pm	09/12/62	*The Big Catch*		APR
8.02pm	12/12/62	**Business Trip**	John Hopkins	
2.30pm	16/12/62	*Affray*		JH
7.31pm	19/12/62	**The Five Whistles**	Allan Prior	
2.06pm	23/12/62	*Friday Night*		TKM
7.45pm	26/12/62	**Search**		
2.30pm	30/12/62	*Team Work*		TKM
7.56pm	02/01/63	**All up by Seven**	Geoffrey Tatlow	
2.50pm	07/01/63	*Suspended*		TKM
7.54pm	09/01/63	**Trumpet Voluntary**	Allan Prior	
2.30pm	25/01/63	*Unconditional Surrender*		JH
7.55pm	16/01/63	**Five and a Match**	John Hopkins	
6.33pm	19/01/63	**Trail of a Gun**		
2.30pm	20/01/63	*Peoples' Property*		JH
7.55pm	30/01/63	**A Simple Case**	John Hopkins	
2.30pm	03/02/63	*Day Trip*		APR
7.56pm	06/02/63	**Act of Vengeance**	Lesley Sands	
2.30pm	10/02/63	*Appearance in Court*		JH
2.30pm	17/02/63	**Further Enquiries**		JH
7.55pm	27/02/63	**The Main Chance**	Keith Dewhurst	
7.55pm	27/02/63	**Follow My Leader**	John Hopkins	
7.55pm	06/03/63	**Members Only**	John Hopkins	
7.59pm	13/03/63	**Matter of Conviction**	Elwyn Jones	
8.00pm	20/03/63	**The Bad Lad**	Allan Prior	
8.01pm	27/03/63	**Enquiry**	John Hopkins	
8.25pm	03/04/63	**Pay by Results**	John Hopkins	
7.59pm	10/04/63	**The Peterman**	Allan Prior	
8.03pm	17/04/63	**The Pigs of the Air**	Keith Dewhurst	
7.29pm	24/04/63	**Train of Events**	John Hopkins	
7.55pm	01/05/63	**By the Book**	Elwyn Jones	
2.30pm	19/05/63	**Nothing Serious**	John Hopkins	
7.55pm	15/05/63	**Alarm Call**	John Hopkins	

From	Date	Title	Writer	Rpt
2.30pm	19/05/63	**Friendly Relations**	John Hopkins	
7.55pm	22/04/63	**A Try by Weir**	Alan Plater	
2.54pm	26/05/63	*Johnny Sailor*		KD
2.05pm	29/05/63	*Looking at Television*		JH
2.30pm		*Extract from* **Pay by Results**		
		Extract from **Search**		
		Extract from **A Simple Case**		
7.55pm	29/05/63	**Quiet Confidence**	John Hopkins	
2.30pm	02/06/63	*Business Trip*		JH
7.56pm	05/06/63	**Bears**	Allan Prior	
2.30pm	09/06/63	*Full Remission*		APR
7.56pm	12/06/63	**Caught by the Ears**	Jason Doran	
4.06pm	16/06/63	*The Navigators*		JH
9.12pm	17/06/63	*Points of View (Extract)*		JD
2.01pm	19/06/63	*Looking at Television*		JH
		Extract from **Navigators**		
7.31pm	19/06/63	*Come on the Lads*	Keith Dewhurst	
2.21pm	26/06/63	*Search*		
7.57pm	26/06/63	**The Whissers**	Allan Prior	
2.23pm	39/06/63	*The Thin Girl*		APR
7.54pm	03/07/63	**Police Work**	John Hopkins	
2.30pm	11/07/63	*Five and a Match*		JH
2.30pm	21/07/63	*Trumpet Voluntary*		AH
2.20pm	28/0763	*All up by Seven*		GT
2.30pm	04/08/63	*A Simple Case*		JH
2.30pm	11/08/63	*The Main Chance*		KD
2.30pm	18/08/63	*The Listeners*		APR
2.30pm	25/08/63	*By the Book*		EJ
2.31.pm	01/09/63	*Follow my Leader*		JH
7.35pm	04/09/63	**Lucky Accident**	John Hopkins	
2.30pm	08/09/63	*Pay by Results*		EJ
7.56pm	11/09/63	**Made for Each Other**		
2.30pm	15/09/63	*A Matter of Conviction*		EJ
7.55pm	18/09/63	**A La Carte**	Elwyn Jones	
2.30pm	22/09/63	*Enquiry*		JH
7.56pm	25/09/63	*Light the Blue Paper*		JH
2.30pm	29/09/63	*The Peterman*		
8.11pm	02/10/63	**A Quiet Night**	Alan Plater	
2.30pm	06/10/63	*Alarm Call*		JH
8.12pm	09/10/63	**Hit and Run**	Allan Prior	
2.30pm	13/10/63	*Quiet Confidence*		JH
8.10pm	16/10/63	**Wide and Go Back**	John Hopkins	
2.30pm	20/10/63	*Scars*		APR
8.11pm	23/10/63	**The Kiter**	Allan Prior	
2.30pm	17/10/63	*Caught by the Ears*		JD
8.10pm	30/10/63	**Special Duty**	John Hopkins	

From	Date	Title	Writer	Rpt
2.30pm	03/11/63	*Train of Events*		JH
8.12pm	06/11/63	**Remembrance of a Guest**	John Hopkins	
2.32pm	10/11/63	*The Whissers*		APR
8.11pm	13/11/63	**Daylight Robbery**	Lesley Sands	
2.31pm	17/11/63	*Members Only*		JH
9.49pm	20/11/63	**Running Milligan**	Keith Dewhurst	
2.38pm	26/11/63	*Police Work*		JH
9.14pm	17/11/63	**Choose your Partners**	John Hopkins	
3.55pm	01/12/63	*Come on the Lads*		KD
8.11pm	04/12/63	**Tuesday Afternoon**	Alan Plater	
8.11pm	11/12/63	*Supper in the Morning*		
2.30pm	15/12/63	*Made for Each Other*		
8.11pm	18/12/63	**Wait for It**	Robert Barr	
2.30pm	22/12/63	*A La Carte*		EJ
7.18pm	25/12/63	**It Never Rains**	John Hopkins	
2.32pm	29/12/63	*Light the Blue Paper*		JH
8.00pm	01/01/64	**And a Happy New Year**	John Hopkins	
2.30pm	05/01/64	*A Quiet Night*		APL
8.00pm	08/01/64	**Happy Go Lucky**	Robert Barr	
2.30pm	12/01/64	*Hide and Go Seek*		JH
8.00pm	15/01/64	**Promise Made**	Alan Plater	
2.31pm	19/01/64	*Hit and Run*		APR
8.01pm	22/01/64	**I Mean – Where Does it Stop?**	John Hopkins	
2.30pm	26/01/64	*Running Milligan*		KD
9.45pm	29/01/64	**A Stroll Along the Sands**	Joan Clarke	
2.32pm	02/02/64	*Daylight Robbery*		LS
8.15pm	05/02/64	**No Malice**	Robert Barr	
2.30pm	09/02/64	*Remembrance of a Guest*		JH
8.04pm	12/02/64	**Profit by Their Example**	John Hopkins	
2.30pm	16/02/64	*Choose Your Partners*		JH
8.00pm	19/02/64	**Question of Storage**	Alan Plater	
2.30pm	23/02/64	*Tuesday Afternoon*		APL
7.34pm	26/02/64	**Fun and Games**	John Hopkins	
2.30pm	01/03/64	*Supper in the Morning*		
8.01pm	04/03/64	**A Man ... Like Yourself** One hundredth edition		
2.31pm	08/03/64	*Wait for It*		RB
8.00pm	11/03/64	**A Straight Deal**	Robert Barr	
2.30pm	15/03/64	*And a Happy New Year*		JH
8.00pm	18/03/64	**Happy Families**	John Hopkins	
2.30pm	22/03/64	*Happy Go Lucky*		RB
8.00pm	25/03/64	**Inside Job**	Allan Prior	
2.35pm	29/03/64	*A Stroll Along the Sands*		JC
8.00pm	01/04/64	**Clues are What You Think**	Elwyn Jones	

From	Date	Title	Writer	Rpt
2.35pm	05/04/64	*I Mean – Where Does It Stop?*		JH
8.00pm	08/04/64	**The Whole Truth**	Robert Barr	
2.35pm	12/04/64	*Promise Made*		APR
8.01pm	15/04/64	**Person Unknown**		
4.59pm	19/04/64	*No Malice*		RB
8.00pm	22/04/64	**Whistle and Come Home**	John Hopkins	
4.44pm	26/04/64	*It Never Rains*		JH
8.00pm	29/04/64	**First-Class Citizen**	Allan Prior	
4.49pm	01/05/64	*Profit by their Example*		JH
7.31pm	06/05/64	**Seconds Away**	John Hopkins	
4.35pm	10/05/64	*Fun and Games*		JH
9.40pm	13/05/64	**Centre of Disturbance**	John Hopkins	
4.46pm	17/05/64	*A Question of Storage*		APL
8.00pm	20/05/64	**You Let All Kinds**	Robert Barr	
4.19pm	24/05/64	**A Man ... LikeYourself**	John Hopkins	JH
7.31pm	27/05/64	**Happy Birthday**	Joan Clarke	
4.45pm	31/05/64	*A Straight Deal*		RB
9.28pm	03/06/64	**Somebody ... Help!**	John Hopkins	
4.45pm	07/06/64	*Inside Job*		APR
8.00pm	10/06/64	**Cage Until Tame**	Robert Barr	
4.56pm	14/06/64	*Happy Families*		JH
8.00pm	17/06/64	**Family Reunion**	Alan Plater	
2.56pm	21/06/64	*The Whole Truth*		RB
8.00pm	24/06/64	**A Place of Safety**	John Hopkins	

4th series

From	Date	Title	Writer	Rpt
8.00pm	09/09/64	**The Dark Side of the**	John Hopkins	
8.01pm	16/09/64	**What A Main Event**	John Hopkins	
4.46pm	20/09/64	*Whistle and Come Home*		JH
8.00pm	23/09/64	**Finder Keepers**	John Hopkins	
4.40pm	27/09/64	*First Class Citizen*		APR
8.01pm	30/09/64	**Lucky Partners**	Arthur Hopkins	
4.42pm	04/10/64	*Seconds Away*		JH
8.00pm	07/10/64	**The Soft Spots**	Allan Prior	
4.42pm	11/10/64	*Centre of Disturbance*		JH
9.31pm	14/10/64	**Somebody Said**	James Doran	
4.40pm	18/10/64	*You Got All Kinds*		RB
9.29pm	21/10/64	**Charity Begins**	John Hopkins	
4.40pm	25/10/64	*Happy Birthday*		JC
8.00pm	28/10/64	**The Hunch**	Allan Prior	
4.40pm	01/11/64	*Cage Until Tame*		RB
8.02pm	04/11/64	**Two in the Bush**	C Wilkinson	
4.40pm	08/11/64	*Family Reunion*		APL
8.00pm	11/11/64	**Welcome Home, Jigger**	Brian Hayles	
4.46pm	15/01/64	*A Place of Safety*		JH

From	Date	Title	Writer	Rpt
8.02pm	18/11/64	**In a Day's Work**	John Hopkins	
4.39pm	22/11/64	*What a Main Event*		JH
8.00pm	25/11/64	**No Stone Unturned**	Elwyn Jones	
4.41pm	29/11/64	*Finders Keepers*		JH
8.01pm	02/12/64	**You Pays Your Money**	John Hopkins	
4.40pm	06/12/64	*Lucky Partners*		AH
8.02pm	09/12/64	**One Day in Spring Street**	Alan Plater	
4.40pm	13/12/64	*The Soft Spot*		APR
8.02pm	16/12/64	**Bring Back the Cat**	Bill Barren	
4.40pm	20/12/64	*Somebody Said ...*		JD
8.01pm	23/12/64	**If He Runs ... Grab Him So**	Elwyn Jones	
3.57	29/12/64	*Welcome Home Jigger*		BH
8.01pm	30/12/64	**First Post**	Alan Plater	
8.03pm	06/01/65	**Think On**	Eric Coltart	
4.30pm	03/01/65	*In a Day's Work*		JH
8.00pm	13/01/65	**The Luck of the Game**	Stan Barstow	
4.38pm	17/01/65	*The Hunch*		APR

5th series

From	Date	Title	Writer	Rpt
8.01pm	20/01/65	**I Love You Bonso**	Keith Dewhurst	
4.42pm	24/01/65	*Two in the Bush*		C Wilkinson
8.01pm	27/01/65	**Brotherly Love**	Alan Plater	
4.41pm	31/01/65	*No Stone Unturned*		EJ
8.00pm	03/02/65	**Matter of Give and Take**	Brian Hayles	
4.41pm	07/02/65	*You Pays Your Money*		JH
8.01pm	10/02/65	**Give a Dog a Name**	Joan Clarke	
4.40pm	14/02/65	*One Day in Spring Street*		APL
8.00pm	17/02/65	**The Long Spoon**	Elwyn Jones	
4.42pm	21/02/65	*Bring Back the Cat*		Bill Barren
8.00pm	24/02/65	**Teething Troubles**	Alan Plater	
4.49pm	28/02/65	*If He Runs ... Grab Him*		EJ
8.000m	03/03/65	**Shame to Take the Money**	Bill Barron	
5.46pm	07/03/65	*Think On*		EC
8.01pm	10/03/65	**Window Dressing**	Ronal Eyre	
4.47pm	14/03/65	*I Love You Bonso*		KD
7.35pm	17/03/65	**Partners**	Alan Plater	
4.44pm	21/03/65	*Brotherly Love*		APL
9.00pm	24/03/65	**The Fanatics**	John Wilson	
4.56pm	27/03/65	*A Matter of Give and Take*		Brian Hales
8.02pm	31/03/65	**You Got to Have Class**	William Emms	
4.46pm	04/04/65	*Give a Dog a Name*		JC
8.00pm	07/04/65	**The Mice Will Play**	Alan Plater	
8.00pm	11/04/65	*The Long Spoon*		EJ
8.02pm	14/04/65	**Z Cars – Sound An Alarm**	Elwyn Jones	

From	Date	Title	Writer	Rpt
4.46pm	18/04/65	*Teething Trouble*		APL
8.01pm	21/04/65	**The Soft Game**	Eric Coltart	
4.45pm	25/04/65	*Window Dressing*		Ronald Eyre
8.00pm	28/04/65	**Snakes Alive**	George McRobert	
4.24pm	02/05/65	*The Fanatics*		John Wilson
8.00pm	04/04/65	**Suspected Murder**	Alan Plater	
4.46pm	09/05/65	*You've Got to Have Class*		William Emms
8.00pm	12/05/65	**The Share Out**	Allan Prior	
9.32pm	19/05/65	**Checkmate**	Robert Barr	
4.45pm	23/05/65	*The Mice Will Play*		APL
8.00pm	26/05/65	**Another Fairy Tale**	Eric Coltart	
4.26pm	09/05/65	*Sound On Alarm*		EJ
8.02pm	02/06/65	**Market Square**	Elwyn Jones	
8.00pm	09/06/65	**Error of Judgement**	Alan Plater	
8.06pm	16/06/65	**Under Cover**	Ray Jenkins	
8.02pm	23/06/65	**One Good Turn**	Eric Coltart	
8.01pm	30/06/65	**Warning Shots**	Alan Plater	

Titles in italics are repeats
Writers of repeats are represented by their intitials

Robert Barr	RB
Joan Clark	JC
Keith Dewhurst	KD
James Doran	JD
Elwyn Jones	EJ
John Hopkins	JH
Joan Clarke	JC
Troy Kennedy Martin	TKM
Allan Prior	APR
Alan Plater	APL
Lesley Sands	LS
Geoffrey Tatlow	GT

Full details of *Z Cars* programmes published as broadcast, are held on microfiche at the BBC Written Archive, Caversham.

Index

Note : Film titles are indicated by date only; other media are appropriately designated